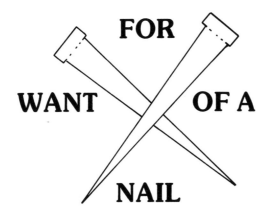

FOR WANT OF A NAIL

The Impact on War of Logistics
and Communications

Titles of related interest from Brassey's

CHAPMAN
Military Air Transport Operations

EVANS
Amphibious Operations: The Projection of Sea Power Ashore

JAMES
Imperial Rearguard: Wars of Empire, 1919–85

LAFFIN
Brassey's Battles: 3500 Years of Conflict, Campaigns and Wars From A to Z

O'BALLANCE
The Gulf War

OXLEE
Air Reconnaissance

PAKENHAM
Naval Command and Control

PERKINS
Brassey's Weapons and Warfare

SAMMES & RICE
Communications and Information Systems for Battlefield Command and Control

WALKER
Air Superiority Operations

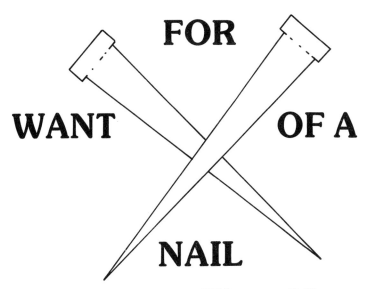

FOR WANT OF A NAIL

The Impact on War of Logistics and Communications

by

Kenneth Macksey

BRASSEY'S (UK)

(A member of the Maxwell Pergamon Publishing Corporation plc)

LONDON · OXFORD · WASHINGTON · NEW YORK · BEIJING
FRANKFURT · SÃO PAULO · SYDNEY · TOKYO · TORONTO

UK (Editorial)	Brassey's (UK) Ltd. 24 Gray's Inn Road, London WC1X 8HR, England
(Orders all except North America)	Brassey's (UK) Ltd., Headington Hill Hall, Oxford OX3 0BW, England
U.S.A. (Editorial)	Brassey's (US) Inc., 8000 Westpark Drive, Fourth Floor, McLean, Virginia 22102, U.S.A.
(Orders) North America	Brassey's (US) Inc., Front and Brown Streets, Riverside, New Jersey 08075, U.S.A. Tel (toll free): 800 257 5755
PEOPLE'S REPUBLIC OF CHINA	Pergamon Press, Room 4037, Qianmen Hotel, Beijing, People's Republic of China
FEDERAL REPUBLIC OF GERMANY	Pergamon Press GmbH, Hammerweg 6, D-6242 Kronberg, Federal Republic of Germany
BRAZIL	Pergamon Editora Ltda, Rua Eça de Queiros, 346, CEP 04011, Paraiso, São Paulo, Brazil
AUSTRALIA	Brassey's Australia Pty Ltd., P.O. Box 544, Potts Point, N.S.W. 2011, Australia
JAPAN	Pergamon Press, 5th Floor, Matsuoka Central Building, 1-7-1 Nishishinjuku, Shinjuku-ku, Tokyo 160, Japan
CANADA	Pergamon Press Canada Ltd., Suite No. 271, 253 College Street, Toronto, Ontario, Canada M5T 1R5

First edition 1989

Library of Congress Cataloging in Publication Data
Macksey, Kenneth.
For want of a nail: the impact of war on logistics and communications/Kenneth Macksey. – 1st ed.
p. cm.
Bibliography: p.
Includes index.
1. Logistics–History. 2. Communications, Military–History,
3. Military history, Modern. I. Title.
U168.M33 1989 355.4'11–dc20 89-7311

British Library Cataloguing in Publication Data
Macksey, Kenneth, *1923-*
For want of a nail: the impact on war of logistics
and communications.
1. Army operations. Logistics, history
I. Title
355.4'11'09

ISBN 0-08-036268-0

Printed in Great Britain by BPCC Wheatons Ltd, Exeter

Acknowledgements

AS ON so many occasions, I am indebted to John Andrews, Chief Librarian of the Ministry of Defence Library, Whitehall, for his encouragement and to his staff for their help and unfailing courtesy over the tracing of the sources of reference without which the research for this book would have been so much more laborious. Also my sincerest gratitude to Lieutenant Colonel Bill Woodhouse for reading and criticising the first draft in his usual thorough and helpful manner; and to Felicity Northover for coping so cheerfully with my drafts while typing it all.

Contents

List of Figures

List of Maps

Introduction

TO THE militarily educated it goes without saying that the most perfectly conceived operational plan is liable to fail if its logistic support is not equally well thought out and implemented. Yet history shows how often the most elegant plans have collapsed due to the failure of logistic services, allied to inadequate or even non-existent, communications to hold a force together. If the defeats of several Great Captains can be explained by their own administrative lapses, few there were who have admitted it, and many were those they blamed for the shortcomings.

It is another seeming truism to suggest that such failures have been the result of inferior peacetime logistic preparations; by omissions through parsimony; by a politically grandiose way of economising through an exercise known as 'cutting the tail'; and by a naive hope that 'it will be all right on the day'. History shows the need for reminders, which is one reason why this book has been written. To show not only how logistic thinking and services have developed over the past 150 years but also to indicate how easily even the best forces slip into the false belief that they are prepared 'to the last gaiter button' when, in fact, they would do well to remember Benjamin Franklin's celebrated maxim:

> *'For want of a nail, the shoe was lost —*
> *for want of a shoe, the horse was lost — for want of a*
> *horse the rider was lost — for want of a rider the battle was lost.'*

It's a lot more complicated two hundred years later. The terminology has changed, but the principles of Administration, formulated in the more scientific, analytical 20th century, apply with equal force. Woe betide the statesman (or woman), military leader or innovator who unheedingly forgets or casts aside the principles of Foresight, Economy, Flexibility, Simplicity, Co-operation and Self-Sufficiency. Foolish are those who overlook the workings of what may be termed 'the logistic equaliser' — that attritional phenomenon which insidiously exhausts the stamina of a superior force as it pursues a seemingly defeated opponent until the moment is reached when the latter has restored its strength and fortunes to the point of equilibrium. It is possible only to give an outline of so vast a subject — an outline which I hope, nevertheless, will encourage students and others to look more deeply into what is arguably the most important subject in the military curriculum, about which least has been specifically written and over which too many people tend to draw a veil for fear of engendering boredom. In the hope that my contribution might stimulate intense interest, may I simply draw the reader's attention to the Bibliography with the hint that most of the books mentioned there contain (sometimes almost conceal) the details this book cannot, for want of space, include.

K.J.M.

Chapter 1

Teeth versus Tail: An Interminable Contest

WHEN THE armoured spearheads of General Ewald von Kleist's Panzer Group reached the English Channel on the evening of 20 May 1940 they made history in more ways than one. Not only was this the first time ever that the army of one first class military power had out-fought another and advanced 200 miles in eleven days, it was also the first time such a feat had been accomplished with hardly a tremor of logistic breakdown. Which was all the more remarkable when it is borne in mind that the German Army, to which Group von Kleist belonged, suffered, as had so many armies before, from the depredations of what is sometimes known as 'The Teeth versus Tail' conflict. That is, the contest which, from the dawn of military history, has been waged between those strategists and operational commanders who desire mainly to put all their assets into fighting, 'teeth' arms and the administrators and quartermasters (whose warnings that to do so courted logistic disaster) who so often had seen the logistic 'tail' services cut to the bone.

That contest reached its zenith in the twentieth century, when two world wars saw the global deployment of huge forces in theatres far removed from their home bases, thereby creating heavy burdens for every facet of the logistic machinery of the combatant nations. The ratio of tail to teeth increased at an alarming rate and savagely eroded the pools of manpower upon which the teeth arms would have hoped to draw for their necessary expansion and reinforcement.

The keys to these revolutionary happenings were to be found, of course, in a sophisticated utilisation by skilled and practised commanders and staff officers of the latest technical and managerial methods. At the heart of it all lay the internal combustion engine and its supplanting of horse drawn vehicles. Dependent though armies remained upon railways for movement of bulk stores, motor vehicles now augmented transport systems' flexibility to an unimagined extent, while the latest high speed communication systems speeded up reactions to rapidly changing situations. As never before, it was possible, by the use of quickly laid

1

teleprinter and telephone circuit cables, supplemented by high frequency 'quenched' radio (made almost secure by Enigma encoding machines), to impose strict centralised control and reduce wastage. As General Guderian, leader of the German armoured forces, remarked, at no time was the advance jeopardised for lack of supplies, even though on one occasion a divisional commander was deluded into thinking his troops were out of fuel when they were not. 'Good staff work can avoid this calamity', he wrote with bland optimism, '. . . it was only a question of transport and easy to solve.'

Yet such a glib answer could not have been given by the Anglo-French armies von Kleist had cut off in Belgium. Still virtually intact, these formations were nearing their last gasp because their land lines of communication had been severed and their command and control system was close to paralysis due to a stroke deliberately aimed at their vitals. Good staff work and ample transport would not solve the logistic problems of a force cut off from its base.

Why was it that nothing like this master-stroke had been achieved in the past? How was it, for example, that in 1914 the mighty, long-planned wheel of the Germany Army through Belgium towards Paris collapsed at the Battle of Marne? Not, it can be said, through defeat of the highly competant German teeth arms. But far more likely due to their physical exhaustion caused in large part by an inadequate logistic plan allied to flawed signal communications, command and control (in modern parlance, C^3). On that historic occasion the fighting troops, upon whom so much had been lavished, outmarched both the railway and the signal services to the point at which they could no longer deliver supplies or messages to the right places in the volume demanded; faults which can be traced back to an initial neglect of attention to these vital matters.

Tracing back through the major campaigns of the 19th century reveals the logistic defects which plunged other armies into disastrous confusion. Held up for derision is the celebrated boast of the French Minister for War in 1870, that, for the French Army, 'not a gaiter button would be wanting'; when, in fact, it was on the verge of utter chaos due to a confused mobilisation plan, dire shortages of weapons and transport, and the wrong positioning of many essential supplies; a disaster largely brought on by pre-war parsimony and myopia. Not that the German Army was so very superior in many of its transport departments or in communications in general. Ample evidence of defects were forthcoming, of which those within the railway organisation occasionally threatened their invading armies with starvation. Win almost every battle though the Germans would, the difference in combat worthiness between them and the French was fundamentally a measure of relative logistic and C^3 capabilities. The men of both sides fought well when given the opportunity; the disparity in weapons was not immense. It was inferior pre-war planning and provisioning by the French which, time and again, spoiled their performance and broke their morale; and similar, though lesser, faults on the German side which delayed a final decision.

Initially the American Civil War which broke out in 1861, had been in a quite different category to the later Franco-Prussian War — if only because its very nature militated against assured pre-war planning. Confronted by unforeseeable situations which both sides would have preferred to avoid (for military even if not political reasons), the spirit of the opening moves was one of improvisation. Not until the collapse of the Federal North's hasty, opening thrust to capture the Capital of the Confederate South, and to end the war by Christmas, did their leaders settle upon a logistically orientated strategy which guaranteed eventual victory. A strategy which, incidentally, was fatally complemented by the South's yielding response. For while the North's naval blockade, allied to concentric land offensives, relentlessly squeezed a deprived victim to death, the South ensured their own eventual defeat by adopting a defensive strategy which assisted the North to establish a stranglehold. If ever a nation managed to conceive a strategy which was balanced between the demands of the teeth and the tail, it was the industrially strong North. More clearly than the rural South, they recognised that the combined action of forces controlled by the latest telegraph systems and supplied by steam-powered railroads and steamships, was a guaranteed match winner. And one which the South's armies, for all their initial superior generalship and wonderfully dedicated panache in battle, never overcame.

In 1861, however, the Americans did at least have the benefit of reading about what had happened in the European wars of the 1850s. They were aware of how the effects (lethal and logistic) of the latest rapid fire weapons, of the telegraph and steam-powered transport had changed the face of war. How British, French and Russian armies, for example, came to blows in the Crimea in 1854 under elderly senior officers whose vision of combat was frozen in small colonial campaigns and the Battle of Waterloo in 1815. Unable though the Americans were to restrict the casualty lists, it was to their credit that they made far better efforts to supply and succour their men than had, most notably, the British in 1854. Indeed, they had but little option, in a democratic society, but to come to terms with the fundamental changes in social outlook which were sweeping the world in the aftermath of the 18th century revolutions (on both sides of the Atlantic) and the subsequent European upheavals and emancipations of the 1830s and 1840s.

All of a sudden, a surge of popular, humanitarian conscience could no longer be restrained by privileged aristocracies. The social impulses which abolished the slave trade and insisted, for example, upon improved public health by the building of sewers, were carried through into the treatment of fighting men. Human life became more highly valued even among the lowest born. By a bitter irony, as weapon power increased, insistence of better care for the wounded became irresistible — a political trend which would have been derided at Waterloo but, at the time of the Crimea, one which brought a government down. Once recognised, in a world being shrunk by the latest communications systems, which rapidly published almost immediate news in volume, there was no going back in the process of breaking down class distinctions. As the works of Florence Nightingale and Henri Dunant were to show, care for the soldier's welfare now placed an unprecedented load upon the tail, such a load, indeed, as might lead, preposterously in some minds, to a paring of the teeth.

In the new humanitarian atmosphere, ironies abounded. As medical science and improved health service raised the manpower available for the fighting ranks, far greater effort had to be apportioned to the logistic services in their support. Rapid fire weapons called for much increased supplies and transportation of munitions. Telegraph systems and steam-powered mechanisation demanded the recruitment of many new classes of technician, besides the supply of all manner of new items, such as hundreds of miles of copper cable and thousands of tons of coal. Any suspicion that increases in the range and power of weapons might allow reductions in the numbers of men at the front in order to hold a given stretch of line were disabused, since greater depths of deployment usually resulted. In any case, more complex and sensitive logistic zones demanded stronger protection than in the past. In effect, the calls upon manpower increased almost in relation to its rising supply; and the logistic zone progressively became merged into interdependence with the combat zone.

Hinterlands, with their swelling populations and burgeoning industrial complexes, were also becoming war zones. No longer was it a matter of despatching men and materials to the campaign to the sounds of cheers and bands, and then sitting back, in cool detachment, to await news of the results long after they had occurred. When the populace could be informed, in a matter of days or even hours, of what was going on, it became involved almost as if under direct attack itself. In much the same way as improved weapons were the product of advanced technology, so were the more sophisticated logistic systems which they and humanitarianism had generated, a product of radically changing social organisation and liberal politics which, in themselves, were stimulated by the impact of advanced technology.

Of course trends such as these had long been apparent. But it was not until the latter half of the 19th century that they took a startlingly revolutionary turn. So it is that period, after a short backward glance at previous events, which one must consider before examining teeth versus tail in the 20th century.

Chapter 2

A Revolution in Complexity: The Price of Neglect

A SEARCH for the origination and meaning of the word 'logistics' reveals several different sources and a variety of interpretations before its now universally accepted definition became accepted. Suggestions that it can be traced back to Roman times need not be taken seriously even though, of course, the armies of Rome functioned under a well-regulated administrative system of supply of men and material and of movement from one place in the Empire to another. Most authorities agree that the word first assumed modern form in General Antoine Jomini's celebrated *Précis de l'art de la guerre* (1836). For although he defined it as 'the practical art of moving armies', he included in that phrase almost everything in military practice except strategy and tactics. Even if the word did not at once come into general use and, but for acceptance by the United States Navy (under the influence of Captain Alfred Mahan in the 1880s), might have been lost sight of, some such expression would in due course have had to be coined to embrace the ever diversifying military ramifications generated by the inventiveness of the Industrial Revolution. It was merely another facet of American creativeness that gradually they broadened the meaning of this word to include not only the supply and transportation of men and materials to the battle zones, but also the procedures of finance and the procurement of war resources. In this book, however, the latter functions will not be considered in detail, although passing reference to their fundamental aspects are inevitable.

Until the introduction into general service of practical steam power-plants, the dependence of transportation by sea and land upon muscle and wind power not only hampered the supply of armies but cramped the evolution of societies and nations. Because there was no satisfactory way of preventing the decay of harvested crops and meat, the size of communities was restricted by their ability to feed

5

themselves from locally raised foodstuffs. Edible produce could not be imported over larger distances than it took time for decay to take place. Similar difficulties of distribution and decomposition seriously restricted the sustenance and hence the mobility of fleets and armies. Wherever armies went they tended to induce famine because, locust-like, they ate up such meagre stocks as communities held. It was impossible for them to be self-contained because herds of livestock slowed movement, horses ate vast quantities of fodder and horse-drawn waggons never could be provided in sufficient number to meet demand.

To avoid starvation, large military forces had to keep on the move from one feeding ground to another, simply because it was rarely possible for poor roads and the vulnerable waterways to carry sufficient supplies. For waterways were usually controlled by fortifications strong enough to prevent capture before the besieger had either run out of food or ammunition, had been driven off by a relieving army, or compelled to avoid assault for fear of excessive casualties in a period of manpower storage. Interaction between engineering, fortifications, ammunition expenditure and food consumption has always been critical to the logistic equation. Its resolution has invariably demanded intricate planning, shrewd calculation and astute administration by staffs to enable commanders to achieve their aim. It is much more precise than the arts of strategy and tactics. It may be said rightly that the commander who makes fewest mistakes in battle wins the campaign. Still more truthfully, let it also be stated that the most resourceful and least wasteful logistician, with the best staff work, is he who wins wars.

Hardly ever in history have fortifications affected logistics to the extent to which they did in the latter half of the 17th and the beginning of the 18th century. So strong were fortresses of the type built by General Sebastian de Vauban that he was a bold commander who dared waste the time, the munitions and the manpower to tackle them — even if he had been able to feed his army at the halt. It is instructive, for example, to compare the Duke of Marlborough's advance from Holland to Bavaria in 1704 with his later campaigns in Flanders.

In 1704, Marlborough could retain mobility with 35,000 men, as he followed the Rhine and Neckar rivers, because, with the initiative in his possession, he could afford to move at a measured pace through rich country and pay for pre-positioned supplies without having his soldiers antagonise the population by ungoverned scavenging. Only at the Schellenberg fortress, dominating the River Danube at Donauwörth, did he feel compelled to make a quick attack, costly in manpower and powder, to achieve his aim. His opponent, Marshall Tallard, by contrast, was ever at a logistic disadvantage: compelled to advance at speed with inadequate pre-positioned supplies for 90,000 men and thwarted in a siege of Villingen to secure his lines of communication, his was a tired, hungry and disgruntled army when drawn to defeat at Blenheim.

After the battle of Oudenarde, among the fortress-controlled river arteries of Flanders in 1708, it was a different story. Here the French had the advantage of reasonably well stocked fortresses whose necessary capture by siege posed classic

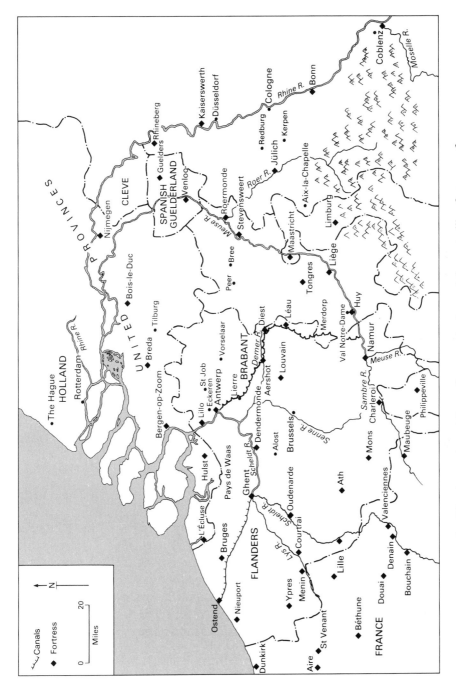

MAP 1. The river and canal lines of communication and the controlling fortresses of Western Europe in the 18th Century

logistic equations. At Lille, for example, between August and December, the struggle centred upon logistics without a major battle being fought. Well supplied by food from the port of Ostend, the joint army of 110,000 under Marlborough and Prince Eugene had only to be kept supplied with sufficient ammunition along the 70 mile road to Lille eventually to prevail; while the French Marshal Vendôme needed to cut that road and somehow also rush supplies (above all powder), into the city. He failed in the first part, but a gallant partially successful replenishment attempt at night in September probably prolonged resistance by a month or more. This battle for logistic supremacy was vital. A continued supply of powder enabled Eugene to capture Lille with economy of manpower. With secure, short lines of communication and ample supply from the sea, Marlborough could capture the fortresses of Ghent and Bruges in winter (a most unusual time to campaign) against the seriously weakened Vendôme; thus gaining control of Flanders and making the French contemplate peace negotiations.

It may seem surprising that it was not until the end of the 18th century that the tyranny of siege warfare, with its attendant logistic handicaps, was shattered. Napoleon takes the credit for exploiting the increased availability of manpower from growing populations through the *levée en masse*. He it was who harnessed revolutionary zeal to strategic concepts which went part way to solving the logistic problems of maintaining mass without inducing starvation. But it took more than a change of doctrine to co-ordinate the advance of several large armies, well separated in space and by-passing fortresses, towards unification on the decisive battlefield. It required the practised management of a well-drilled organisation, functioning through an Empire-wide communications network (of which Claude Chappé's high speed semaphore system was an important part), to handle swiftly a far greater volume of signals traffic than ever before.

These assets Napoleon possessed — along with Louis Berthier, his brilliant Chief of Staff, who knew best how to actuate the supply and transport departments. To such effect, indeed, that within 36 hours of being told by his master on 23 August 1805 to redeploy the Army from the English Channel coast to the Rhine, orders were ready for despatch. Not that Napoleon gave Berthier a logistic free hand. He insisted always that the operational scheme must take precedence. Nevertheless the eight army corps, despite scant warning, were crossing the Rhine, in dispersed columns, five weeks later, fresh and well supplied, to arrive on 6 October at Donauwörth on the Danube poised for battle. Failures in supply there were but none so serious as to upset operational balance; nor so crippling that scavenging (which even Napoleon's armies found necessary to a lesser or greater extent) was much worse than 20 per cent — and usually paid for quickly. The pay-off came in battle at Austerlitz on 2 December, making the culmination of a campaign in which, for the most part, the system worked so satisfactorily that few among the troops felt the temptation to breach discipline by unauthorised pillage.

Why then was there so complete a breakdown of this proven system in Russia six years later after Napoleon and his staff had gone to greater lengths than ever to guard against it? How was it that the French Army, having reached Moscow after defeating the Russians at Borodino, was compelled to make a disastrous retreat in deep winter with the loss of a quarter of a million men and nearly all their equipment? Fundamentally, it would appear, because Napoleon put teeth before tail. His logistics were less well geared than those of his opponent to satisfy the demands of operational concentration. Because the Russians deliberately denied Napoleon battle and withdrew from the poorer frontier zone into the richer interior (and wasted much of the land as they retreated), the French masses were reduced to scavenging the farther they out-reached their transport columns struggling forward along the ill-founded roads. The greater the rapacity of the soldiers, the faster their discipline declined. By the time Napoleon reached Vitebsk, which was the farthest point at which it was calculated his supply system could cope, he had been defeated by the enemy's strategy of denials of both battle and sustenance.

At this point Napoleon had either to obey the rules of logistic sense or admit defeat with all its political consequences. If he hoped to compel the enemy to give battle by extending the advance towards Moscow, he risked, as he well knew, serious deprivations. He therefore gambled in choosing to go on, pitching the stakes still higher by concentrating his columns far too closely. As his formations entered a wasted land, the men's discipline automatically deteriorated still more as they began also to plunder in addition to scavenging. Win the costly Battle of Borodino though Napoleon would (the only occasion in which large quantities of ammunition were expended), it was at the price of lost French cohesion and morale, abetted by unflagging Russian self-sacrifice in the tightening of their logistic stranglehold, by determined government as well as shrewd Generals. The denial of winter shelter to the French by the burning of Moscow was simply another dividend for the Russians to whom counter-logistics, so to speak, had been the cornerstone of their defence. Moreover, the counterstroke they could now launch was made in the comfortable knowledge that the French would receive no help from an angered populace in a winter wasteland. Napoleon's supply system had been defeated as much by the sheer, timeless inability of his available transport resources to cope with the needs of large military forces as by his own boundless ambition, which clouded his judgement of logistic reality.

Quite different distractions were at work, however, when the Anglo-French armies attacked the Russians in the Black Sea in 1854, to find themselves beset by factors very different to those of 40 years ago in the Waterloo campaign. It was not simply that the latest breech-loading weapons had vastly multiplied firepower, or that the replenishment of artillery ammunition was more difficult because bursting shells, unlike cannon balls, could not be salvaged for re-use. Far more revolutionary were steam-powered ships and railways — which not only carried men, horses, artillery and supplies at high speed in great quantity but also hastened the despatch of information and orders — the latter function supplemented by simplex (one way working) telegraph networks as they spread across Europe, rendering semaphore stations obsolete.

Among the Anglo-French and Turkish forces engaged with Russia in the Black Sea in 1854, it was the French who, most recently, during the 1848 disturbances had acquired experience of the latest logistic revolution. Moreover their Intendance, the commissariat organisation which co-ordinated supply and transport for 30,000 men with operational demands, ran a practised system, adequately financed by government. It was quite the opposite with the British, whose successive governments over the years on grounds of economy, in the pursuit of popularity and from a national lack of interest in the Army, had disbanded the efficient waggon train built up during the Napoleonic Wars and permitted the Commissariat, which arranged supply, to fall into decay.

Whenever military organisations come under financial constraint, they tend to make disproportionate economies in the logistic services compared to the combat arms. This is especially likely in an army, such as the British, where the combat arms are founded upon the 'family' type, Regimental system. Lacking much influence, the under-privileged services have no political muscle and so can only plead and usually lose in the teeth versus tail tussle. By 1854 the tail had lost both at sea and on land. The protection of British interests overseas had been largely handed over to the semi-military private companies such as the East India. The Army, in the hands of aged Generals who were out of date, was still run on 1815 lines but without the means to fight even Waterloo, let alone a modern campaign. Aged admirals still obstinately resisted the introduction of steamships. Equipment in both Navy and Army was in desperately short supply. There was an almost complete absence of trained logisticians. The work of mobilisation and the ordering and movement of supplies for a far off foreign theatre of war fell largely into the hands of a few clerks. Small wonder that there was chaos and that there were crippling shortages: remarkable that, despite Admiralty prejudice, the Army did at least charter fast steamships (mostly from the P & O Line and which, if armed, were superior in combat in some respects to many sailing ships of the Royal Navy) for transport to Scutari, Varna and the Crimea.

Blameworthy as the military commanders were for much that was wrong with the British war effort in 1854 and 1855, their plight was caused, at root, by governments. Without much consideration of the inadequate state of the forces at their command, they insisted, as an open secret, upon the immediate seizure of the Russian naval base of Sevastopol. It is often over-looked that Lord Raglan, the much maligned British Commander-in-Chief, protested that his Army of 26,000 men, wasted by cholera, typhus and dysentery when staging at Varna, was in no fit state for an amphibious operation which would pitch it into inhospitable terrain off which scavenging would be impossible. Lacking sufficient supplies and transport and compelled initially to maintain his force across unsheltered beaches, he knew he was courting disaster. But told to get on with it he declined to resign since others were sure to be appointed who would do as they were told.

With no fodder available (and his urgent request for 2,000 tons unsatisfied until 1855) he left all the animals behind except for the few needed to pull 300 waggons

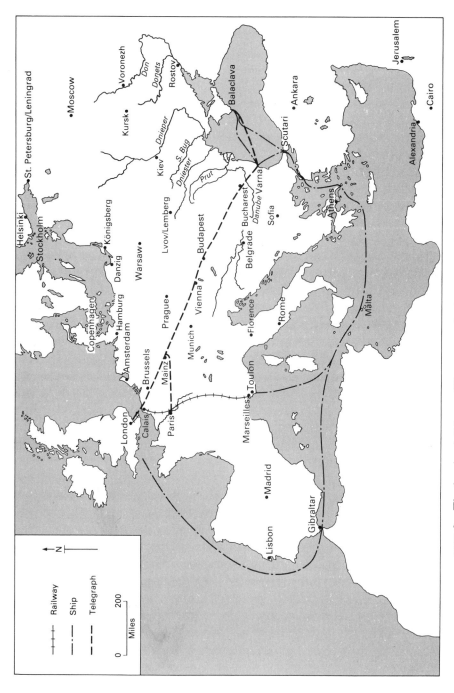

MAP 2. The 'modern' Crimean War communication system. Only a few very high priority messages went by the low-capacity telegraph. The rest went by sea and land

which, somehow, had been scraped together. It was bad enough that all the medical stores and much else besides had been dumped ashore in confusion at Varna and Scutari; that for want of cooking equipment the men were further weakened by under-nourishment; and for lack of fodder the cavalry horses were soon dying from hunger; or that after the Battle of the Alma the surgeons were without bandages, splints, morphia and chloroform and, for want of lamps and candles, were operating by the light of the moon. It was far worse that the Government was unable to put matters right at once. An inefficient logistic machine cannot be rebuilt overnight. Meanwhile, as the wounded and sick were shipped back to Scutari in their thousands, the under-staffed base hospital broke down completely because most of the stores and medicine needed had been dumped at Varna. Amid the most appalling squalor and filth, the fighting men rarely received proper treatment and died by the hundred.

It was one thing for the reports of William Russell of the *London Times* to be read in all their impassioned, detailed immediacy within nine or ten days of the Alma, and that as a result the Government was brought down. It certainly helped that despatches which travelled fast by sea to Marseilles and thence by rail to Calais, and onwards again by sea and rail, significantly hastened action. But there could be no systematic and organised rectification of what was wrong until the Commissariat was properly staffed and what became known as the Land Transport Corps was formed and sent out. But even then there would be scant improvement because, for one thing, the Commissariat and Land Transport Corps were inhibited by bureaucratic rules and sheer obstinacy from collaborating with each other; and the officers, recruited from all manner of pastimes and occupations, were for the most part neither expert, energetic nor competent. It is rarely sound to transfer failed combat officers or untrained civilians to administrative duties in the field, as now was done. Dynamic administrators of Florence Nightingale's knowledge and zeal, in putting the care of the sick and wounded on well founded lines, were few and far between. But, like Colonel McMurdo (who put the Land Transport Corps right) she played a leading part in the creation of better logistic services at the same time as the Board of Ordnance (which was no better than the Commissariat) was abolished. Waste and corruption by inefficient civilian contractors, principal among them in roguery the sutlers who sold food to the soldiers, were out of hand. Yet, as all genuine reformers such as Miss Nightingale discovered, one might form a new Army Hospital Corps, but it did not mean that previous malpractice would be dispelled at once or that old gangs would not cling to past malpractices.

Nevertheless, it is to the Crimean campaign that it is possible to trace the real beginnings of modern logistic systems as practised by most armies in addition to Britain's. To begin with, through a chain of reforms gradually — so very slowly — identified and implemented by innumerable government inquiries, can be observed the establishment of military medical, supply and transport services in which the civilian element was progressively removed from the lower levels of organisation. As established corps were formed under full military discipline, regulation became easier. Between government bureaucracies, military head-quarters and the formations at the front can be detected the multiplication of better communications and the development of military engineering as an essential logistic service. Just as it was true that the weakened state of the Anglo-French force made it impossible to invest Sevastopol completely in 1854, thus enabling the Russians to pour in supplies and extend the siege, so it is evident that, without the Engineers, the besiegers' build-up would have been impossible. Largely by last minute improvisations, the wharves at Balaclava and the roads and light railway to the siege lines were put together. The Engineers also had to take over the running of a 340-mile submarine cable link which was installed early in 1855 by the English Electric Telegraph Company from Balaclava to the front. Just one more complica-tion of the logistic process, along with provision of the gutta-percha insulated cable which soon was ruined by soldiers who found the insulation made useful smoking pipes.

It is a tribute to those who struggled against the sloth of the past that the British Army was able to resume offensive operations in the summer of 1855, after a truly terrible winter of deprivation, and eventually, with the French, capture Sevasto-pol. It is still more interesting to record that, by 1856, British logistic support was far better than that of their ally. National competition may have had something to do with it, along with a logical French assessment that the whole war was a great mistake. But at least, from that day forward despite numerous backslidings, the care of the soldier in most armies of sensitively democratic nations was placed on a higher plane of consideration than ever before.

Yet although the logistic legacy of the Crimea was never to be lost, the immediate aftermath demonstrated how incorrigible were governments in putting short term economy before long-term prudence. Of course it can be argued that, in 1856, the outbreak of the great Indian Mutiny in 1857 or the war between France and Austria in 1859 could not be foreseen. But it was patently ridiculous, for example, for the British Government to abolish the Land Transport Corps (which had at one time comprised 14,000 men and 28,000 beasts) in 1857 and cosmetically to rename it the Military Train, with an ability to supply only a single division of the British Army. A direct consequence of this ploy was that when large-scale help had to be sent to rescue the East India Company from its dire predicament (much of which could be ascribed to poor administration and its treatment of the native soldiers), there occurred another desperate hunt for the qualified logisticians who had been dispersed so recently. Nor was the new Military Train really up to its task. Sir John Fortescue commented upon a remark that the officers were too much suited to the combatant branches of the Army: 'Being military it looked down upon the Commissariat, which was civil, and being mounted, it gave itself the airs and graces of the cavalry.' Indeed, on one occasion the Train did charge enemy batteries with distinction!

As for the French and Austrians, it was their opportunity in Piedmont to discover that although the railway could deliver masses of men and materials speedily to the battle front, that was far from the end of the matter. For one thing control of dense railway traffic along what amounted to a single artery was much more complex than with river transport. Sidings were needed to sort and shunt trains at their destination. And the destination of a train did not always coincide with a point at which bulk loads could be transferred to waggons even supposing sufficient labour was available for handling. All too easily, full rail waggons either stood where they awaited labour to unload them; or they had to be unloaded and their contents left to be spoiled or looted because the road waggons had not arrived. Sometimes, rail schedules were thrown out of gear when cut by the enemy — the only saving grace being the discovery that, as yet, it was easy to repair such breaks when the enemy neglected to do the job thoroughly.

Since large numbers of men could now be transported quite close to the front at such great battles, such as Magenta and Solferino, the system also offered up more men to wholesale slaughter by rapid fire weapons. It mattered not in the eyes of humanitarians who had won or lost each battle. The neglect of the wounded again aroused great indignation, yet instigated another series of reforms which, in the future, would bear heavily upon logistics. Out of the aftermath of the bloody Battle of Solferino, where 40,000 casualties out of 320,000 men present were incurred, came the movement under Henri Dunant which eventually saw the formation of the Red Cross Society and the Convention of Geneva. After 1864, there appeared a gradual acceptance by an increasing number of powers that they had to perform specific duties in the treatment of wounded and prisoners — along with many diplomatic and administrative complications previously quite uncatered for.

The time was approaching when the number of men dedicated to logistic support would far out-number those in the firing line.

Chapter 3

Railways: A New Strategic Factor

IN THE midst of two decades of frequent large wars a chain reaction of logistic development linked to technical progress was irresistible and with strategic repercussions too. In the aftermath of the Crimean War, for example, as navies rapidly abandoned sail in favour of steam, those with empires, such as Britain and France, had to take account of the fact that it was no longer possible completely to provision (except for water) a ship for a round the world voyage lasting a year or more, as once had been the case. The need to refuel and therefore to establish coal stocks at previously out of the way places was one aspect of the new order, and all the more so since coal took up so much of the space aboard a ship which previously was filled by stores and ammunition. Conversion to the new arrangements was delayed by a need to retain sail to some extent for economic reasons, but by the end of the century it was complete. By then, islands such as the Falklands and several in mid-Pacific, besides mainland ports, had assumed a vital strategic and logistic importance.

The American Civil War: Sherman's Touch of Genius

On land it was the railway which, both strategically and logistically, began to displace waterways as the dominant transport artery. Everywhere it was commercial interests which impelled the construction of the latest fast transport systems and the telegraph networks which were so vital to efficient railway operation and, more often than not, followed their tracks. Wise military leaders took note, encouraged those projects which were to their advantage, and recognised the need to adopt them in war, along with recruitment of the civilian operators required. Yet when the American Civil War broke out in 1861, neither side fully understood the impact of the latest communications technology.

Although the war's coming had long been foreseen, it was by no means clear, until after the first shots had been fired, how the states would divide. That was hardly conducive to accurate planning — and all the more so because both sides tended to think the war would be a short-lived limited affair, 'over by Christmas'. Neither was on a war footing. The entire United States Army before the split was a mere 17,000 strong and the Navy, with only 90 sailing ships, each capable of manning only 40. Weapons and war material, reserve stocks and supplies in general fell short of the requirements of a Federal army initially planned at 140,000 and soon greatly expanded. The Confederates aiming at 170,000 were no better off, although their Army's further expansion would later be curbed by manpower shortages, despite the extensive use of slaves to dig numerous fortifications. Those who became sick or wounded also faced a bleak future. Urgent requests were being made to Florence Nightingale for help in organising hospitals and in creating a Federal medical service which hardly existed. To Dorothea Dix, who became the Federal Superintendent of Army Nurses, (and once said 'All nurses are required to be plain-looking women') she sent full information about her records and proposals. Meanwhile, in the South, similar measures were put in hand, though not with Miss Nightingale's collaboration it seems.

Looming over every activity was the naval blockade which bore down heavily upon the Confederates because, although many sailors had joined their ranks, they had no warships to begin with. Thus General Winfield Scott's blockade strategy, imposed by the Federals on the eve of war, was not only logistically a strong weapon, it was one which the Confederates had no hope of defeating. The best they could manage, as very well they did in the first two years, was evasive blockade running by fast ships, and a limited series of pin-prick attacks by commerce raiders against enemy shipping.

From start to finish the American Civil War was a logistically controlled struggle of the sort ingrained in the people after two hundred years pioneering in the wilderness. Like the indigenous Indians, the settlers knew that survival in mobility depended upon ensuring food supplies and on reliable transport. Instinctively experienced travellers and fighting men carried with them enough to live upon in sparsely populated or undeveloped country. They always went armed. But neither transport nor weapons were in sufficient supply for a big war in 1861. Needing 100,000 rifles a year for replacements alone, the Confederates had only 200,000 at the start and were entirely dependent on imports because they lacked sufficient manufacturing capacity. The Federals were little better off in terms of stocks but possessed far larger manufacturing potential. Therefore, at the start, there was little difference in strength between opponents who expanded as best they could and paid full attention to transport requirements.

Only after 1862 did the Federal blockade impose a telling effect — that is after the vital port of New Orleans had been seized in April and the Confederate hold upon the Mississippi River was loosened by concentric Federal advances on Vicksburg from north and south. Even so this implementation of Winfield Scott's master

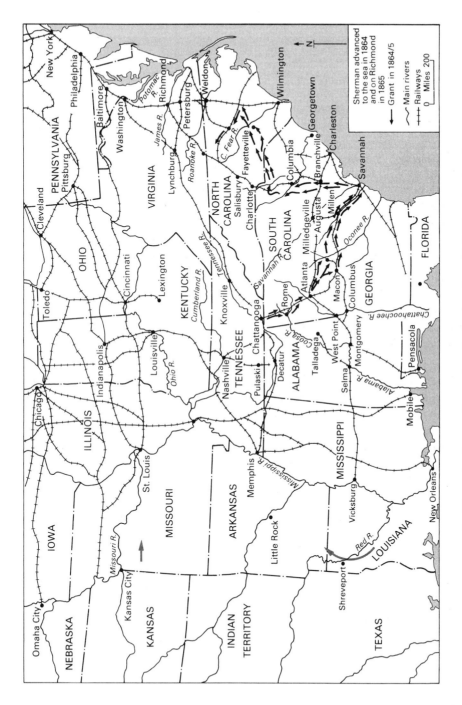

MAP 3.   The main theatre of operations in the American Civil War, showing the principal rail and water communications open to interdiction

plan was incomplete so long as the ports of Mobile, Charleston and Wilmington remained open. For it was from there that blockade runners maintained a regular traffic, exporting what little cotton was allowed into Europe in face of a crippling embargo; importing the greater majority of cannon, arms and ammunition supplied to the Confederate Army, thus extending the war by many months if not at least a year.

A glance at the map of communications networks — densest to the east and north, much more attenuated to the east and south and thinning out to open space the farther west the eye moves — shows how the Federals held the whip hand. Only the railway lines had anything approaching high capacity and even they, for the most part, were single track. Roads and tracks, no matter how profuse in the east, were poorly founded and unreliable, particularly in bad weather. Rivers retained their old importance, chiefly the Mississippi which divided the eastern Confederacy from the west; and the Cumberland and Tennessee rivers, pointed like daggers at the Confederate heartland of Georgia and Alabama. By seizing the fortresses controlling these rivers, in addition to those on the north Mississippi when captured by General John Pope, General Ulysses Grant was able not only to tighten the blockade but also open up lines of communication which promised best to support a thrust into the enemy's vitals, via the key railway junction at Chattanooga. In this terrain, which was still largely primitive and off which it was almost impossible for anything other than small parties to subsist, armies were channelled narrowly along rivers and railways. But both were controllable by fortifications and the latter were easily interrupted by demolitions. Few, too, were the bridges; so waterways were considerable tactical obstacles.

Histories of warfare tend to be written about battles. Those of the American Civil War seem to concentrate rather more on those fought in the approaches to Washington and Richmond than elsewhere. Yet politically important as these heavy attritional battles might have appeared because both capitals were threatened, they were nothing like as strategically critical as the smaller encounters in the West and at sea. Strategy, above all the negative defensive strategy adopted by the Confederacy at the will of the militarily trained President Jefferson Davis, was naturally all-important. For Davis, correctly appreciating that the Federals were too strong to be defeated by battle and hoping that war weariness would bring his opponent to terms, handed the initiative to the Federals — though, at the same time, obliging the militarily ignorant President Abraham Lincoln to aim at the total conquest of the Confederacy. Costly in men and material as this conquest would be, and close as Davis came to achieving his aim when the peace parties of the North shook public nerve in 1863 and 1864, the final result was put beyond doubt, perhaps as much as by anything else, because, except during the brief Confederate advance to defeat at Gettysburg in 1863, the North was spared the sight of war's horrors. And also because, at no time, were the Federal logistics under any sort of serious or prolonged threat, while those of their opponent were being steadily eroded or permanently eliminated.

The most the Confederate Army was ever to accomplish in attacks on lines of communication were isolated cavalry raids of limited duration and range. A few stores depots destroyed here, a few miles of railroad ripped up there along with bridges blown, were mere pin-pricks, easily replaced or repaired by efficient Federal engineers. The brilliant handling of cavalry units under command of such Generals as 'Jeb' Stuart, Nathan Forrest, John Morgan, Benjamin Grierson and Phillip Sheridan, much praised as they are for advancing scores of miles while living off the country and the enemy, achieved, in the final analysis, little more than diversions. Once when a Confederate General claimed that the extensive damage he had done to a length of Federal communications would take at least two weeks to repair, the work was completed by engineers so quickly that a train's whistle was heard as he was reporting.

Nor, for that matter, did the intensive battles of attrition which repeatedly ravaged the land between Washington and Richmond do more, logistically speaking, than hasten the wearing down of failing Confederate resources. Operating at relatively short range from main bases along shorter, reasonably well-developed lines of communication, neither army was in serious logistic difficulty here. It was very different in the West, however, once the Confederates had been pushed off the Mississippi and where the Federal Army, advancing through Tennessee into Georgia, had its main base in hostile territory at Nashville. Here its tenuous lines of communication were not only vulnerable to cavalry raids but also to sabotage from local Confederate sympathisers. Because of this, the most original, strategic-cum-logistic campaign of the war was contrived.

General William Sherman, whose task was to exploit the weakening of the Confederacy in the west after the fall of Vicksburg, was a regular soldier with experience of fighting in Mexico, and in civil administration in California. His concentration upon supply matters, with their elevation over strategic considerations, was therefore a natural product of practical experience. In compliance with General Grant's intention in 1864 to tackle the enemy on two principal fronts — by himself in Virginia and with Sherman's Army in a thrust through Georgia to the Atlantic Ocean — it was Sherman's task to exploit the defeat in 1863 of the Confederates at Chattanooga, by seizing the vital railway junction and manufacturing centre of Atlanta, as the first step in an advance to the sea. Out-numbering his opponent's army of 60,000 men, Sherman's main problem was the almost insoluble one of making and keeping open the railway link from Nashville to Atlanta via Chattanooga in order to maintain the momentum of his army of nearly 100,000 men. Beg, borrow and steal locomotives and rolling stock as his staff would from all over the Federal system; upset both friendly and hostile populaces as he would by denying them the use of the lines; and despite employing as much road transport as possible, there was always the chance of a supply shortfall made worse by rail accidents or enemy interdiction. The latter threat, moreover, posed difficulties out of proportion to the relatively few numbers of men committed by the enemy to raiding. As the Federal Army advanced, driving the Confederates from one stop line after another, the number of men who had to be detached to guard the 250 miles of track from Nashville to Atlanta far exceeded those lost in battle. So, when Atlanta fell on 2 September (after over a month's manoeuvre and counter-manoeuvre cutting across the railway lines radiating from the city), Sherman, whose strength had been unequal to a formal siege, stopped in order to rethink his next step. With his army reduced to 68,000, he now lacked the strength to accomplish the projected 300 mile advance to Savannah.

For one thing, it was calculated that the railway capacity would be as much a liability as an asset. And all the more so, he might have reflected, when the track and what rolling stock he captured was delapidated from lack of replacement and maintenance during almost four years of war and blockade. Also, the enemy's extremely bold movements under General John Hood had to be taken into account when, of a sudden, instead of positioning to confine Sherman's move to Atlanta, he began a series of manoeuvres aimed at the Federal lines of communications, moves allied to persistent attacks upon railway key points and the garrisons guarding them. It was a strategy well judged, all the more to embarrass Sherman logistically; and reasonably secure, too, since Hood was operating in friendly territory against a much disliked enemy. But Sherman by now knew there were only small, light enemy forces to the east and that, go where Hood might to the north west, it should be possible to spare men enough to neutralise him and simultaneously to reach his own objective at Savannah — providing he solved his own logistic problems.

The genius of Sherman's plan was contained in a telegraphed signal to Grant on 9 October:

> 'I propose we break up the railroad from Chattanooga forward and that we strike with our waggons for . . . Savannah . . . it is useless for us to occupy [Georgia] but the utter destruction of its roads, houses and people, will cripple their resources. By attempting to hold the roads we will lose a thousand men a month . . . I can make this March and make Georgia howl! . . . We can find plenty of forage in the interior of the state.'

Even as Sherman was setting out on 15 November, Hood was thinning the opposition by setting forth with 40,000 men in the opposite direction, aiming a diversionary blow towards Nashville. By some sets of rules, this should have made Sherman turn back to catch him, Grant thought. But in these unusual circumstances Sherman reasoned that Hood's army was not up to the job — and he was right. With time enough to gather fresh, well supplied troops at Nashville, General George Thomas was able to contain Hood (who had logistic problems of his own when far from his base and adrift from a wrecked railway) and finally destroy him in battle at Nashville a week after Sherman reached the sea.

Sherman's raiding column of 62,000 men was stripped to the essentials. All sick, wounded, non-combatants and servants were shipped back by rail to Chattanooga before the track to that place was thoroughly destroyed by twisting the rails into knots over the heat of their burning sleepers. With 2,500 waggons, mostly containing 200 rounds per gun but also ten days food, and 600 ambulances he set forth with four corps in two wings at an average speed close to ten miles per day. His army's frontage was about 50 miles, usually marching along four roads adjacent to the railway, which for 160 miles of its length, he wrecked. Each corps was self-contained in waggons. Each man carried his pack, 40 cartridges and a few emergency rations. To make up the balance and, at the same time, rip out the enemy's heart, the army was told to 'forage liberally on the country' — but in a disciplined manner. That in many instances this was far from the case was inevitable. Unauthorised looting was widespread, atrocities by no means unheard of. Yet the veteran Army, on the whole, retained the discipline which Sherman insisted upon.

That discipline extended well beyond control of the men's behaviour. There was also strict traffic control discipline whereby the men marched off the road to leave room for the waggons and ambulances to move freely. Commendable care of the wounded was usually the case in this war, the lessons of recent European wars had been well learnt by a democratic nation which understood only too well the political penalties which might be paid if scandals were permitted in that sphere. Nurses trained in Florence Nightingale's methods were given proper opportunities to practise her methods, although treatment of prisoners of war was not always so enlightened. Most Generals concerned themselves with care of the wounded, Sherman's provision of 600 ambulances demonstrating his concern.

For the most part, too, his orders that '. . . each brigade commander will organise a good and sufficient foraging party . . . who will gather near the route travelled, corn or forage of any kind, meat of any kind, vegetables, corn-meal . . . to keep in the waggons at least ten days provisions . . . and three days' forage' were obeyed, although permission for the rest of each brigade to forage within sight of a halt, but not to enter buildings or to trespass, was not universally complied with. Likewise it cannot be said that the injunction that corps commanders only were permitted to authorise the destructions of 'mills, houses, cotton-gins etc' was upheld entirely. Vast destruction there was, whether or not provoked by hostile acts. Not only the 'hostile' rich but also the 'poor and industrious' forfeited their horses, mules and waggons.

A swathe was cut across Georgia as the 'bummers' of the foraging parties systematically put to the torch strategic materials and manufacturing premises and carried produce to roadside collecting points for the waggons. The barns were filled with corn which was now denied to the rest of the Confederacy. Threats by some Confederates to burn their own corn in order to deny it to Sherman came to little when it was pointed out that this was cutting off the nose to spite the face. Make the enemy howl, as intended, it was not Sherman's intention to create famine. In any case, hardly ever opposed on the march, he was soon within striking distance of Savannah where the Navy would at once establish his new base. And, indeed, as his leading troops came within sight of the mouth of the Ogeechee river on 13 December, a friendly steamer was spotted approaching.

Sherman's march had achieved surprise far more by means of logistic unortho-doxy than by strategic direction — vital as was the latter in striking a crippling blow at the Confederacy's political will, while the logistic blow wrecked the economy. It had never occurred to the Confederates that Sherman would detach himself from his main base so long as Hood was at large in his rear, or that he would make himself totally self-supporting for such a long advance. It is the first example of true strategic logistic surprise in the railway era and has been seen by some commentators as setting the example for future deep penetration exploits in motorised operations of the 20th century. The validity of these claims will be examined later. All that need be said here is that Sherman's advance to Savannah, and his subsequent northward sweep to Raleigh in April 1865, had very long-term effects which out-weighed even those of the Federal blockade with its deadly threat to the rear of General Lee's army where it held up Grant near Richmond. Sherman's march had pronounced social and economic consequences. By the severity of treatment dealt to the Southern States the already backward nature of their economy was further retarded for years to come, along with a creation of an animosity among the people which would last for generations.

Such is the fundamentally destructive nature of warfare waged on predominantly logistic lines, especially when directed against highly populated countries.

1870: A Faltering Success: Far Too Late by Rail

It is said that the Great Prussian General Staff was dismissive of the lessons to be learnt from the American Civil War when it came to their application to European campaigns. Tactically and technically this, if really true, would have been unwise and it is to be disputed that their observers on the spot throughout the war totally ignored evidence of the power of modern weapons and communication systems — patronising though they undoubtedly were then, and in wars to come, of American combat prowess. Arguably, however, they were correct to discount the strategic and logistic lessons from campaigns fought over vast, undeveloped distances, so very unlike most of Western and Central Europe. For by 1861 the whole of Europe, with the exception of its eastern provinces (notably Russia and the Balkans), was covered by the completed network of main railways which played so prominent a part in the evolution of German unification under Prussian dominance.

When King William I appointed a Mecklenburger, Helmuth von Moltke, to be Chief of Staff of the Prussian Army in 1857 he promoted a studious General with modern ideas, but without command experience. Yet he was one who, before a single railway was built in Germany, recognised (as many did not) their strategic and logistic importance. Partly in order to speed visits from Berlin to his bride in Holstein, he riskily invested money in the proposed Berlin to Hamburg line. Von Moltke envisaged the coming of the railway as a promised extension of Napoleonic strategic mobility. By moving massed, yet dispersed, armies, with their supplies at six times the speed of marching troops, he foresaw the possibility of achieving rapid, surprise concentrations on a chosen battlefield as well as the feasibility of maintaining long sieges or unbroken frontages of several hundred miles, even in the depths of winter. To facilitate this new logistic and strategic liberty, he allowed higher commanders considerable freedom of action, within the framework of a broad operational instruction. Meanwhile he co-ordinated affairs from the centre by telegraph *currently* to guide dispersed formations towards a rendezvous on the battlefield instead of *beforehand*, as Napoleon once practised.

It well suited von Moltke that, when planning the convergence of the Prussian armies into northern Bohemia from Saxony and Silesia in June 1866, he had at his disposal five routes as against the two available to his Austrian opponents marching up from Moravia. But it was to the Prussian disadvantage that, as the start of this so-called Seven Week War, they were misinformed of the Austrian movements. This made it all the more difficult to control a convergence of armies to the decisive place when reconnaissance units failed to indicate where that might be. As a result the Prussian Army commanders, misusing their freedom of initiative, approached the enemy in a rather erratic manner. Both sides began to suffer logistic difficulties as they moved on foot towards a meeting in the vicinity of the road and rail junctions of Sadowa and Königgrätz, neither having made extensive use of the railways since entering Bohemia. For though each army used the railways admirably to mobilise and move their forces towards the frontiers — von Moltke's deployment into Saxony and Silesia from the hinterland being notably impressive — neither was able to exploit them to deliver troops on the battlefield (as sometimes the French and the Americans had done in earlier wars). However, neither received much logistic benefit due to poor organisation.

When two confused opponents, of roughly equal numbers and in similar logistic trouble, collided at Königgrätz on 3 July, the ensuing struggle was decided more by chance and superior Prussian firepower than by any exhibition of deft tactical skill. And while the Prussian needle gun, with its far greater rapidity of fire, completely outclassed the unfortunate Austrians with their old-fashioned muzzle loader, the rate of ammunition expenditure was well below estimate — a mere seven rounds per man. Yet, driven from the field with 20,000 dead and wounded, plus 20,000 prisoners with their equipment, to add embarrassment to Prussian logistics (against 15,000 on the Prussian side), the Austrians were permitted to make a disorderly withdrawal without undue hindrance. For von Moltke's troops were stranded temporarily on the battlefield in disorder, their pursuit delayed by chaotic movement arrangements. As a result, there was no further major engagement while the Austrians retired on Vienna, where an armistice was arranged on 22 July.

For this state of affairs the Prussians had mainly themselves to blame. While still fairly close to the railheads, where they had detrained, the marching columns had subsisted well, supported by the Train Battalion of each Corps which von Moltke had been developing as regular units of a special logistic arm since 1856. Even

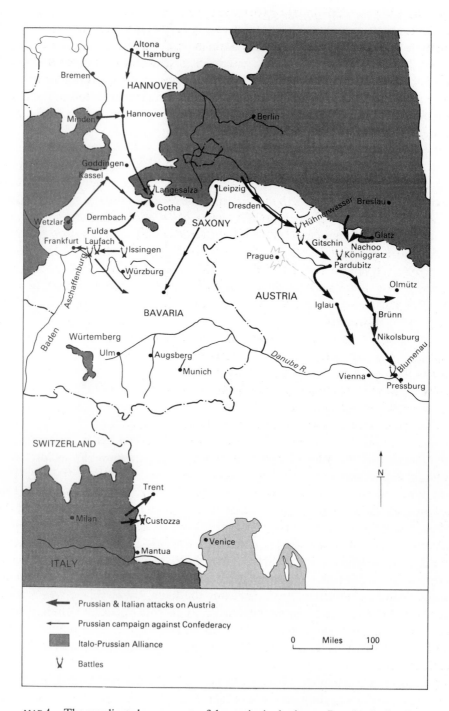

MAP 4. The coordinated movements of the armies in the Austro-Prussian-Italian War
of 1866

when these logistic battalions (to give them a modern name) failed to keep up along the choked roads leading to the battle, the troops still managed to subsist, to obtain remounts and receive the hospital treatment which these administrative units provided. Scavenging and local purchase made good deficiences in the traditional manner, ammunition supply was never a problem since adequate quantities were carried in limbers and on the men. But if von Moltke had studied closely Sherman's methods in the march to the sea in 1864, he might have done better after Königgrätz than he did.

At the heart of the trouble lay the inability of the three Railway Battalions, formed since 1859 by von Moltke, to carry out their task. Capable of carrying out minor repairs, they were ill-equipped rapidly to construct emergency loop lines or sidings. Nor could they smooth out recurrent difficulties with the civilian railway authorities, which, so far, had provided only 24 per cent of double track in the German network. Operational inflexibility ruled as 18,000 tons of supplies rotted in hundreds of waggons which, from lack of arrangements by the staff and insufficient labour to transfer their loads to the Train Battalions, stood idle. Enormous was the wastage as the advancing troops scavenged increasingly when the Train Battalions failed to deliver. For not only were those battalions unable to make contact with railheads, they were held up because the teeth arms claimed absolute priority on the roads — an anarchy condoned by von Moltke from the beginning because, instinctively, he conferred higher priority on the teeth arms than on the tail — to the extent that, when working out the mobilisation plan, totally insufficient space on the railways was allocated to supplies, with a resultant imbalance of delivery at the front.

At the root of the road congestion lay the traditional arrogance of combat troops — among whom the cavalry and Guards looked down on the Artillery and the Infantry and everybody looked down on the Engineers and the Train Battalions. In a free for all, formation and unit commanders who were among the first to inflate their own columns with unauthorised waggons, were also the first to push Train waggons off the roads and compound traffic indiscipline by blocking roads at the halt and hampering the field police when exercising their authority.

Another cause of failure was the inability of the railways to function beyond the frontier. Enemy rail cutting had something to do with it although this was easily overcome since the Austrians were anything but thorough in the work. Far more handicapping were fortified towns blocking the route. Until the war was over the main lines to Prague and Vienna remained closed to the Prussians — indicating to von Moltke that his celebrated remark, 'Build no more fortresses, build railways' had its contradictions. Yet, at the war's end, no matter how desperately short of supplies many units of the pursuing Prussian Army were, they remained in command of the situation. This was in part because the demoralised Austrians failed to recuperate as they fell back on their sources of manpower and supply but also because the Prussians held ample ammunition and, by sensible improvisation in the time-honoured fashion, just sufficient supplies with their columns to nourish marching men and animals — while medical services coped with what few casualties now came in.

Even so, as a slightly chastened von Moltke reflected when mulling over a campaign in which he had referred to 'our very difficult supply situation', something had to be done to impose logistic and traffic discipline. The under-developed railways had been disappointing. The habit of combat commanders behaving scornfully to lowlier administrative mortals, to their own detriment, had to be curbed before the newly formed North German Confederation went to war again, — as predictably it would within the next few years, as France waxed belligerent in dread of Prussian dominance.

★   ★   ★   ★   ★

With but few reservations, it may be said that France's defeat by the Prussian-led North German Federation in 1870 was as much as the result of experience gained by Prussia in the previous decade as it was the product of logistic chaos in France. Strategy and tactics, along with the martial enthusiasm of both sides, came into it of course — but logistics dominated planning and execution. Even so, anomalies and contradictions abounded in the prewar concepts of each side. For while von Moltke believed that enhanced strategic mobility conferred an advantage on the defensive, and also conceded that the French railways system (some 60 per cent of which was double track) was superior to the German one, he nevertheless felt constrained to attack France instead of standing on the defensive and waiting for the French to oblige. Which, until the last moment, the French had no intention of doing, preferring themselves to await the correctly anticipated German thrusts from the Prussian Rhenish Province, the Palatinate or Baden. But while it was contributory to French discomfiture that, a bare two months before the outbreak of war, Napoleon III acceded to Austrian wishes by consenting to an offensive into Baden based on Strasbourg, the real causes of French weakness were administrative rather than a sequence of orders and counter-orders leading to disorder.

In the realisation by 1866 that Prussia must inevitably soon challenge them to a battle, the French had been reorganising and rearming their army. Predominantly, and with ammunition expenditure as well as tactical implications in mind, they chose to increase their fire-power by the adoption of a new *chassepot* rifle (which was superior to the Prussian needle gun) and the multi-barrelled *mitrailleuse* machine-gun (a mere 194 of them), but did so to the neglect of their artillery. In so doing they overlooked the devastating power of bursting shells which were far more destructive of material and enemy morale than a rain of bullets which might scythe the air almost unnoticed. Yet although the French made this notorious, psychological misjudgement (and thus cast a doubt, which lasted several decades, upon the battlefield effectiveness of machine-guns in general) it was as nothing to the disastrous consequences of their muddled mobilisation plans with closely related logistic ramifications.

Quite unlike the Germans, whose mobilisation scheme will be described later, the French chose to implement the final stage of mobilisation in war deployment areas. Recalled reservists would find their way via depots, to their units which, when possible, were located adjacent to the Army Corps to which they belonged. There, if all went well (which it rarely did) they would marry up with weapons and supplies and be put through refresher training. Also, if all went well, the process would take only two weeks (one week quicker than the Prussians), thus stealing a considerable march on the enemy. But to accomplish this General Edmond Leboeuf, the Minister of War ordered mobilisation to take place in one single phase. Thus, when the order to mobilise was given on the 14 July, everybody began rushing at once in every direction with an inevitable choking of the transport systems which were totally inadequate to cope with so much traffic at once. For weeks on end, chaos reigned supreme throughout France while men, horses, vehicles and supplies criss-crossed from one place to another, each searching for its proper place in the order of battle. Wildly enthusiastic civilians who cheered men supposedly on their way to the front (and occasionally removed items of equipment as souvenirs) may not have known that some, for example, would be shipped from Marseilles to their regimental depot at Oran before being shipped back to join their corps in Alsace.

Several never reached their destination at all, so long did their wanderings last. Units which had never met before were assembled in formations without the slightest chance of devising collaborative plans. Most damaging of all, it was the vital technical arms and services which suffered worst. Out of 3,000 artillery pieces available, less than 1,000 could be taken into action (against some 11,000 Prussian) because insufficient associated equipment and trained gunners had been allocated to the task. Almost as bad, the *Intendance* was unable to feed, clothe and arm the men as they reported. And without a hope of rectification, for the clearing of stores from railway trucks, was as inefficient as it had been in Piedmont in 1859 and in the more recent Prussian campaigns. Once more, loaded waggons stood idle in sidings and the system began to grind to a halt. For one thing nobody had yet thoroughly tackled the problems of integrating the old system of bulk-broken supply by road in slow, horse-drawn vehicles with the rapid bulk transport of railways which could only deliver to a few carefully chosen and prepared marshalling yards. For another, the French transport columns, deprived of the majority of their men, horses and waggons, were little more than improvised ghosts of what the *Intendance* intended.

Strange to relate the logistic arrangements of the Germans were only slightly better. For while the phased call up, embodiment and despatch of fully equipped troops from the hinterland to the Rhine went forward with clockwork precision, reception arrangements in the concentration areas left much to be desired. Benefitting from the dress rehearsal of full mobilisation during the 1859 Piedmont crisis, and the full dress war performances of 1864 in Schleswig-Holstein and of 1866 (plus several peacetime exercises, the practical like of which the French never emulated, after 1859) it was to be expected that movement and supply, carefully planned and watched over by von Moltke's chosen experts of the Quartermaster

General's Department and the *Intendance*, would have everything in hand. Not a bit of it! Once again, the combat arms received or grabbed what they could, often landing themselves in concentration areas without logistic units (which had been deliberately left behind) and running short of food. Once again the railways were over-burdened and, due to labour shortages, waggons became trapped in sidings with a back-log of traffic piling backwards into Germany. Fortunate it was that all this took place on German soil where improvisations and local purchase could make good deficiencies — but it was nothing to be proud of.

And all the more to be deprecated because the latest logistic organisation, as further developed by von Moltke since 1866, was much improved. Each field Army had acquired considerable numbers of horse-drawn waggons through impressment. These could transfer stores to the Corps Train Battalions, which had been greatly expanded from the original 292 officers and men to consist of 40 officers, 84 doctors, 1,540 men, 3,074 horses and 670 waggons. With local labour or men from combat units added, an ample service capable not only of organising and transferring stores from railway trucks to horse-drawn waggons, but also, if given the opportunity and space on the roads, of lifting many of those supplies to the combat troops' supply echelons in divisions and units. Yet, although a steady flow of supplies was envisaged, it only happened sporadically because effective control was not imposed and the combat units, far from being prepared to assist with menial tasks, snobbishly rode as roughshod as ever over the waggon trains. Only the hospitals seem to have been accorded reasonable treatment — and for the quite obvious reasons of educated self-interest by individuals. Medical treatment cannot be scavenged.

In point of fact, and as almost invariably is the case prior to war, both armies were reduced to improvisations before the first shot was fired by the French as they advanced on Saarbrücken on 31 July. The principal differences lay in the comparative measure of each side's improvisations and that, within four days, the French began a prolonged retreat which would strain resources in a dissimilar way to those of the advancing Prussians. For although the French were embarked on one of the most ignominious debacles of their history, they were at least withdrawing into friendly territory where supplies could be obtained willingly when, as was often the case, the *Intendance* failed to deliver. Whereas the Prussian combat units, moving ever deeper into a hostile land and daily becoming further detached from their railheads and the Train Battalions, were at once, in varying degree, logistically embarrassed. Though never starving nor short of ammunition.

It was to the greatest benefit of von Moltke that Napoleon III gave battle close to the frontiers — as politically, if not militarily speaking, he had to do. Nearly all the August battles, in which the French were ground down and pushed back, took place within 40 miles of the frontier and some railheads. Admittedly the advancing German troops at once began to draw ahead of their corps and divisional supply columns, while the French fell back upon depots and the fortress city of Metz. Yet the Prussians were much better off than their enemy, for while they could scavenge whatever food they were short of from a well-stocked countryside, the French were to discover that neither Metz nor the other principal fortresses were properly stocked. Like so much else, that matter had been left too late, due to inefficiency and because not only the military but also the commercial distribution of supplies had been stopped because of the disruption to mobilisation and the clogging of railways and roads. An anarchy, so familiar in many campaigns of the past, began to corrode the French Army long before it entered action. Popular enthusiasm for the war soon evaporated, due to the accumulated ailments of defective mobilisation. Disgruntled men, wrenched away from their homes to an uncertain future, inevitably undermined discipline. Soldiers who, from the start, often came and went from their units as they chose, dressed in a slovenly way, cared little for their weapons and paid scant attention to their officers, and were among the first to pillage when food was not readily available.

The series of defeats inflicted on the French from Weissenburg on 4 August to Mars-la-Tour/Vionville on the 16th, which were instrumental in forcing the defeated Marshal François Bazaine to retire into a state of siege in Metz, merely accelerated the demoralisation induced by logistic collapse. Meanwhile, the Germans, buoyed up by a quite apparent overall superiority and with no serious supply problems, now conducted a war of movement which allowed them to live freely off the country even after they had long out-stripped the railways and the road supply columns. A notable relief in this connection was freedom from worry about ammunition supply in six battles up to and including Gravellote on 18 August. The infantry fired about the same quantity as in 1866. The artillery, which even at Mars-la-Tour fired its highest number of rounds (88 per gun) in any single engagement, was only ever temporarily short when its own indigenous waggons could not reach and replenish the batteries in the heat of battle. Apart from that, each corps, with holdings of 157 rounds per gun, came easily through a six months' campaign in which the average number of rounds per gun fired throughout the Army was only 199.

Fortunate this was for the Germans, whose railway was tediously slow in operating westwards. If there had been heavy demand for ammunition or if their armies had not captured quite substantial French military stocks, besides living off the country, things might have been serious indeed. As it was, despite many shortcomings, the German Army was able to advance without fear of logistic collapse to overwhelm Marshal MacMahon's Army at Sedan on 3 September (with the capture of 83,000 men and 449 guns, plus Napoleon III) and could begin a pursuit to Paris in the confident belief that neither operational nor logistic problems would intervene. The reasons for the political and strategic difficulties which then arose to delay the quick imposition of peace are outside this book's scope, but the logistic events are of immense importance in the context of campaigns to come. For while it was demonstrated that large bodies of troops advancing into rich country were as capable as ever of feeding themselves so long as they kept moving, it was also shown how ineffectual were the railways — even

29

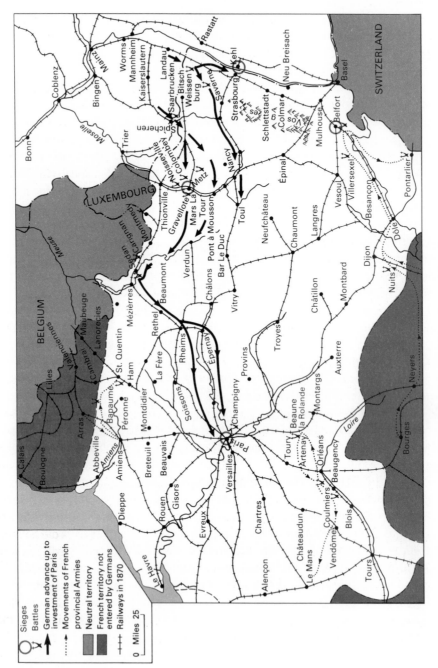

MAP 5.   The Franco-Prussian War of 1870. The advance to Paris

though von Moltke had done so much to provide for repair and operation deep into enemy territory.

Certainly von Moltke's concept of prolonged siege operations guaranteed by the railways was proved correct. Sieges at Metz, Belfort, Strasbourg, Verdun and, in due course, Paris were sustained with relative ease — even though rail deliveries to Metz did not begin until 15 September. Yet the Army which reached Paris on foot on 19 September was taking a nicely calculated logistic risk, though safe in the knowledge that the French were in utter disarray. The real problems came later, with the onset of winter and the distressing inability of the single railway line to be extended to within 15 miles of Paris until December, linked to quite irrational (in some German minds) French unwillingness to surrender. For by then, as the citizens of Paris held out, though quite unprepared for siege and living under dreadful privations as they were, the Germans were compelled to employ a high percentage of combat manpower in the good old-fashioned task of finding and garnering food while reserve stocks were laboriously built up. Thus it was that nothing like a sustained 'Political' bombardment of Paris could begin until 5 January, the heavy guns and their shells having been so long in arriving. Which raises the question of what went wrong, when one recalls how, in the war's aftermath, von Moltke spread the myth of the wonderfully decisive railways.

On his part, no doubt, this was a cover-up. He had backed railways in order to enhance strategic possibilities and simultaneously to solve the logistic problem. His candidate had not come up to scratch in the logistic field and his reputation was at stake under criticism of Chancellor von Bismarck and War Minister von Room, who rightly blamed him for lack of foresight and inability to impose disciplined movements. So severe were shortages of rolling stock and locomotives at home that the civilians were complaining bitterly about curtailed services (which were raising prices and affecting standards of living). At one time, indeed, the cavalry in France had been tasked to go hunting for enemy waggons. But the German railway organisation in not only failing to control movement at home, was equally incompetent in adapting French railways and their communication systems. Initially delays were the result of demolitions of track, bridges and rolling stock, mostly by the French but also sometimes by over-enthusiastic German cavalry raiders whose broad instruction to hamper the enemy communications did not take account of later German requirements. Nor could the German Railway Battalions cope sufficiently with their task. Much praise was accorded to them by von Moltke for rapidly building a pre-planned by-pass line round besieged and starving Metz — but he was merely taking credit for his own foresight. Far less credit was their due for being the cause of a rash of accidents when their hasty repairs failed to stand up to working conditions. Of course there were also numerous interruptions of the lines by the quite unexpected outbreak of guerrilla warfare behind the German lines, but the effect of this almost spontaneous uprising was far less effective in its reduction of supplies than in the manner in which it over-stretched the German Army. For von Moltke now discovered what Sherman could have told him, that guarding several hundreds of miles of track and road against wholesale destruction consumes armies. Von Moltke never admitted it, but he may well have reflected upon how much easier it was, in some ways, to maintain smaller forces in the old way instead of finding himself irrevocably committed to feeding vast hordes by an inflexible and vulnerable linear system.

Be that as it may, fortresses would continue to be built while railways were fitted into their proper role as just another tool in the logisticians hands — one which, within two decades, would have a rival — the internal combustion engine vehicle.

Chapter 4

The Impact of
Emerging Technology

THE WARS of the 1850s and 1860s, which had boosted a flourishing technological dynamism, innately stimulated war-making techniques at a pace in excess of anything before. Surprisingly the response of logisticians to the prospects of immense improvements to supply, transport and communications had not been as impressive as the welcome by strategists and tacticians to the latest weapons and signal communication systems. But that has often been a stumbling block of communication in the teeth versus tail contest, how to change attitudes and marry revised techniques to new technology.

Resistance to Change

Some new technology, such as rapid fire weapons, achieved high notoriety because of their noise and dramatic impact. But as often as not, the most important advances were achieved quietly and almost imperceptibly: as, for instance, in the vital matter of food preservation to simplify supply in the field by making it possible to hold large reserve stocks without undue concern about rapid deterioration. For many generations, of course, spicing, smoking, drying and salting had helped delay spoilage at a price in palatability. It took a French *Intendant* initiative in 1795, with a prize of 12,000 francs, to inspire new radical research, although it would not be until 1809 that Nicolas Appert, a Parisian confectioner, would devise a bottling process of heat-sterilised preserved food. Without Appert or anybody else understanding how his methods worked organically, manufacture was begun, notably in France and Britain, and with particular benefit to navies. By 1814, bottled foods were being issued to ships of the Royal Navy and in 1825 were taken in HMS *Erebus* on a polar expedition. In 1839 Peter Durand, an Englishman, found a way of using tin-plate canisters instead of heavier, bulky and fragile bottles.

Nevertheless, it was not until the culmination of Louis Pasteur's brilliant research into fermentation in 1864 which showed how scientific control had to be applied, that the long-term storage of canned foodstuffs became safe. At last logisticians could begin to calculate much more accurately the quantities of supply needed by any stated number of men, without resort to guesswork over wastage or the need to rely upon uncertain provision of locally acquired fresh rations. Until then there had been an unacceptable unreliability due to scientifically inexplicable instances of putrefaction and food poisoning, caused by inadvertent contamination or sheer negligence in factory processing. Henceforward, not only navies and armies but also mankind would benefit as scientists, spurred on by food manufacturers and retailers, developed 'pasteurisation' for all manner of products. Furthermore, refrigeration, which had come into use during the 1850s, entered general commercial practice at sea in the 1870s, thus disposing of the need to take on board farmyards to supply passengers on long sea voyages with more attractive menus. Simultaneously, during the American Civil War, notable advances in dehydration made possible the issue of 'dried' eggs, fish and vegetables as a basis for better stews for the Federal Army.

The easier handling of preserved foods enormously simplified storage and movement at a time when transport systems were on the verge of yet another revolution in the wake of the railway one. It was so much easier to carry preserved foods in vehicles and, if necessary, dump them in forward depots rather than drove and feed herds and flocks. At the same time, the utility of old transport systems was being amplified as railway networks spread outwards from western and central Europe into Russia (the trans-Siberian railway would be completed via a detour round Lake Baikal, in 1904); across the United States by 1869; and at a much slower rate, due to capital shortage, in the under-developed parts of Africa, Asia and South America.

In parallel, and essentially so as to keep up with fundamental developments in all spheres of technology, the emergence of duplex telegraph systems, with their traffic capacity vastly increased by the Wheatstone system of mechanically-driven perforated tape transmissions, were being incorporated in the growth of a world-wide communications network. The invention of the 'repeater' (to boost signal strengths along a cable route) and the laying of the first successful trans-Atlantic cable in 1866, were merely milestones in an accelerating march of communications progress which were vital to transport control, among other things. For example, the development of economic tramp shipping was only initiated because shippers were provided with a way rapidly to locate cargoes and send ships to ports of loading.

Communication systems, be they the more rapid transit of printed paper through faster rail and maritime links, or by the even quicker sending of messages by telegraph, all sharpened the spur in the exchange of intelligence between users, manufacturers and inventors. For example, no sooner had the telegraph taken root as part of everyday life in every civilised country, than work had started on the telephone to enable people to speak directly one to another. All this when printing techniques were in revolution after the introduction, in 1866, of mass-production rotary presses and, in 1874, of the first practical typewriter — just two years ahead of the invention of a practical telephone by Alexander Bell.

At this quite early stage in the latter 19th century technical explosion, a natural resistance to change can be detected. It reflected an inertia related to man's increasing difficulty in assimilating the potential of one new invention before it was superseded by something apparently better. For example, the capital expenditure of laying cable once telegraph was accepted, was a deterrent to immediate development of the telephone on a large scale. Not until 1885 would the telephone be used by German Gunners to direct artillery fire; and for several decades it was commonplace for British Army staff officers to avoid speaking on the telephone, that infra dig duty being delegated to lowly signalmen — thus forfeiting the telephone's advantage as a means of personal contact between executives.[1] In essence, although military officers of many nations were quite quick to see the strategic and tactical advantages of the latest communication systems, they were far slower to incorporate them into command, control and staff activity — with as much loss of benefit to the logistic services, which had dire need of such facilities, as to the tactical handling of combat units. Lacking the spur of profit, the military community tended to lag behind their commercial counterparts in calling for extensive telephone links to improve the efficiency and flexibility of their operations.

As a general rule, however, it was the highly capitalised nations which generated the infrastructure required by logistically well-supported armed forces. Thus, to a greater extent than before, the division widened between those nations which were capable of waging highly sophisticated war and those which, at best were cast in the Middle Ages and, at worst, with the Bronze or Stone Age. The European and North American nations achieved a quite overwhelming martial superiority over the rest of the world, because of their ability to make dominant weapons along with being able to move and supply powerful, yet relatively small forces to most parts of the accessible world and here impose their presence by force.

Tribal Wars of the 1870s

The significance of this gap was all too apparent when, for example, small forces armed with rapid firearms met North American Indian or African tribes. It took a monstrous tactical error on the part of Colonel George Custer in 1876 to give the Indians a chance to massacre his meagre but well-trained and better armed cavalry column at the Little Big Horn. And for similar reasons, in 1879, when 1,300 out of 1,800 well-armed British soldiers, under Lord Chelmsford, were routed by 20,000 Zulus at Isandhlwana when caught in the open, with insecure flanks, after reconnaissance had failed to discover the true enemy threat. Nevertheless, at Isandhlwana it was a local logistical failure in ammunition supply, (not a problem for Custer at the Little Big Horn), which contributed substantially to the

Zulu victory. For while there is no clear authentication of the theory that screwed down ammunition boxes could not be opened in time when the Zulus pounced, it is all too apparent that the British ran out of bullets because quartermasters either refused to supply men from other units, because they judged their own soldiers had a greater need ('the infantry have a greater need than you,' one cavalry unit was told) or simply because loyalty to their own unit was pre-eminent. ('Go and get it from your own people' went one fatal rebuff.) With soldiers reduced to searching dead comrades for live cartridges, the crackle of rifle fire was reduced to a splutter and then silenced as the enemy charged to the slaughter with their assegais.

But Isandhlwana suggested logistic lessons of a more fundamental kind than those of simple human culpability. Notwithstanding that 1,800 British with about 50 cartridges apiece had killed some 3,000 Zulu, there were clear indications that the latest, breech loading weapons were blasting off far more ammunition to smaller effect than once had been normal from slower loading muzzle loading weapons. Not only did each rifleman's aim deteriorate at the longer ranges of engagement, his chances of a hit were further reduced against dispersed, faster moving targets than had been the case against the slowly shifting, old massed formations (themselves adopted to maximise disciplined fire effect). Yet the lesson that for the latest weapons, scales of reserve ammunition might have to be increased compared with those of the wars of the 1860s, was slow to be assimilated — despite the incentive to learn thrust home by implication after the invention by Alfred Nobel in 1885 of the more powerful and tactically significant smokeless powder, and the invention in that same year of the automatic belt-fed machine gun by Hiram Maxim. The fact is that nobody detected the underlying tactical and logistic importance of these developments because it was not the habit of industry or the military to engage in profound scientific analysis of the effects of new developments once an inventor had disclosed them for sale; operational research was an investigative activity as yet unthought of. It was a period in which the rate of technical progress was fated to catch armed forces unready for any future campaign to which they were introduced for the first time.

The Spanish-American War of 1898

The American Army which, to its surprise, found itself pitch-forked by popular demand and political miscalculation at short notice into war against Spain in 1898, was in no way fit for a big amphibious invasion and war on land in Cuba and the Philippines. So it was fortunate for them, as well as the Government, that the Navy was sufficiently ready to outclass a Spanish Navy which was also unprepared for a major confrontation. From the Army's point of view, however, it was a demonstration of a quite remarkable ability to organise adequate logistic support within an astonishingly short time which was impressive — a talent for improvisation by the USA which certain European and Asian nations, many decades later, should have recalled. For though, within a week of the American Declaration of War on 25 April, the Spanish naval squadron in Manila Bay had been destroyed and within a month the Spanish Atlantic squadron was bottled up in Santiago in Cuba, the Army looked to its political prestige as well as the need, with an available force of 28,000 men, rapidly expanded to 60,000, to win a victory on land in Cuba. This it achieved by mid-August, despite crippling losses from beriberi, malaria and yellow fever.

Studies of the political and logistic precautions of the United States Army in its campaign against Cuba make fascinating reading indeed. Post-war reports from the various departments indicate shortfalls in the provision of many essential combat items, with remedial over-insurance measured against the risks of damaging political possibilities. For example, while there was a great shortage of all weapons for the field armies, which were assured of combat in the planned invasion of Cuba, immense effort was expended upon the design and construction of complicated coastal fortresses against the possibility of attacks upon United States soil — a danger which had diminished almost to vanishing point once the Spanish Atlantic squadron had been penned in Santiago. The attention given to these unnecessary works might well have been better employed remedying the deficiencies in weapon and ammunition supply by stepping up manufacture and the production of smokeless powder, an absence of which prompted the purchase of such improvised ingredients as cocoa.

Under political, as well as humanitarian and morale-building, pressures, praiseworthy energy was thrown into the establishment of medical services by the creation of several hospitals and the purchase and fitting out of two hospital ships. Nothing was to be left to the chance of a single sailor or soldier not receiving the best possible treatment. Doctors were recruited from all over the place and no less than 1,700 nurses engaged on contract — rather more than the number of Americans eventually killed or wounded in battle. Unhappily many, less emotive, yet vital, items were somewhat overlooked. When the troops landed in Cuba only two ambulances were at first put ashore; and as time went by not only was it found that the ambulances were too heavy but there was a lack of mules to draw them and a worsening shortage of drivers due to disease.

Disease, indeed, was the greatest menace, inflicting far more casualties than battle. Dysentery, a fairly common complaint in battle zones where hygenic standards fall off, was rife. It weakened the resistance of those who contracted the most serious and, arguably, avoidable pestilences — malaria and yellow fever — the likelihood of which in the beachhead areas was suspected. Their contraction therefore was a distinct calculable risk (though little prior calculation seems to have been done) and no attempt made to mitigate the consequences. Malaria, in fact flourished in that part of Cuba but a complete antidote unknown; though in the event, with the aid of the dubious suppressives of the day, was contained within limits. The presence of yellow fever, on the other hand, was not only known but also the fact of its carriage by mosquitoes, of which there were swarms in and around Daiquiri where the first, unopposed landing was made at the end of June. There is no evidence to indicate whether the operational plan took account of the relative merits of landing against enemy opposition in less infected areas or chancing medical casualties instead. Be that as it may, the losses from the killer diseases were catastrophic; sufficient, within a few weeks, to oblige a strategically premature withdrawal of the Army from Santiago in the immediate aftermath of the Spanish surrender on 17 July. Indeed it is almost certainly the case that if the Spanish commander, whose garrison's health was in reasonable shape, had been aware of the rapid disintegration of his besiegers, he might confidently have held on and, perhaps, won a victory which was beyond the capability of his force in battle. As it was the American decision to withdraw, simultaneously with shipping out the Spanish prisoners, was an entirely logistic one; quite unavoidable, and yet also politically as well as morally controversial. For there was much heart-searching as to where to send and isolate the infected army in the United States in trepidation of communicating the disease to the population in general. Eventually a secluded spot on Long Island, whence they could be shipped direct, was chosen.

These things apart, the extent and energy of the American assembly of improvised administrative resources compels admiration. Within a few weeks, no less than 48 ships had been chartered or purchased by the Army Department's Transportation Service and, in many instances, retained after the war. Numerous camps, hospitals and depots were built or requisitioned throughout the country; and large quantities of men, animals and stores moved by rail and road to ports of embarkation, and thence to one or other of the theatres of war. In the four months duration of the war, the Quartermaster's Department recorded the transport of no less than 709,000 persons, 60,000 animals and 1,529,580 tons of stores. Of people, 453,432 travelled by rail and 92,836 by sea.

Perhaps the most dramatically significant statistics of all are those concerning the Signals Corps (which had achieved that permanent status in 1880, well in advance of such recognition in the British Army, for example). At the outbreak of war it comprised 10 officers and 50 specialists for a central role in a conflict in which, as officially noted, 'The existing organisation and skills of men was often inadequate to cope with so much modern equipment — artillery in particular'. Worst off among the technical arms, the Signal Corps, within four months, expanded twenty-fold, far more than any other corps. It is scarcely to be wondered that line communications broke down at the start because never, at any one place, were there more than two signallers. The officers therefore, were worked off their feet, not only in finding equipment and arranging connections through the multifarious civil companies to and within scores of widespread headquarters, depots and transport facilities, but also in scouring the Army and the civil populace for suitable technicians and administrators. Almost overnight, a number of ordinary regular soldiers found themselves undergoing crash courses in telephony and telegraphy while men from the communications industry and enthusiasts from ordinary walks of life volunteered as specialists. In a war which generated much more logistic action than combat, by far the higher proportion of the traffic handled by the Signals Corps was logistic — without which the improvised military machine, expanding helter-skelter at top speed, would have been in chaos. Moreover, the work of the Signals Corps (which guaranteed its future leadership in American technology) provided much that was to be useful in post-war times, including the charter of a ship to lay undersea cables in Cuban and Philippine waters.

Nothing, in fact, was more revolutionary in the conduct of this war than the imposed awareness of electricity upon the Navy and the Army. Both found themselves handling numerous electrical generators for searchlights and certain components of that latest of power-plants, the internal combustion engine. Not only the Signals Corps, with its telegraphs and telephones, lived by electricity, but also the Gunner's, Engineers, and Ordnance organisations which had to understand and maintain so much electrical equipment. It was they, therefore, who were among the first to discover that much that might have been satisfactory in civil use, was hopelessly unsuitable or unreliable when exposed to rough handling by semi-trained soldiers and technicians in the field.

Most appropriately, indeed, as the 19th century drew to an end, the style of warfare with which it had started almost disappeared at the same time as several innovations of the 1880s became of questionable value in the first decade of the 20th century. If technical progress had seemed fast between 1850 and 1880, its speed through invention and development in the ensuing 30 years was breakneck, with staggering effects on people as well as equipment. No longer could admirals, generals, staff officers and the rest sit back in cosy contemplation of a *status quo* in the military balance. Some vital weapons and equipment, along with ways of using them, were becoming obsolete almost upon introduction. To an unheard of extent, the pressure for change was being supplied by technical and logistic services in collusion with entrepreneurial inventors and industrialists. In a manner of speaking, the 'tail' was dictating irresistibly to the 'teeth', no matter how obdurately classically educated members of the ruling classes and the Operational staffs resisted ideas which, to them, were both obnoxious and beyond their conservative and often bigoted comprehension.

Significant Advances at the End of the 19th Century

How diverse, all embracing and vital these technical changes were may be judged from a resumé of major inventions with a military function since 1870. To begin with, and fundamental to most machines, stood metallurgy, with the manufacture of cheap mild steel by the Bessemer and Siemens processes at the core of vast demand for increased production. Expansion of steel works, as time went by, promoted new uses for this basic ferrous metal as well as encouraging research into alloys for higher performance tasks. As a result, demand rose for such metals as nickel, chromium, tungsten and manganese for steel alloys; and copper and silicon steels for its good conductivity in electrical devices.

Highlights of the application of the new metallurgy upon military equipment was in the construction of ships and fortifications. As the fabric of ships swung almost entirely away from wood to metal; as sail propulsion gave way to mechanisation; and as artillery became both heavier and semi-automatic, a wholesale revision of logistic as well as strategic and tactical considerations unavoidably took place. Dockyards and ships which, under the old regime, had been equipped mainly to store and work with timber, cloth and rope, had to convert to metals, steam engines and electric motors. Programmes to establish coaling bases at strategic locations became extended for every navy, be it for world-wide voyages or simply coastal defence. An almost complete reraining, as well as an expansion of the labour force, both ashore and afloat, had to be undertaken, causing much disruption and discontent when traditional practices had to give way to new methods. Moreover, no sooner had one new type of power plant been adopted and the men trained to accept and get the best out of it, than another began to take its place. When, by the 1890s, the marine compound steam-engine had been developed to a state of reasonably higher power and economy to meet the ambitious requirements of admirals, Sir Charles Parsons improved the output and economy of existing steam and water turbines to the point at which, in 1897, the 44-ton *Turbinia* was propelled through the water at 34 knots and demonstrated in trials such reliability that the old types of propulsion were made obsolete overnight.

Likewise, as naval guns mounted in armoured steel barbettes and turrets supplanted ancient broadside firing ships in the line of battle, land fortresses were fitted with similar turrets in place of the old, exposed battlement emplacements. Fortresses, like warships, were at a turning point in their way, though not in their functions of providing shelter for armies and supplies, while denying freedom of access to vital routes and ground for the enemy. The difference between the latest forts, pioneered by the Belgian General Henri Brialmont, and their predecessors, was in far stronger underground protection, provided by steel, masonry and earth. To which was added the immensely increased striking power of bigger and, in due course, semi-automatic weapons to restrain the enemy at a distance. Yet an admission of a fort's weakness was to be seen in the need to build far more than in the past, placing rings of them round vital centres instead of incorporating a single fort at the centre. A weakness inherent in the enormously increased cost of complexity, as well as numbers, when it became necessary to incorporate complicated communication systems for command and co-ordination. Small wonder that this additional drain upon military budgets, to the detriment of the other arms, produced vehement doubts about the cost effectiveness of a dubious form of immobile deterrent. Yet, among the protective items soon to be available for most static defensive positions, was one of extremely low cost and simplicity — the steel, barbed wire fence which originally had been produced for agricultural purposes in 1874.

The invention of the telephone in 1876 and its demonstration by the Germans as a link between a forward observer and gun positions as a way of directing fire, was but one way of harnessing the latest communications to multiply fire support and thereby increase ammunition expenditure, on the eve of the invention in the 1880s, of much more powerful explosives. Whereas, in past campaigns, the use of artillery had been restricted by the necessity for the gun-layer to see the target before opening fire (thus imposing economy of ammunition expenditure) it had now become possible to indulge in indirect fire against all manner of previously inaccessible targets. The guns could now engage over the hill, using an observer equipped with flags or, in due course, the telephone, to provide corrections on fall of shot. Far more ammunition than in the past could be expended on long-range counter battery engagements. Nevertheless, although the latest more powerful and better constructed artillery pieces had improved accuracy, their beaten zone was far too large to guarantee hits at the longer ranges — thus redoubling ammunition expenditure and upsetting once more previously assumed stock and production requirements. When the French Schneider 75mm gun came into service in the 1890s everything was thrown into the melting pot. For this field piece and others of its kind, with fixed, quick-fire ammunition and a sprung recoil system, could fire six rounds a minute. A startling upwards demand for ammunition and the transport to move it was so inevitable as to give the logisticians a violent nudge — of which few took sufficient notice.

The conundrums puzzling Army logisticians were simple, however, compared with those confronting their naval opposite numbers. The latter had to cope with even more complicated gunnery matters and acquire the latest communication systems for fitting into warships. These soon developed as a honeycomb of compartments demanding telephones to connect them to the Captain and his staff, while the latest gunnery methods associated with long-range shooting called for a host of expensive new instruments, including optical range finders. Yet, mechanically and logistically speaking, gunnery promised in the near future, to be in complexity and lethal pay-off, as nothing when compared with the gyroscopically guided torpedo, proved feasible by Robert Whitehead in 1864. To the moored mine, with its limited, static application in shallow waters, was added, for the far more deadly below waterline attack, a mobile weapon with immeasurable potential against all manner of targets in deep waters, launched from the latest surface and underwater craft which were showing their paces at the turn of the century. All at once the admirals were compelled to create entirely new classes of torpedo-carrying vessels — submarines and fast, turbine-driven torpedo boats — which would revolutionise tactics and demand an entirely new sort of logistic support. For to man the shore and seagoing bases needed by these small craft, a new class of depot ships, fitted with machine shops manned by technicians, would have to be built. And at considerable cost — possibly also to the detriment of traditional gunnery, when it was shown that battering a ship to pieces at long range, with hits difficult to obtain, was sometimes a dubiously economic way of winning a battle.

Logisticians tended to stand politely aside whenever the deities of the gunnery and torpedo worlds, along with the protagonists of battleships, cruisers, destroyers and submarines, squabbled over funds for their competing requirements. Whatever the outcome, there was more work for them to do and many more problems of maintenance and storage to solve. All they could offer was advice in trying to persuade the fighting men to adopt vessels and equipment which would get the priorities right and ease the logisticians' task. In some ways it was more important to all concerned that means of propulsion and of communication should be rationalised. It was desirable to be rid of coal fuel, that filthy material so laborious to handle and store, which begrimed every corner of a ship and threatened delicate machines and instruments whenever all hands turned to 'coal ship'. Nothing was more attractive, particularly to crew members, than the cleaner, thermally more efficient, more easily purified and bunkered oil fuel. Since 1859, when a first successful oil well had been drilled in Pennsylvania, it had gradually become available in volume. Yet it would take nothing less than a decision by the French Navy, as late as 1909, to abandon coal in favour of oil, to convince all others of the need; and intensive exploration by the oil producers to demonstrate that world stocks were considerably larger than previously envisaged.

This decision for oil, with its immediate transformation of strategic emphasis by the creation of vital oil bearing areas urgently demanding defence (as well as connection by land and sea to storage places) would probably have proved irresistible to armies, even if the navies, for fear of crippling shortages, had delayed their interest indefinitely. The demonstration by Gottlieb Daimler in 1885 of a practical, liquid-fuelled internal combustion engine, left armies little alternative but to adopt oil fuel. By the late 1890s, it was no longer a question of if, but when the already useful coal fired steam traction engines replaced animals as the best shifters of heavy loads. This inevitably stirred a lurking realisation among the open-minded that quite soon the far lighter automobiles and trucks already on the market might eventually do away with the horse and all other beasts as traction power for lighter war loads, including man himself. The Anglo-Boer War of 1899–1902 would point the way, as will be seen.

Meanwhile there was another even more exciting technical development which had to be dependent upon the compact internal combustion engine with its liquid fuel and high power-to-weight ratio. Since balloons had made their military debut in the 18th century, the hunt had been on for a practical, steerable, powered flying machine, the feasibility of which in lighter-than-air craft had been demonstrated in 1887 by the French *La France* non-rigid ship, driven by an electric motor. But the true way ahead was shown by those who built heavier-than-air winged gliders and suggested they could easily be engined for sustained flight. With the military possibilities of such machines plain, it was not surprising that most armies kept touch with progress in this field, or that the United States Army, for example, in the immediate aftermath of the Spanish–American War, contracted Samuel Langley to build a powered aircraft.

The stimulus of war, with the extra funds released by governments, would ever be crucial in opening doors into the future, particularly when existing weapons, communications and logistic systems were shown to be deficient in practice. In no field was this more provocative than that of signal communications which held the golden key to accelerated progress on land, sea and, in the immediate future, air. No sooner had Guglielmo Marconi transmitted a morse code 'wireless' (radio) signal over a mile in 1895 and extended that range repeatedly in the days to come, during a series of experiments, than every commercial and military organisation worth its salt became interested. Not unnaturally, it was marine mercantile companies who headed the enquirers since the advantages of radio at sea were obvious. For fifty years cable connections had only marginally helped ships in port or in visual touch with shore signal terminals. At last tactical and, perhaps more important of all, logistic information and guidance could be sent over the so-called ether. In constant touch with their shore controllers, ships would enjoy lucrative advantages by an extension of flexibility in programming their operations. It was by no means a coincidence that Marconi's first long-range experiments were conducted across water because he realised that commercial advantages could be won more quickly in a medium where it had no competition from cable trans-missions. Navies seized upon the new invention with keen experiments, but armies were by no means lagging. Already by 1899, for example, the American Army was transmitting experimentally with what was called 'space telegraph'; and in that same year the British Army was shipping some of the first 'spark', undamped radio sets to the war in South Africa. There, it was hoped, this new way of sending messages without laboriously laying vulnerable cable, would solve pressing problems in communication along extended lines of communication which traversed difficult and hostile country.

The Anglo-Boer Wars

It was fortunate for the British Army that nearly 20 years before their first intensive war in 40 years, it had managed to rationalise its doctrine on something approach-ing modern lines. Lagging behind the Germans, the French and the Russians (who had formed a General Staff Corps', early in the 19th century, based on the Quartermaster General's staff), the British did not open a Staff College until 1858 and delayed until 1906 the formation of a General Staff. Nevertheless, although the Army Corps they assembled in September 1899 to fight the Boers reflected current European trends, in that its artillery and logistic service content was significantly generous in proportion to the infantry and cavalry, its command and control organisation was defective and amateurish because attending the Staff College was unfashionable and far too few officers had received the benefits of its course. In heart and mind, the British Army functioned as a loose amalgamation of individual regiments whose first loyalty tended to be inward looking and to whom the Army as a whole was of secondary importance.

The logistic story of the British Army since the Crimean War had been of repetitive chop and change. One committee after another had recommended changes to organisations as, at root, attempts were made to resolve the long standing struggle about by, whom and how Supplies and Transport were to be acquired and moved. Not until 1888 was a lasting stability achieved by the creation of the Army Service Corps (ASC) responsible to the Quartermaster General for the technical handling of supplies and transport, leaving equipment stores (excluding Engineer items) to be cared for by the Ordnance Corps. It says much for the forethought behind this organisation that it coped magnificently in the opening phase of the Anglo-Boer War — until, that is, uneducated officers changed it.

When after years of brooding hostility and two previous resorts to arms, diplomacy broke down in the summer of 1899 between the Boers, who occupied the Transvaal and Orange Free State, and the British in Natal and Cape Colony, the drift into war took place in a state of military and, notably on the Boer's part, logistic unreality. With only about 14,500 men and 69 guns (none of them quick-firers) guarding Natal, and a mere 5,000, without artillery, in Cape Colony, the British unwisely involved their forces on the frontier and got them locked up in Ladysmith, Mafeking and Kimberley by a Boer Army which never exceeded 48,000 men. Yet the ensuing sieges, which inflicted the usual deprivations on the garrisons, were beyond the Boers to resolve.

The Boers had, indeed, miscalculated ludicruously in embarking on war. Not only did they mislead themselves politically by reckoning upon practical support from assumed sympathetic nations such as Holland and Germany, but they based their hopes of victory on a commando militia whose fieldcraft was excellent, but whose logistic support was sufficient only for a short war. It was therefore disastrous when, partly due to transport deficiencies, they were incapable of driving deeply in hot pursuit of the beaten British before the latter's Army Corps on its long and unimpeded voyages from Britain and India, arrived. Self-deception lay at the root of the Boer tragedy. Skilled marksmen in the commandos, who knew well how to fight, as in ambush, from prepared and camouflaged positions, and who could manage large scale hit-and-run raids, were at a loss when it came to sustained operations against a fully equipped and well supplied opponent. Lacking more than a few pieces of heavy artillery and progressively shorter of ammunition of all natures, the Boers condemned themselves, in the long run, to a wasting, two year guerrilla war they could not win.

It was a bonus for the Boers when the British repeatedly, in the opening encounters, made mistakes, in over-confidence, of blundering head-on across unfavourable ground into the deadly fire of a concealed enemy. And that in many subsequent engagements the more mobile Boer commandos, living off the country and, whenever possible, pillaging material and supplies abandoned by the British, maintained themselves in the most enterprising manner. But, in a prototype of many such guerrilla wars to come, it was the side which put its logistics on solid ground supplied from uninterruptable sources which prevailed in the end.

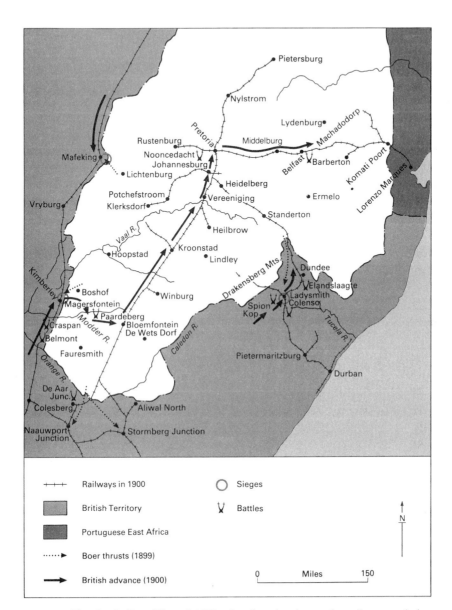

MAP 6. The Anglo-Boer War of 1899, showing the sieges, the railways and the principal related battles

Deplorable though British generalship was from the outset, the same charge cannot be levied against the logisticians of their Army Corps (see Fig. 4.1) which, under General Redvers Buller, began disembarking, towards the end of October at Cape Town, Port Elizabeth, East London and Durban, prior to inland movement by rail. The arrangements were admirable from the outset by the inclusion of substantial ASC (Army Service Corps) companies among the arrivals to obtain and organise the thousands of oxen and mules which, experience had shown, required little forage, and were far superior to horses as draught animals in the difficult hinterland. It was systematically done. As each unit stepped ashore it found waiting, according to long-conceived regulations, its First Echelon transport containing ammunition, entrenching tools and so forth, plus two days rations and forage. Backing them was a second Echelon ASC column to support each Cavalry and Infantry Brigade, the Divisional Troops and the Corps Troops. And behind them moved a Third Echelon with so-called Supply Parks and Ammunition Parks which acted as a 'travelling Depot or Rolling Magazine, organised to carry at least three days food and forage' for the entire Corps, plus ammunition. And lastly a Fourth Echelon of Auxiliary Transport to meet the need whenever a railway was not available.

The requirements for oxen is indicated when it is realised that each waggon load of 600 lb required 32 slow-moving oxen (which subsisted entirely by grazing) and three men, and that each company consisted of 100 waggons. But how uneconomic this was by comparison with a single steam tractor, which could pull 30 tons at 5 mph on the roads, and also operate across country, was remarked upon very critically at the time. Furthermore, a tractor required at most only two men, an easily obtained quantity of fuel and simple routine maintenance to keep it going; whereas animals could be tempermental and demanded much bulk fuel and most careful attention and care if they were not to founder. Mules, of which 50 were usually hitched to a heavy waggon or 20 to a light one, suffered immense losses from a population of 100,000 due to overwork and mismanagement. The cavalry's and mounted infantry's horses fared even worse; throughout the two year eight month-long war the average daily wastage was 300 — a sad commentary on slip-shod horsemanship and poor supervision by officers. Steam power, of course, on three main, single track railway lines converging on Pretoria was the cornerstone of the British transport system. Without it, the rapid advance of a division to the relief of Ladysmith would have been impossible because the entire British build-up in the months to come would have taken on a very different, slower form. Small wonder that the Boers recognised the railway as a prime target for attack and all the more remarkable that they did not put more effort at the outset into this sort of disruptive raid, along with cutting of the telegraph lines which parallelled the tracks. Inevitably, as had been so noteworthy in the American Civil War, the British were compelled to detach an ever-increasing proportion of their manpower to railway protection. Without so doing their speedy concentrations against the Boer main forces would have been seriously delayed. Thus defence of the long lines of communication evolved into a largely silent struggle which tied down considerable resources.

Let it be added, however, that the undeniable British logistic success in Natal was by no means repeated in Cape Colony — and for that General Kitchener, the Chief of Staff to Field Marshal Lord Roberts, the Commander-in-Chief, was mainly to blame. A Royal Engineer, with brilliant and ruthlessly achieved military successes against Arabs in Egypt and the Sudan behind him, he was among those senior officers who might have benefitted from a Staff College course and whose knowledge of logistics was mainly acquired from small campaigns in the Sudan. Like Roberts, he brought with him in December a preconceived notion that the British Army (with which he had for years been out of touch) was lumbered with a disorganised logistic service demanding his personal attention. When the system of supply was explained to Kitchener he is said to have stared blankly and ejaculated, 'I don't know what you mean.' Nor did he attempt to learn, but instead, whilst retaining unit First Line transport (out of respect for each Regiment's traditional sanctity), he pooled the rest of the transport belonging to the Engineers, the ASC and the Ordnance Corps. He also reverted to the old-fashioned Crimean model of supply (which presumably he did know about) by separating control of Supplies from Transport. Most disruptive of all, he imported Regimental officers, few, if any, with staff or technical knowledge, to supplement and often override the trained ASC specialists. To reorganise so radically in the midst of a campaign was bad enough, but to introduce a purely theoretical system without proper discussion was nigh upon criminal.

Then, to compound the evil, Lord Roberts decided that after relieving Kimberley (on the western railway line), he would plunge 100 miles across country to capture Bloemfontein, on the centre railway — a line which remained closed to the southward, in Boer hands. In the name of tactical elegance, he thus imposed an overbearing strain upon the already disorganised transport and supply companies, many of which had been further dissipated by uneconomic 'loans' of their transport to artillery and other units whose real needs were not always paramount. By surrounding General Cronje at Paardeberg on 18 February 1900, Roberts did indeed win a fine tactical victory (made easier by Cronje's self-imposed immobility due to unwillingness to abandon his waggon train when envelopment threatened.) But it was not decisive due to his inability to exploit beyond Bloemfontein because, for two months, the Army lay marooned, living hand-to-mouth due to logistic collapse. Thus haste in winning one battle gave the Boers a chance to make a strategic recovery.

Harrowing are the tales of logistic chaos which lasted from March until May — when some conscientious officers broke down under the strain of their unnecessarily unequal tasks and the havoc wrought by Kitchener's incompetence foisted upon them. One amateur transport officer insisted, for example, that it was his sole duty to see his drivers moved as one, with each vehicle at the correct distance and dressing. Supply did not concern him. Due to men such as he, innumerable

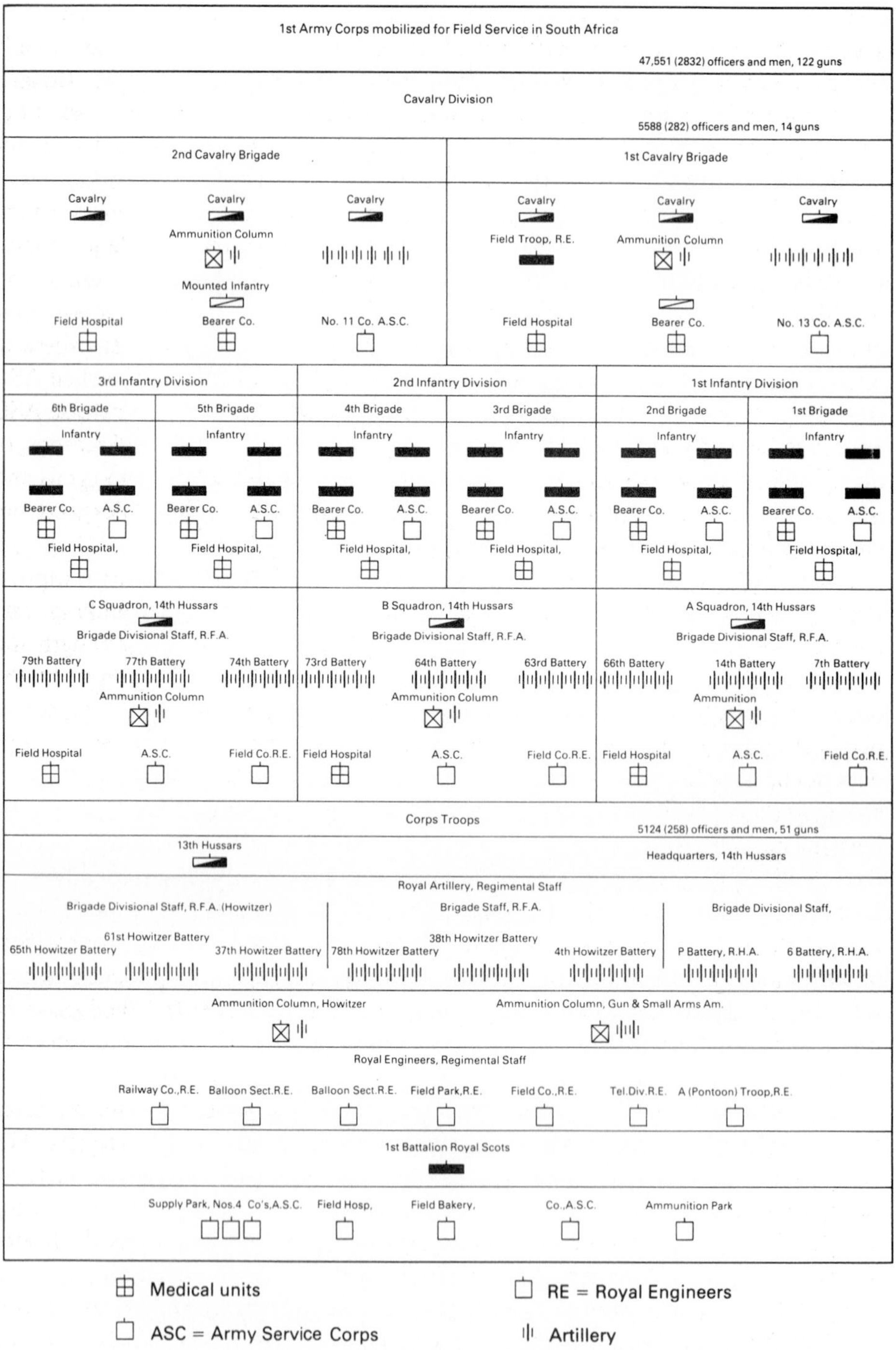
1st Army Corps mobilized for Field Service in South Africa
47,551 (2832) officers and men, 122 guns
Cavalry Division
5588 (282) officers and men, 14 guns
2nd Cavalry Brigade
1st Cavalry Brigade
Cavalry
Cavalry
Cavalry
Cavalry
Cavalry
Cavalry
Ammunition Column
Field Troop, R.E.
Ammunition Column
Mounted Infantry
Field Hospital
Bearer Co.
No. 11 Co. A.S.C.
Field Hospital
Bearer Co.
No. 13 Co. A.S.C.
3rd Infantry Division
2nd Infantry Division
1st Infantry Division
6th Brigade
5th Brigade
4th Brigade
3rd Brigade
2nd Brigade
1st Brigade
Infantry
Bearer Co.
A.S.C.
Field Hospital,
C Squadron, 14th Hussars
B Squadron, 14th Hussars
A Squadron, 14th Hussars
Brigade Divisional Staff, R.F.A.
79th Battery
77th Battery
74th Battery
73rd Battery
64th Battery
63rd Battery
66th Battery
14th Battery
7th Battery
Ammunition Column
Ammunition
Field Hospital
A.S.C.
Field Co.R.E.
Corps Troops
5124 (258) officers and men, 51 guns
13th Hussars
Headquarters, 14th Hussars
Royal Artillery, Regimental Staff
Brigade Divisional Staff, R.F.A. (Howitzer)
Brigade Staff, R.F.A.
Brigade Divisional Staff,
61st Howitzer Battery
65th Howitzer Battery
37th Howitzer Battery
38th Howitzer Battery
78th Howitzer Battery
4th Howitzer Battery
P Battery, R.H.A.
6 Battery, R.H.A.
Ammunition Column, Howitzer
Ammunition Column, Gun & Small Arms Am.
Royal Engineers, Regimental Staff
Railway Co.,R.E.
Balloon Sect.R.E.
Balloon Sect.R.E.
Field Park,R.E.
Field Co.,R.E.
Tel.Div.R.E.
A (Pontoon) Troop,R.E.
1st Battalion Royal Scots
Supply Park, Nos.4 Co's,A.S.C.
Field Hosp.
Field Bakery.
Co.,A.S.C.
Ammunition Park
Medical units
RE = Royal Engineers
ASC = Army Service Corps
Artillery

FIG 4.1 British 1st Army Corps in South Africa in 1899, showing the allocation of its logistic units at all levels

instances occurred of units being sent on forced marches without transport to accompany them. Human malaise and sickness flourished; mules were totally incapacitated and oxen worked off their feet with little time to graze, Roberts would only admit that in the advance to Bloemfontein 796 mules were lost out of 11,362 (7 per cent) with horse losses as bad. But, in fact, so emaciated were the beasts that in one division, because of the time it took to restore over-worked beasts to working strength, 50 per cent were out of use. It was this which paralysed the army at Bloemfontein for two months. At the same time, although adequate local native labour had been engaged to transfer waggon cargoes in bulk, the destruction of the pre-war methods which Kitchener had abolished, crippled the orderly issue of stores at the distribution centres. It was every unit for itself, regardless of operational priorities. Anarchy prevailed, as units hoarded surplus attached ASC transport. An artillery unit which, for example, had been ordered to release ASC ammunition waggons by dumping their contents, refused, for technical reasons, to do so, instead they sent back the mules alone — thus marooning the waggons and seriously reducing load capacity for an essential task because the mules were not equipped for pack working.

The British, however, won the first conventional phase of the war to capture Pretoria and Johannesburg, relieve Ladysmith, Kimberley and Mafeking, and overrun the Transvaal and Orange Free State because inherent Boer strength and logistic arrangements were even poorer than those of their opponents. At the outbreak of war, the Boer Republic was equipped and supplied for an intensive war of short duration only and, apart from an ample supply of food, was largely dependent upon outside sources for weapons, ammunition, explosives and other war material. Waggons and draught animals, along with horses and ponies for the mass of mounted infantrymen, were plentiful and the railways working well, to begin with. But resupply by import was virtually impossible through Portuguese East Africa (due to the British naval blockade) and, in any case, was nullified due to the indifference of potential suppliers. Medical Assistance was let through from other nations and the Red Cross. But ammunition and explosives, stocks of which were barely adequate in October 1899, were cut off and rapidly dwindled since the Boers lacked manufacturing capacity themselves and were unable to create it in time.

Small arms ammunition supply was complicated by having to cater for three types of rifle, plus a few Maxim machine-guns, firing a variety of cartridges. The very efficient regular artillery branch was even worse off by having seven different calibres in service. But if general incompatibility, linked to an ever-threatening ammunition famine, was not bad enough, grossly wasteful shooting by the troops most certainly was. Riflemen whose well-earned reputation in earlier campaigns as crack shots had made them so formidable, fell into disrepute as the veterans were eliminated and as it became increasingly difficult to spot British soldiers, whose improved fieldcraft was augmented by the recent issue of khaki uniforms in lieu of red jackets. Although neither side's ammunition expenditure was immensely in excess of anticipated scales, the Boers were perniciously wasteful due to poor discipline. They just loved shooting things. Officers who attempted to stop the practice of blasting off thousands of rounds against ant-hills from moving trains were ignored. Majuba Day was celebrated with a *feu de joie* of heroic but quite reprehensible exuberance.

As with so much else in the Boer military organisation, transport was improvised and on less than the scale of their enemy. A further handicap was the general use of very heavy waggons which had been sound on trek in the pioneering days, but by no means ideal for mobile operations. So long as the Government deemed it politically essential for their cause to maintain formed armies in the field, dependence upon rail and waggon transport was unavoidable, since traditional foraging was impracticable. Like the British, difficulties arose over divided responsibility between Supply and Transport — and muddling through was very much a characteristic of Boer maintenance in the field, so long as the army fought concentrated. The fatal result of Cronje clinging to his waggons, and being eventually compelled to use them as a besieged laager fortress at Paardeberg, was the beginning of the end of formal resistance and a signal to the Boers either to sue for peace or change their strategy and tactics.

Shortages of transport also impinged upon the Boer Medical Service, which lacked a central Authority until January 1900, being dependent until then upon the Artillery for such meagre arrangements as were made! In the Transvaal there were only 287 surgeons, doctors and vets. Overall there were far too few nurses, ambulances, hospitals and supplies. Without outside help on the large scale provided, the most dreadful conditions (and perhaps a quicker end to the war) would have occurred. As it was, the British made no attempt to block the sending in by the Red Cross and foreign governments of extensive aid, including hospitals. Moreover, they did all in their power to alleviate the suffering of the Boer wounded. Indeed, but for characteristic intransigence on the Boer's part at Paardeberg, a British hospital might, by agreement, have been set up between the opposing lines, Cronje's army had virtually no medical cover of its own, yet he made impossible conditions. When his army, out of food and desperately short of ammunition, surrendered, it at first became dependent on the British to care for its men, women and children who had endured intense fire throughout the siege.

Ironically, when the war reverted to guerrilla raiding by Boer commandos, who lived wholly off the country (moving by night and grazing by day) it was in the nature of the logistic struggle waged by Kitchener (when he took over as Commander-in-Chief) that women and children became among the greatest sufferers. For the Boers, by striking at isolated British positions (mainly those securing lines of communication) compelled the British to tie down nearly 500,000 troops on guard duties and in repressive counter-measures. Immense engineering effort was put into the building of blockhouses along the railways and at key points elsewhere. But an elusive opponent, who required little ammunition and who helped himself to British stocks whenever possible, seemed capable of staying at large, almost indefinitely so long as he was at liberty to draw food from his own farms. Kitchener's ruthless response in organising British hunting troops on Boer lines was also to starve out the enemy by destroying the farms and removing their occupants. Concentration camps were built hastily and 120,000 women and children incarcerated behind wire fences. But in over-crowded conditions of primitive sanitation and minimum medical care, outbreaks of disease, of which cholera and typhoid were by far the deadliest killer, were inevitable. By the war's end some 20,000 women and children, plus many volunteers sent to their care, had died due to non-existent preventitive measures.

It was not the plight of these families or the thousands of sick which eventually brought an end to the war, however. Logistically squeezed and hunted as they were, the Boer commandos survived and attempted to raid deeply and often into Natal and Cape Colony. As their farms were put to the torch, they took reprisals which, they hoped, would be politically persuasive, against their enemy's farms. But it was the increased difficulties of living off the land while unwillingly and undesirably compelled to concentrate against Kitchener's extremely effective counter-measures which brought the Boers to their knees. Nothing they could do in all their fervent, patriot zeal, would weaken an enemy whose logistic arrangements were now running to a smooth rhythm. Cut railways as often as they might, the Boers would not make inroads into the stocking of depots established at well protected strategic centres. Well practised British engineers, with ample materials, soon repaired tracks and bridges.

The final stages, as the Boers' resistance was gradually worn down, provided a clear indication of how far logistic services had progressed in the past century, let alone how Kitchener's depredations had been overcome. While the British had demonstrated how mechanisation, allied to improved organisation and methods, could sustain both mobile and static operations (even in difficult country), the Boers (with fanatic determination alone on their side) had shown how large guerrilla bands could subsist in friendly territory for a disquieting length of time, despite heavy enemy pressure. It had also been shown that although arrangements to care for the wounded were adequate, the prevention of disease was overlooked through lack of knowledge: Sanitary organisations to check their spread did not exist and would not have known how to tackle flies, lice and the other carriers of pestilence. An anti-typhoid vaccine, for example, was not generally available until 1898. In these circumstances a far larger load was placed upon medical services by disease than by weapons — a state of affairs which would persist almost unchecked throughout the next major war in Manchuria.

The Russo-Japanese War of 1904: The Power of Logistics Demonstrated

If, as some called it, the Anglo-Boer War was 'The last Gentleman's War', the struggle between Russia and Japan which erupted in 1904 was 'The First Modern

War'. Both sides in this contest used the latest weapons to their fullest extent and fought with a ferocity unheard of in South Africa. Whereas, in South Africa, motor vehicles, the latest quick-firing artillery, Maxim machine-guns, barbed wire and radio made but little impact, in Korea and Manchuria they all contributed to enormous loss of life and a profligate expenditure of material — particularly of ammunition. It goes without saying, therefore, that from the moment of the undeclared, surprise attack by the Japanese Navy upon the Russians at Port Arthur on 8 February (when several shore batteries fired blank rounds because only saluting ammunition was to hand) this war was almost entirely controlled by logistic factors.

To begin with, the Russian 'diplomatic' removal from Japan of the spoils of their victory over China in 1895, and construction of an ice-free naval base at Port Arthur, was a provocative threat to Japan's future influence beyond her shores. For another thing, the building of the 5,500 mile long single track Trans-Siberian Railway (which was finished by 1904 except for the Lake Baikal gap) brought close the day when the Russians would be able to send an unchecked flow of men and material to the Far East. Japan's best hope of continued expansion thus seemed to rest upon securing a strong foothold on the mainland, seizing Port Arthur and inflicting a deterrent defeat upon the Russians before Port Arthur became impregnable and the railway was completed.

Everything hinged upon an early defeat of the Russian Pacific Fleet as a guarantee of Japanese sea lines of communication to Korea and Manchuria. Hence the importance of the surprise attack on 8 February, when so many Russian warships were hit by torpedoes, and the significance of the lack of a dry dock capable of berthing ships above 6,000 tons. Some severely damaged battleships and cruisers were beyond local repair. Inevitably there were demoralising effects upon a fleet which, from the outset, was under-trained and well below combat readiness, mainly due to mechanical defects caused by poor maintenance. With small fear of interference, the Japanese could transport the bulk of their 280,000 strong army (modelled on Germany's) with its 870 guns and logistic services, to Korea as the first phase in driving off a Russian force which, initially, consisted of only 80,000 men and 200 guns.

Regardless of the withdrawal of the Russian Fleet into Port Arthur and its subsequent routing when it emerged to fight and lose the Battle of the Yellow Sea to Admiral Togo on 10 August, the Russian General Kuropatkin had, by February, only one sound course open to him. Until his army could be heavily reinforced, it was vital to avoid a major battle, even to the extent of allowing the Japanese to besiege Port Arthur for several months. Logistic factors dominated his appreciation. While the Japanese Army built up its forces along the short sea route from Japan to the east coast ports of Korea, prior to invading Manchuria, Port Arthur's ring of modern but incomplete forts was substantially reinforced and improved by a phenomenal amount of engineering work, made possible by the release of resources which, thanks to peacetime economies, had previously been witheld. By the time the siege began in May, ample stocks of ammunition and sufficient food for 40,000 soldiers and the populace of 18,000, to last at least six months, had been stored. Meanwhile the capacity of the railway to transfer 40,000 men, with supplies, each month from the west had been virtually assured by a remarkable 'transport' re-adjustment.

The ferries which sailed on Lake Baikal in summer were unable to cope with the vast increase in traffic anticipated. Furthermore only enough locomotives and rolling stock to run three pairs of trains a day were positioned east of the lake; and coal stocks were not only too low but quickly would be exhausted since they were imported, along with other commodities, through Port Arthur. This Quarter-master General's nightmare was solved by Prince Khilkov, the Minister of Ways and Communications, with commendable energy. In February he constructed a railway, across 30 miles of ice, by which rolling stock could be repositioned in the east. In three weeks, after many hitches (including a locomotive through the ice) waggons were being towed by horses while the locomotives were transferred in pieces for reassembly the other side. By mid-March, no less than 65 locomotives were across along with 1,600 waggons. Thereafter the capacities of the railway and the ferries were increased to overcome what might have been a fatal choke to the Russian reinforcement plan.

It was Kuropatkin's misfortune that, having got his calculations right, his strategy was overturned by impatient superiors in Moscow. Ordered to attack, his hopelessly inadequate army suffered a series of rebuffs from a Japanese Army which, despite poor roads and, to begin with, no railway, solved its access to Manchuria by seizing several ports intact. Of these Dairen, within 40 miles of Port Arthur, was vital since, without it, the maintenance of General Nogi's 80,000 men and nearly 500 guns in the siege of Port Arthur would have been impossible; and Field Marshal Oyama's advance inland to Liaoyang, with necessarily increasing numbers to meet the Russian built-up, fatally impaired. That they did not demolish Dairen docks and thus impose a logistic barrier was merely another example of fatal Russian command incompetence.

Nogi's breaching of the three main lines of Port Arthur defence was notable as the first such attempt on a ring of modern forts protected by barbed wire and covered by searchlights and machine-guns; as well as for his rejection of traditional sapping methods in the interest of speed. The urgency of bombarding the Russian ships at anchor, before they could put to sea again, drove him to attack without siege artillery — contrary to the lessons learnt against the outer defences, which had showed how ineffective field artillery was against the simplest wired entrenchments. It took two months to ship and drag forward sufficient manpower, guns and ammunition for the first major assault on 7 August. The price of 1,280 killed and wounded paid for only limited gains was a taste of far worse to come. A fortnight later, when Nogi tried again to extend his gains (still without heavy artillery, in the interest of speed and logistic economy) the repulse cost 15,000 men and further-more, it added to the logistic problems by piling up heaps of dead which magnified the dangers of pestilence and caused a terrible stench and disposal problem. Nogi now had no option but to ship in the siege train — a laborious, time-consuming operation which took over a month. Meanwhile, Kuropatkin's strength had grown so that in August he had reached numerical equality with Oyama's field force — a change in balance which continued to move in the Russian favour, despite successive defeats at the hands of a more skilful opponent who, nevertheless, was approaching exhaustion from several causes.

As more and more ammunition was demanded to prepare the way for infantry assaults at Port Arthur and as gun barrels wore out, it took all the longer to dump sufficient shells at the gun sites and accumulate sufficient reserve stocks to sustain a bombardment of deteriorating accuracy. Japan's declining reserves of ammunition and guns however could barely be replenished by production. Of manpower there was plenty, imbued with sacrificial enthusiasm to die for the Emperor. But even the best men could be debilitated by beriberi, that all too familiar Asiatic disease (caused by an unbalanced diet of too much unpolished rice stripped in milling of its Vitamin B content) which ravaged the Army.

Inside Port Arthur, conditions were no better. True, the garrison's battle casualties were considerably fewer than those of the Japanese, but conditions in the hospitals, many of which had been hit by shells, were appalling. True also, ammunition was still plentiful and food was lasting out well — well enough to suggest that, with the aid of a few blockade runners, resistance could be extended well into 1905, by which time, it was hoped, the Baltic Fleet would have arrived, after its 20,000 mile voyage, to lift Admiral Togo's blockade at the same time as Kuropatkin came to the relief from up north. But, despite all these high hopes, the health of General Anatoli Stössel's garrison was far worse than that of Nogi's besiegers. A deficiency in diet of Vitamin C (the existence or importance of which, like Vitamin B, was unknown) had permitted an outbreak of scurvy which appears to have affected some 20 per cent of the garrison at the beginning of December, rising to 40 per cent by Christmas Day, with a virtual certainty, therefore, that almost everybody would be suffering from it by mid-January. In other words, in January 1905, the total deficiency of fruit or green vegetables in an inevitably depleted diet was on the verge of overcoming some 40,000 people (in the way that it had crippled ships' crews in the past). There would be no need for Nogi to add to his already terrible list of 59,000 battle casualties and 34,000 sick, including 21,000 with beriberi. Stössel surrendered.

Mutual exhaustion loomed large as Kuropatkin, with 300,000 men, tried on 26 January to overwhelm Oyamas' 220,000 at Sandeput — and failed, by the narrowest of margins, in a snowstorm. Now a futuristic scenario was unveiled amidst the long fierce struggle for Mukden, between 21 February and 10 March, when the Japanese discovered how logistically difficult it was to maintain mobility in trench warfare. No matter how deeply their troops, supported by intense artillery fire, penetrated, a moment soon would arrive when further exploitation fizzled out due to local artillery ammunition shortage. Kuropatkin eventually withdrew from Mukden with his army intact because the Japanese were unable, for logistic reasons, to prevent it. Military stalemate had been reached at the moment when the Russian Army had achieved overwhelming preponderance in numbers and supply, and the Japanese economy and war making capacity was close to collapse. The Russians had won a great logistic victory but, ironically, the failure to translate it into anything other than defeat in battle (which bred rising unrest at home) would make them withdraw from the war — a withdrawal made inescapable in the aftermath of the crushing defeat of their Baltic Fleet at Tsushima on 27 May, after one of the most extraordinary maritime logistic improvisations of all time.

The Baltic Fleet, which had began sailing to the Far East by squadrons from mid-October onwards, was in no shape for battle with anybody. Although during a voyage of 20,000 miles, which would take over seven months, it was to be expected that training, inferior morale and poor mechanical state might be improved, logistic factors, in addition to inadequate leadership, ensured the reverse. The harm done by an outbreak of typhus, due to water distillation problems at the outset, was almost incidental to the tyranny of supply. International law which proscribed use of neutral ports for periods of over 24 hours, raised diplomatic problems all along the course of the battleships, which sailed round the Cape of Good Hope, and for the smaller vessels, which went through the Suez Canal. Had it not been for the blind eyes of some nations, and the outright support of the French (in compliance with a Dual Agreement with Russia which made possible replenishment in Madagascar and Indo-China, among other places); the voyage could have been impossible. As it was, the over-complicated arrangements (which could not have been made in time without modern signal communications) imposed, for prime example, extremely difficult coaling from colliers in sheltered waters. To make matters worse, the need to pile every inch of cabin space, as well as the decks, with coal had a disastrous effect on morale and operational efficiency. A sense of doom among weary, begrimed men attended a voyage which lacked strategic justification after the fall of Port Arthur; a sense which convinced Admiral Rojestvensky that battle with the experienced Japanese fleet could have only one outcome.

No sooner had the Russian warships been destroyed at Port Arthur than Togo was free to withdraw his Fleet to Japan for a much needed dockyard refit. Informed by telegraph of the arrival of the ships of the Baltic Fleet in Shanghai and later made aware, by radio intercept, of the enemy's intention to break through the Straits of Tsushima, his interception and crushing of an inferior and demoralised foe was simplicity itself.

★   ★   ★   ★   ★

In the nine years between the end of the Russo-Japanese War and the start of the First World War in 1914, scant attention was paid by European armies to many basic lessons. The logistic implications of extensive and prolonged siege type operations, to the minimising of mobile warfare, were virtually and with perverse logic, ignored. All the main contenders had adopted offensive doctrines, on the 1870 model, which envisaged face-to-face encounters by cavalry and infantry in which artillery (the largest logistic consumer) mainly engaged direct and played a subsidiary role. The importance of powered aircraft, in the immediate aftermath of the Wright brothers' accomplishment at Kitty Hawk in 1904, was belittled. Nothing like enough thrust was applied to the introduction of large quantities of motor lorries to amplify the espoused doctrine of mobility. Indeed, of the crucially important inventions of the period, only radio received due attention. True it had failed on land in South Africa because of aerial array trouble and bad static interference, but at sea, in its first successful wartime use, it had been of immense help in the Royal Navy's blockade of Boer supplies through Portuguese East Africa. Later, the Japanese had demonstrated its infinite number of strategic, tactical and logistic functions throughout the naval war against Russia — to the extent, indeed, that the German Army which invaded Belgium and France in August 1914 placed a sort of misplaced reliance upon it.

Note

1. Incredibly this same aversion was reflected until comparatively recent times in the failure of many Infantrymen to maintain officer-to-officer communications after the general introduction of radio — a shortcoming finally overcome by force of necessity and some years of experience.

Chapter 5

Overload in the First World War: 1914-16

FROM THE torrent of ink spilt about the causes of success and failure of the opening campaigns of the First World War, only a trickle has been diverted to the examination of certain decisive logistic and communication factors. Dramatically important as were strategic and tactical planning; vital as the attributes of commanders; and fascinating the quirks of fate in shaping a confrontation of unprecedented scope and dimensions, one is drawn to the conclusion that it was logistics and communications which handed their early successes to the French and British and that, thereafter (like the Russians and Japanese at Mukden) neither side possessed the sinews to sustain a decisive mobility.

Penalties and Gains

Famous as is General Count von Schlieffen's concept of an envelopment of the French Army by a gigantic wheel by the German Army's preponderant right wing, curling round Paris, less well renowned are his flimsy calculations of logistic feasibility (without allowance for enemy interdiction) or how such an immense force could be commanded and controlled. And while Marshal Joffre received just praise for the stroke which won the Battle of the Marne, it is rarely underlined to what extent superior French communications and a scientifically organised logistic service made this possible. Yet, many as were the differences between the German, Austro-Hungarian, French, British and Russian armed forces in this war, only by their common underestimate of ammunition expenditure, creating dire shell shortages, were they logistically on common ground. Regardless of the lessons of 1870, of the South African War and the Manchurian conflict, there were numerous repetitions of past logistic shortcomings, and too little effort put into the motorisation which would have averted them.

Despite the possibility, given the will to possess large fleets of motor lorries, the Germans had only 4,000 trucks and did but make little use of them for logistic purposes; the Russians had all too few of military usefulness; and the British and French, while paying as much attention to mechanisation as the Germans, were largely still dependent on railways, a few tractors, and animals for supply. The armies of General Helmuth von Moltke the Younger, as they advanced through Belgium into France, were still dependent upon horse drawn transport between railhead and the marching spearheads. So once again there was deprivation when the railways fell behind logistic schedules; once more troops received priority of movement; and waggons and supplies stood idle in sidings for insufficient labour to transfer loads, while horse transport could not maintain a service much beyond a 40 mile radius. Inevitably, therefore, when the French demolition of railway lines and bridges effectively retarded the restoration of links, a fodder famine struck the leading German formations because, in due course, railheads became some 80–100 miles in rear (see Map, p.59). Animals could not cope; dispirited, hungry men were close to exhaustion. And it was just one more indictment of the fallibility of horses in war that, at a crucial moment, when a German cavalry corps was on the eve of breaking through the enemy front, they were held back because the horses were 'off the road' in need of re-shoeing.

Even if the Germans had assembled resources to keep their mobile arms moving, it is still unlikely that the plan would have worked. For, with typical arrogance, their General Staff had refused to bring the Chief of Signals into its confidence during planning. As a result, it was impossible to position adequate resources to amplify and restore broken cable communications from, to and between the fighting formations and among the logistic services. With each day's extension of the front from von Moltke's headquarters in Luxembourg and from the German base, chaos multiplied. Over-loaded telegraph and telephone links could not take the traffic generated. Tempers flared as control of both teeth and tail units began to slip. And radio, of which there were high hopes, did little to help since the German system of making contact from front to rear (instead of the other way about) broke down.

As the French and British retreated upon their sources of supply, their logistic services functioned reasonably well. By falling back in a rich countryside as the harvest came in, with balanced transport systems which worked, nevertheless, as well as might be expected, and with cable communications which never failed, they were poised quite nicely to riposte when the German command, control and logistic system broke under the strain. Yet the point of balance would soon be reached when the Germans, once again amply supplied from nearby railheads with ammunition and engineer stores, were able to hold fast on the River Aisne and the Allied horse drawn transport was unable to build up resources to overcome them. And so it continued during the so-called Race to the Sea when neither side was quite able, at the culmination of each out-flanking attempt, to assemble sufficient manpower and supplies to overwhelm an enemy who kept pace logistically.

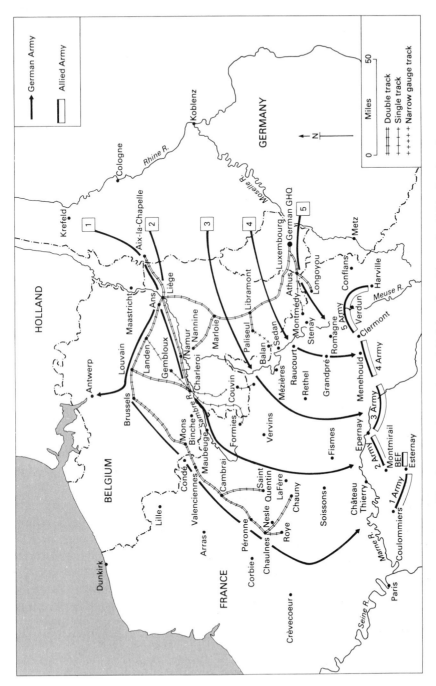

MAP 7. The German advance through Belgium into France in 1914, showing the furthest extent of the railheads at the time of the Battle of the Marne

Stalemate on the Western Front was as inevitable as it had been at Port Arthur and Mukden.

So it was, too, on the Eastern Front, even though there it was the German Eighth Army which benefitted from withdrawing through difficult terrain upon their base while the Russian First and Second Armies, with feeble supply echelons, forfeited their chances. Paradox intruded. After General Rennenkampf's First Army had, without at first realising it, won the Battle of Gumbinnen on 20 August, it failed to press a retreating enemy because its ammunition replenishment was delayed by the troubles of horse transport and the wider Russian railway gauge which prevented use of the good German railway. And if Rennenkampf's inability to advance had not been advertised to German radio monitors by messages in clear or in compromised cypher, it is unlikely that the Germans could have left Rennenkampf to his devices so confidently while they first concentrated against and then crushed the logistically embarrassed Russian Second Army at Tannenberg.

The struggle in East Prussia was merely a foretaste of what was to come throughout the emptinesses of the Eastern Front. Most battles were fought for possession of key railway junctions. Axes of advance necessarily parallelled railroads. The situation was similar to, but on a vastly greater scale, that of the American Civil War — nothing decisive could be achieved in a semi-wilderness without secure railway communications. For example, the Austro-Hungarian armies, whose first ill-conceived offensive in Galicia failed in August as also did their combined attack with the Germans against Warsaw in October; all came to a halt with combat success in sight when communications broke down. On this front with its few, foundering roads and railways, failure to concentrate sufficient strength in order to capture some single key route centre was usually fatal.

In the West, where logistic privations had permitted an unbreakable siege stalemate from the Swiss frontier to the North Sea, the compulsion for both sides to introduce radical solutions in order to overcome overload, and so to restore mobility, were irresistible. Figure 5.1 shows how, in principle, both sides moved stores to the front and evacuated casualties and salvage to the rear. They also highlight the fundamental weakness inherent in the fact that only horsed transport was employed forward of railhead. Before the war motor enthusiasts, who knew how much more cost-effective and reliable than horse-drawn waggons were lorries of up to 3-ton capacity, suffered in frustration the parsimony and bigotry of those in charge of the purse strings, for whom the horse was a 'civilising influence'[1] (I quote from a post-war document). That horses failed to deliver the goods when motor vehicles had already demonstrated their capabilities to do so; that the wounded suffered excessively (because horse ambulances could not do the work and the handful of returning empty ammunition lorries had to be hijacked for the purpose); and the appalling suffering of terrified, temperamental animals were matters seemingly brushed aside, as was the all-too-obvious economic factor.

As conditions changed and the front consolidated and became more static, so did the use of horse-drawn transport diminish. Forward of Second Line, light railways, which tended to be both vulnerable and inflexible, took its place, with porterage by men for the last few hundred yards becoming the norm — a task which was not only exhausting for the infantrymen and gunners but deflected them from their battle tasks.

As transport horses began to disappear from the battle zone, only the cavalry and field artillery (to whom mechanisation would be anathema for the next decade or more) clung to the horse — a discredited mount against modern weapons. Meanwhile the medium and heavy artillery was left no option but to use steam and motor traction engines to move their unwieldy pieces.

As motorisation permeated the lines of communication, prompting an ever-increasing demand for road building works, it drove horses off the roads which they so easily clogged by their slow pace. Base areas ceased to look like farmyards and grew to resemble industrial complexes. Fodder began to be superceded by petrol and coal, each requiring mechanical handling and special storage. To service the machines and the communication systems, farriers, wheelwrights and waggon builders gave place to motor mechanics working in workshops to keep so much machinery running — inanimate equipment which received rougher handling than animals but without suffering. Almost overnight, this great variety of machines — including aircraft being purchased from the new, burgeoning industries at home — had to be supplied with an almost limitless quantity of spare parts — creating a need for warehousing, accounting and economy on a scale to which the transport, supply and ordnance branches of pre-1914 armies were quite unaccustomed. To manage and man these new organisations came a horde of qualified civilians extracted from commerce and industry. Many, but by no means all, wore uniform. Together they created vast bureaucracies, as improvers of the old commissariats. And as their numbers rose in proportion to the strength of the combat areas at the same time as these were suffering fearful losses, a fresh dimension to the teeth versus tail competition was introduced.

By mid-1915, nearly all the combatant nations were encountering manpower problems, with the acutest labour shortages more pronounced on the Allied side than that of the Central Powers. Impetus was given to still greater mechanisation but, above all, to better utilisation of man and woman power. As women filled numerous posts which once were the exclusive province of men, the men were persuaded or compelled to undertake work best suited to their mental and physical calibre. As part of a series of reallocations, the higher grade people who had found their way into the logistic services were removed to the combat arms, while wounded and medically down-graded people took their places in base jobs. Simultaneously, new ideas imposed greater efficiency such as, for an incidental example, the minimising of dumping stores on the ground allied to the prevention of double handling by the transfer of stores from one vehicle to another by tail board-to-tail board loading.

In no other department of the logistic conglomerate was manpower economy more sought after than by the Medical Services, among whom perhaps, the British

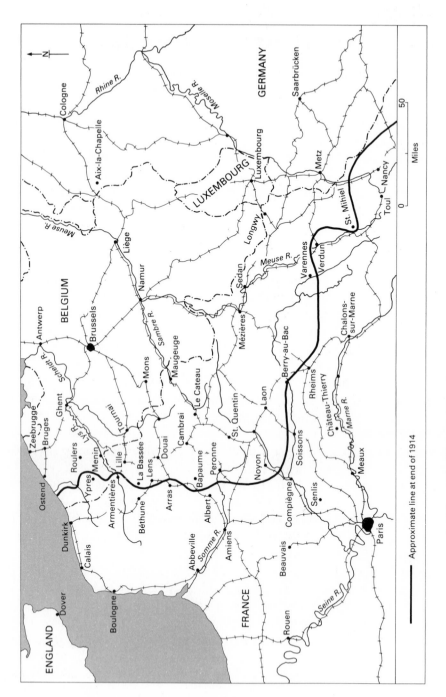

MAP 8. The static Western Front in 1915 with its extensive railways and water transport arteries

— Approximate line at end of 1914

OVERLOAD IN THE FIRST WORLD WAR: 1914–16

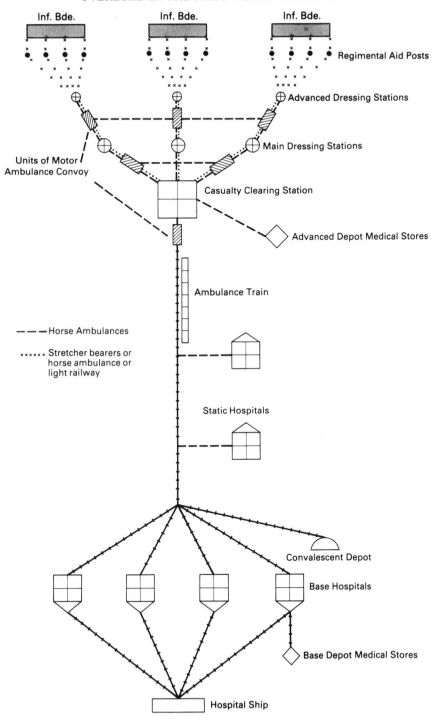

FIG 5.1   The British system of Casualty Evacuation during the First World War as mechanised transport took over

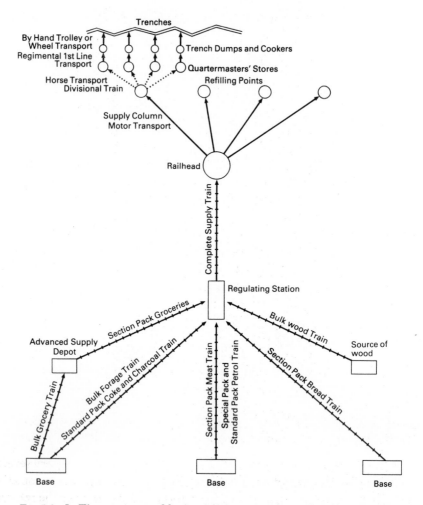

FIG 5.2   In Theatre system of food and fuel supply during the First World War

(after the recent wastage in South Africa) were leaders. By enforcing preventative sanitation and hygiene, they managed to reduce the percentage of losses from pestilence to a fraction of what it had been in 1900. Though, to begin with, there was only a gradual improvement in the percentage of survival from wounds (as young surgeons used the latest ideas about the elimination of infection by cleansing instead of the old-fashioned antiseptic treatment) there were commendable advances in preventative medicine in the trenches, where the chances of respiratory and stomach complaints, along with trench foot and exposure in damp and

64

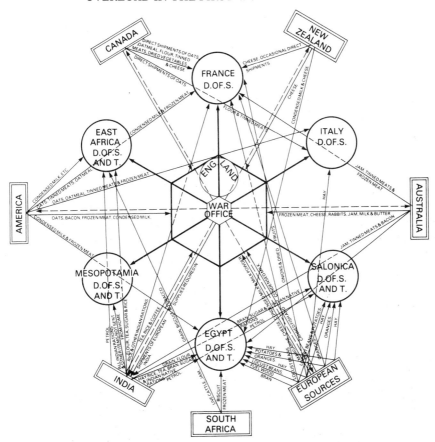

FIG 5.3 Diagrammatic representation of the complex British arrangements for the control of movements and supplies to the many Theatres of War during the First World War (*Reproduced by kind permission of The Institution of the Royal Corps of Transport*)

cold, were high. Outbreaks of disease there would be, some of them very severe in less well-cared-for theatres of war where, as will be seen, standards sometimes deteriorated. But, until prolonged blockades and poor diet weakened the resistance of entire populations, the incidence of killer diseases was kept in check.

Blockade and Sea Raiding

A tightening blockade was, of course, the virtual monopoly of the Allies until the Central Powers, spurred on by the Germans, developed underwater attack as an effective weapon against maritime commerce. Only for a very short while at the outset of war did the German Navy in any way seriously threaten the Allied lines of communication between theatres of war. Not only were the Central Powers' merchant ships swept from the oceans by Allied sea power but, along with a handful of raiding warships, they were also denied sources of fuel. The temporary triumph of Vice-Admiral Graf von Spee's East Asiatic Squadron in staying at large for some five months in the Pacific and defeating a British squadron at Coronel; and the highly effective and romanticised feats of the raiding light cruiser *Emden* in the Indian Ocean were activities forever inhibited by the spectre of running out of coal or betrayal to a superior enemy by radio reports of their movements. It was the rapid capture by Allied and Japanese forces of German coaling and radio centres throughout the Pacific which forced von Spee to move to his doom off the Falklands and for *Emden* to run out of luck in her hunt for fuel as well as targets — the *Emden's* problems being further exacerbated by the humane disposal of numerous captured enemy crews. Yet, despite the fuel problem, the feasibility of a single, elusive raider surviving by living off its victims, was demonstrated as an encouragement to those who visualised blockade by even more elusive submarines.

For a squadron the size of von Spee's, with two armoured cruisers, three light cruisers and a train of colliers, to vanish into the ocean wastes was an almost impossible feat; in due course it had to reappear inshore to refuel. When this occurred, it would be likely to be reported by radio to the British, whose ships were closing in. In the event there were delays to the converging squadrons. Vice-Admiral Sir Frederick Sturdee's two battle cruisers, having been delayed in departure from Britain by dockyard snags, steamed unnecessarily slowly as a fuel economy on the way to the Falkland Islands. Von Spee not only also wasted time with over-insurance by a three day stop for coaling from colliers at Picton Island, but also advertised his intention to make for home via the Atlantic. His detailed requests for the positioning of coal and supplies at Port Santa Elena and New York were soon known to the British, enabling Sturdee to head for a refuelling at the Falklands as the best base for his search for von Spee. Hence it merely required a misleading report to von Spee, saying the coalstocks at the Falklands were unguarded, to lure him thence a few hours after Sturdee's arrival. It was inconsequential that the British had not completed coaling when putting to sea again to catch von Spee. They still had enough in their bunkers to catch and sink an out-classed opponent before returning to the nearby Falklands base which already had paid for its setting up in the previous century.

Gallipoli: The Fatal Flaws

Notwithstanding the inspired, though confused, strategic nature of the British plan to force the Dardanelles in 1915, to establish a naval presence off Constantinople and endeavour to knock Turkey out of the war, the logistic consequences were of fundamental importance to the evolution of the war, even after the invasion was halted and later abandoned. As so-called Easterners would argue, it was essential to gain direct access to Russia through the Black Sea in order to help replace that nation's equipment losses which were threatening to lose her the war. Equally they maintained that, in the face of stalemate in France, it would be strategically advantageous, as well as logistically vital, to establish a major base in Egypt as a springboard for operations in the Mediterranean and throughout the Middle East. Not only was it essential to preserve the link to India by removing the Turkish threat to the Suez Canal, it was also highly desirable to protect the Persian oilfields, which had begun production in 1908. The so-called Westerners retorted that, politically, it was essential to free French soil of Germans by a concentrated effort demanding of so vast a logistic outlay that it would be unthinkable not to utilise it to the full. In the end both policies were pursued with fluctuating enthusiasm.

The drift into a phased naval, followed by an amphibious, assault upon the entrance to the Dardanelles need not be recounted here, except to underline that the purely naval aspects were inherently workable within the meaning of sea power once the fortifications were seized, and once Constantinople and the Bosphorus were in Allied hands. That it was a serious tactical error on the British part, (perpetrated by First Lord of the Admiralty Winston Churchill) to attempt to force the Dardanelles without, first, seizing the forts, is beyond doubt. Not only was the surprise of Allied intentions lost, the Turks were given time to reinforce and resupply the forts which could so easily have been captured at the time of the first successful bombardment. The time it took the Allies to assemble sufficient land forces and a forward base at Mudros, on the Greek Island of Lemnos, was better spent by the Turks in preparing a welcome and nourishing their forward bases and cargo handling facilities on a peninsula which, to this day, is somewhat inaccessible.

The massacre of exposed troops during insufficiently prepared beach landings on the Gallipoli peninsula on 25 April is etched in history and properly portrayed as a tactical and communications muddle of incredible dimensions. When none of the first objectives were reached and those ashore were, for the most part, penned in four shallow bridgeheads overlooked by enemy artillery observers, survival became the order of the day. The British plight would have been far worse had not the Turks run out of ammunition at a critical moment and been unable to prevent the invaders consolidating; but it might have been another matter if Lord Kitchener, now Secretary of State for War, had been permitted to indulge in his characteristic ignorance of transport matters by denying the infantry any at all because they 'would only have to walk across the peninsula' which was up to six miles wide. It was merely another example of muddled thinking that, initially, lorries were sent for use over tortuous terrain which was known to lack roads.

From start to finish, the British were in logistic peril through being wholly dependent upon supply across open beaches which were prone to storms. The infantry, who led the assault, carried three days hard rations but many threw these away during the landing. Two hundred rounds of ammunition per man was barely sufficient, bearing in mind that its supply over the first four days was difficult due to beach conditions, the competing priorities of ferrying reinforcements ashore and the need for man porterage, since so few animals could be landed. Amidst the extremely cramped conditions of the bridgeheads all were within artillery range. There was nowhere for hospitals to be established, and the nightly evacuation of wounded and sick was a harrowing business. Tens of thousands left that way as already high battle casualties were multiplied by those weakened by dysentery and other complaints, caused by a hygiene problem beyond normal control. The place stank from a multitude of unburied corpses and other waste matter, upon which flies bred in swarms. Water was nearly always polluted although only occasionally in short supply, due to the unexpected discovery of wells.

It was much the same for the Turks, of course. Admittedly, until a few submarines and aircraft began operating against their ships in the Sea of Marmora, they were reasonably supplied, though never in abundance. Like their enemy, they were reduced to improvisation to make ends meet. But while the Turks were always struggling to bring in sufficient artillery ammunition, the British barely encountered that problem since, so small were their bridgeheads and so close to hand their warships that they had but little requirement ashore for any weapon bigger than machine-guns.

A Port Arthur-like situation evolved, except that the Turks were never besieged, and the British had many options of out-flanking them. Of these, their landing at Suvla Bay, in the Turkish rear, on 6 August was the one adopted. Although far better organised than the first landings and, with the forces ashore built up to a 15 to 1 numerical advantage over the Turks within a few hours of its start, it still failed. Blame for this has been distributed pretty fairly between a Corps commander without energy; subordinates who lacked drive; raw troops; and a shortage of drinking water. Criticism of the fact that a mere 160 mules were brought ashore in the first 48 hours receives less attention, although this was the basic cause of lost mobility, which impaired exploitation of the initial success. Not only were the tired leading troops diverted to porterage, in place of mules, but there were instances of those who stood on the brink of success at the front, returning to the beach for water. These were the fatal flaws which doomed the Suvla Bay attack and ensured the ultimate British withdrawal from Gallipoli at the year's end.

Attenuation in 1915

Throughout 1915, while both the Allies and the Central Powers sought a decision by offensives in all theatres of war, the realisation grew that, with the resources at their disposal, hopes of doing so were extremely remote. Over-shadowing the fighting, the accompanying heavy casualty lists, the retreats and the advances, loomed the universal shortage of shells. All the combatants suffered from this because nobody had foreseen the voracious appetite of what had become an artillery war.

When the French and British launched all-out offensives in Champagne and Artois to drive the Germans out of France, they made little progress because, for one thing, they lacked sufficient heavy artillery and ammunition stocks to overcome both the German artillery and the wired-in trench systems. The stocks had been accumulated pre-war within estimated consumption rates. Suddenly it was found they could not be replaced at a rate to keep up with the immense expenditure by rapidly expanding forces. Numerous were the occasions when the infantry were denied even a modicum of support from guns which had been rationed to a few rounds per day. Often the guns actually ran out, due to local over-expenditure. Both sides were also to discover that, as production was increased by prodigious labours on the Home Front, as much as 25 per cent of new production could be defective. By the end of 1915, when the Western front had moved only slightly, the first signs of a serious manpower shortage became noticeable. Yet at this time of attenuated resources, the menacing word 'attrition' came into vogue to describe the concept whereby an enemy might be brought to his knees by the pulverisation through unlimited bombardment of infantry. To this we will return.

A form of attrition had already brought about a Russian collapse when the Germans and Austro-Hungarian armies advanced in May 1915 in an attempt to relieve the strain on Turkey and to deter the Italians and Romanians from joining the Allies. It was a hallmark of the thorough realism of the Central Powers' offensive that its strategic and tactical objectives rarely exceeded the logistic means available while wearing down those of a weaker opponent. The German Chief of Staff, General Erich von Falkenhayn, resisted the ambition of those who wished to smash Russia with one mighty blow, realising that a deep advance into Russian space was far beyond his forces' capability. Instead, he authorised a series of relatively local offensives, supplied by sound railway communications and launched with just sufficient artillery support (commensurate with shell supply) to seize nodal points and force the enemy back. He merely wished 'to cripple the Russians for an indefinite period'. By winning a series of battles of limited dimensions, the German and Austro-Hungarian army commanders achieved economic successes and made space for mobility against an already demoralised opponent. Capture of territory for its own sake was unimportant. Over a period of four months the longest advance was 300 miles with others much shorter than that. The aim was to keep the Russians on the move and wear them down. It started a rot from which they never recovered.

Creditable as von Falkenhayn's achievement was in keeping within logistic support at all times, he owed much to a Russian decay which stemmed in large part from a national administrative degeneration which ate deeply into the Army's logistic support and seriously infected morale. The poor quality of Russian officers and NCOs was a major weakness, and the losses they had helped to cause, ruinous. It was a sign of amorality that a ration scale of 4,000 calories a day (almost twice the requirement) was authorised in order to appease the soldiers — who merely wasted it. They might have been much more impressed with more ammunition in the pouches and the sound and support of far larger numbers of guns well-supplied with shells. As it was, Russian industry was unable to meet vast paper orders, and imports were neither sufficient nor properly co-ordinated to the requirement; in 1915 barely 10 per cent of orders were honoured. Likely as not, moreover, the logistic services would have failed to deliver at the right time and place to the front.

So von Falkenhayn had only to achieve his aim of crippling the enemy by keeping him on the retreat in a spirit of abject despondency. This he did to such good effect that, by 1916, he felt strong enough to turn his attention upon the French and British in an attempt to do rather more than just cripple them.

Mesopotamian Outrage — 1915

That attrition could have serious detrimental effects upon its initiator was demonstrated by the over-ambitious commanders of the British Indian Army who made a strategically dubious attempt to capture Baghdad in 1915. For while it was true that the Turks in Mesopotamia were weak because the railway to Baghdad from Europe was still incomplete, their plight was no worse than that of the enemy, who had landed at Basra in November 1914, with a view to safeguarding the Persian oilfields, and then began moving up the Tigris and Euphrates. The port of Basra was of limited capacity and the great rivers, which were to be the main arteries of General Sir John Nixon's army, were very shallow at certain times of the year. Since the land transport allocated was quite insufficient, with few motor vehicles, all manner of transport (such as camels with calves, donkeys and cows) had to be purchased to maintain an advance which, by miracles of tactical endeavour, threw the badly handled and supplied Turks back on Ctesiphon. But there the logistic balance swung the other way. The British were held in November 1915, and thrown back on Kut-el-Amara where, quite unnecessarily, Major General Sir Charles Townshend, allowed himself to become besieged.

By this time the logistic state of the British forces beggared description and attrition had set in. In a desert scorched by burning hot winds, and which harboured swarms of flies and mosquitoes to spread all kinds of disease including dysentery, malaria and bubonic plague, the health of the troops was further undermined by a vegetable deficiency which encouraged scurvy. In a land where sanitation was at a premium, the medical services could not cope even with the wounded — let alone the sick, whose number was the greater. With only a few motor ambulances at last available, the patients whose lives were saved at field dressing stations and hospitals had to suffer the tortures of slow transit down river, often untended, invariably in filth and often short of water.

Attempts to relieve Kut broke down as a result of stiff Turkish resistance and continuing British tactical and logistic shortcomings. A steamer sent to replenish Kut came to grief on sandbanks. The efforts of a few aircraft (which could barely lift pilot and fuel, let alone a sack or two of flour) were of significance only because they represented the first ever attempt at battlefield supply by air. Townshend might have held out longer had he not squandered supplies without making any attempt for two months to conserve supplies; had he at once ejected the 6,000 Arabs to remain within the town; and not persuaded the relieving force to advance to disaster, before it was ready, by falsely announcing that he was almost out of supplies when he had three months in hand. And by making no attempt to breakout towards a relieving army which was without motor transport and as short of supplies and medical support as he. The only redeeming feature of this episode of Crimean misconduct and horror was the performance of the men of the combat arms and logistic services who did all in their power to compensate for the cynical incompetence of their senior commanders, most of whom were sacked while Townshend lived in high-luxurious captivity.

Attrition on the Grand Scale — 1916

By 1916, all the combatants, with the notable exception of the Russians, had largely overcome their ammunition shortages and were determined on renewed offensives. The failures of 1915 had induced a mood of desperation in national leaders who visualised frightening escalating economic and social changes the longer the war continued. The damage armies inflicted on each other by hard pounding, the effects upon life at home and the direct involvement of entire populations in total war were attritional of leaders' senses as well as the people's morale and national resources. To supply the armed forces every civilian sinew had to be strained, every source of energy tapped. It was therefore all the more worrying that competing blockades were beginning to undermine the roots of logistic services.

The involvement of Italy and Greece on the Allied side almost completed the encirclement of the Central Powers. Their material and food shortages began to impair munitions manufacture and sap each nation's health and stamina. Though production was raised, quality fell steadily. Try hard, though the Central Powers would, to fix an equally effective stranglehold on the Allies, the attempt failed in 1915 with the initial submarine campaign — an undertaking which was damaging in every sense to the German cause through the sinking without warning of such passenger ships as the *Lusitania*. It was paradoxical that on the eve of Germany's blatantly attritional project, to bleed France white quickly at Verdun (see below), the Allied boa-constrictor's squeeze was slowly achieving an even deadlier effect.

Blockade and counter-blockade placed such additional demands upon logistic services that, quite often, they were counter-productive. The Allies, for example, were compelled to maintain large numbers of ships and craft at sea to intercept cargoes for the enemy. Ships' maintenance drew heavily upon manpower, material and industrial resources. At the same time, a rising proportion of naval effort had to be diverted to combatting enemy submarines which sailed with impunity through the English Channel into the Western Approaches. The eventual construction, laying and manning of extensive net and mine barrages in the Channel (as well as in the Straits of Otranto to prevent similar egress from the Adriatic Sea into the Mediterranean), plus the expansion of port facilities to service them, were colossal. Short of range as all submarines were (and therefore restricted in operational impact due to lack of sea-going supply craft), their early depredations in small numbers paid a justifiable dividend, in terms of stretching Allied resources, if nothing else.

The Germans, on the other hand, were acutely aware of the poor cost-effectiveness of their High Seas Fleet whose crews ate their heads off in port and whose boilers consumed coal despite the fact that no direct attack was made on the enemy to relieve the blockade. Of course, by tying down the Grand Fleet in the classic manner of a 'Fleet in being', a significant logistic service was being rendered. It was preventing the diversion of Allied escort vessels to submarine hunting and, most vital of all, denying the enemy access to the Baltic and the desperately needed supply link with Russia. But that was not considered to be sufficient. Justification in battle was demanded and led to the Battle of Jutland — an encounter which Vice Admiral Reinhard Scheer intended to be of a limited nature but which turned into a major engagement with all forces involved — all due to logistic and communications ramifications. Had the Germans not given away their intention to sail by the clear indications of getting up full steam and by transmitting radio signals which were duly intercepted by the British, the Grand Fleet might have been caught in port with insufficient steam raised while the Germans enjoyed a momentary supremacy off the British coast.

Jutland was a drawn battle with the balance of losses in the German favour after Scheer had been completely out-manoeuvred by his adversary, Admiral Sir John Jellicoe. It was also balanced in its economic and logistic repercussions, which were immense. Because the German Fleet remained strongly 'in being', an end was put to any prospect of an Allied naval presence in the Baltic, thus extinguishing Russia's hopes of significant material aid, making inevitable her slide into military impotence, her demoralisation and the eventual collapse into revolution in 1917. However, the Grand Fleet, thanks to outstanding work by its logistic services and replenishment with about 4,500 heavy shells, was ready for sea within 48 hours of returning to port, whereas the High Seas Fleet was not fit for action until mid-August. And whereas Scheer did take the High Seas Fleet to sea twice more in 1916 (without contact), it was in the realisation that '. . . a high sea battle will not compel England to make peace . . . a victorious end to the war at a not too distant date can only be looked for by the crushing of English life through U-boat action against English commerce'.

Thus the strain upon all Home Fronts by indirect means would be increased at a moment when the Allied peoples were undergoing a novel direct assault aimed almost wholly against civil morale — attack from the air. From the outset the Germans had dropped a few bombs from rigid airships against targets in Belgium, France and, in 1915, England. To begin with their 'air arms' logistic problems had been simplified because operations could be launched, for the most part, from existing bases. Difficulties were imposed, to illustrate the transient immobility of airpower, only when it became necessary to construct and defend advanced bases in occupied territories in order to strike deeper against enemy territory, including industrial targets. But a far greater load was placed upon defenders who, for the most part, lacked the initiative. Entirely new and all-embracing defences founded upon anti-aircraft guns and fighter aircraft, supplied with information from early warning systems (chiefly listening, observation posts), controlled by land line and (much later) radio communications, had to be created, installed and supplied. It was impossible to ignore a threat which, although it did little physical damage, was immensely harmful to civilians who tended to panic and had to be placated.

Indeed, by mid–1915 air warfare was beginning to absorb a significant slice of the logistic cake as its capabilities were extended from simple reconnaissance to a wide variety of roles at sea and over land. Soon bombing attacks and air combat were commonplace. Senior officers who had once derided aircraft potential came to realise their importance and that air power was a main factor. Behind every front a complex of airfields, headquarters, anti-aircraft artillery, communication networks, maintenance and repair depots sprang up and was imposed upon the traditional logistic services — to raise further the demand for skilled, high grade personnel in competition with the other combat arms and services.

In the light of the knowledge that a swelling volume of munitions from an already antagonised American nation was being shipped across the Atlantic to the Allies, General von Falkenhayn was driven to conclude that Germany might lose the war if she did not knock out France in 1916 and thus dissuade Britain from continuance in the war. That was what drove him to apply blatant, artillery-orientated, mincing-machine tactics against the French Army at Verdun in the hope that the French Army would be 'bled white'.

Von Falkenhayn's choice of Verdun stood on the grounds that the French, for any number of emotive, as well as strategic, reasons were bound to defend it to the bitter end. But he was almost as strongly influenced by the ease with which that front could be supplied. Rail and road links with Germany were good, along with reasonable terrain in which to conceal the full magnitude of preparation which began before the end of 1915. Naturally it was impossible totally to hide the 1,400 guns (including 26 super-heavy pieces) along with the $2\frac{1}{2}$ million shells needed at the gun sites for six days' expenditure. But even though the French were forewarned long before the hammering began on 21 February, they laid themselves open to the very fate von Falkenhayn had in mind. Not only had they stripped Verdun's many fortresses, in the belief they were useless against super heavy artillery, they also allowed the trenches to fall into disrepair and denied adequate logistic support to artillery units which were by no means strong. Moreover, the supply of Verdun's outerworks was made all the more awkward because nearly everything had to be carried along one railroad (which at once was put out of action by shelling), plus a single main road of shaky foundation and limited traffic capacity.

Yet it was this road (now solemnised as the *Voie Sacrée*) which, through the most frenetic and well-organised engineering work, saved the situation. Nearly every reinforcement (and every wounded man returning) every gun, every round and every item of store of all other kinds sent forward to inflict counter-attrition on the

Germans, came that way. Night and day, streams of lorries, at an average of one vehicle every 14 seconds, moved along it, by courtesy of some 15,000 men constantly engaged in its maintenance. Often shelled but rarely bombed, it provided a superb example of the superior flexibility and reliability of motor transport. When the railway demonstrated its hopeless vulnerability and horse transport could not have carried 10 per cent of requirements, the lorries just kept rolling — and were easily dragged or pushed off the simply repaired carriageway if they were either damaged or broken. At the end of February, the *Voie Sacrée's* excellent traffic control organisation had helped to show von Falkenhayn that he had backed a loser. Attrition was mutual; no breakthrough would take place, even if he ever hoped for one. Yet he could not now halt the process because personal and national prestige was at stake. The slogging match, sustained by logistic services which moved the men, the guns and the ammunition to their doom, was maintained until July when the British attacks on the Somme provided an excuse to call it off.

This British attack under General Sir Douglas Haig was as monstrously attritional in concept as von Falkenhayn's. There was no stated strategic objective for an advance by overloaded infantry following a seven days, yet none too damaging bombardment. By having each man carry up to some 60 pounds of personal kit and ammunition, combat ability was severely reduced. Yet there resided the dilemma of generals who launched men into shell-disrupted ground which denied immediate access to even motor transport. Unless the infantry bore sufficient supplies on their backs they would be starved of the means to hold objectives and would be thrown back on their supports. Yet until objectives on commanding ground were secured there was no hope of the engineers pushing through roads or light railways to make good deficiencies. So the struggle on the Somme, like its counterpart at Verdun, festered on into the autumn because of the interaction of man's vulnerability to a devastating firepower and his inability to sustain supplies at the front.

Unrecognised at first, the solution to the dilemma was to hand, and would be unveiled on the Somme on 15 September, when a tracked, armoured and armed motor vehicle called 'tank' crawled across no-man's-land to raise the curtain upon a revolution of war in all its aspects.

Note

1. As, indeed, would the armies of his successors be, to a considerable extent, in both Russia and north-west Europe in the Second World War (see Chapter 8).

Chapter 6

The Rise of Mechanisation: 1916-18

TO THE credit of attrition, with its enormous artillery overheads, there had to be posted a contribution, in the negative sense, to the war's turning point in 1917. Had it not failed to bring an end to the war in 1916, either by attacks in the West or in the East (where the Russian offensive under General Brusilov stalled), the Russians might have avoided the plunge into revolution in March 1917.

Brusilov's attempt in June to crush the Austro-Hungarian armies by firepower and manoeuvre across a wide front south of the Pripet Marshes, deserved better of its initial smashing of a demoralised enemy. By prodigious efforts, Brusilov managed to save up sufficient artillery and ammunition to break through in several places and put the enemy to flight. But as usual exploitation broke down once the spearheads had moved more than 40 miles beyond railheads, the predominantly animal transport being unable to keep up. And, as usual, time for the enemy reaction was provided as the Germans, moving in fast by rail with just sufficient troops at the right places, stopped the rot. Inevitably a moment had to arrive when, even with superior manpower, the Russians lacked the firepower to dislodge a few well supported defenders who, incidentally, derived notably indirect support from air straffing of Russian transport.

Without the rage stirred up by the unrestricted submarine warfare launched by the Germans in the winter of 1917, it is possible that America's entry into the war in April might have been delayed, if not avoided. But when the German decision was taken the Russians were still in the war and the Central Powers with their backs to the wall were forced onto the defensive everywhere. Logistically they could not allow the Allies to draw uninterruptedly from an American arsenal, a flow which restricted submarine attacks and sporadic sabotage had no hope of cutting off.

When von Falkenhayn was replaced in September 1916 by General Paul von Hindenburg and General Erich Ludendorff, the duo was given virtually absolute power to control the German war effort. Almost their first act was to call a halt to offensive action in 1917 in order to recuperate. Associated with this economic strategy was the decision to shorten the Western front by constructing an extremely strong trench and wire barrier — the Siegfried Line — and, in February and March, withdraw into it. Like so many radical economy measures, expenditure on implementation was considerable — in labour and materials to dig three lines of trenches, to emplace deep, prefabricated shelters and to erect four foot high belts of wire. The short-term payoff would take the form of savings in combat manpower, along with the frustration of the Allies, who, when they followed up the retreating Germans, entered a devastated zone — a discovery which not only hindered their own logistic arrangements but, as will be seen, curtailed their offensive operations planned for April.

Amazed as they were by the German withdrawal, the Allies also drew benefits from it. The propaganda exploitation of such ruthless destruction was yet another argument to turn American opinion against Germany at a time when the sinking of ships was also causing much public anger, as well as threatening a vital Allied line of communication. Naturally, at this moment when their manpower resources were falling and industrial output almost at a peak, the Allies welcomed the prospect of having the vast American potential on their side with open arms. But there were snags. It would be more than a year before a totally unprepared American army could arrive in strength. And apart from an immediate naval contribution to help secure the sea lanes, logistically America was an embarrassment. Her munitions industry had expanded to meet Anglo-British requirements and was not geared to equip or supply balanced forces of her own. Until 1919 the Americans would be dependent upon the Allies for the heavier or more sophisticated items such as artillery, tanks and aircraft.

Meanwhile the submarine war had to be won in a contest which the British Chief of Naval Staff (now Admiral Jellicoe) tilted in the enemy favour, by his refusal to introduce the convoy system for protection of commercial shipping. Lacking trained staff officers (due to the Royal Navy having done without a Staff College until April 1917), Jellicoe was not presented with scientific information to formulate a reasoned strategy. In consequence, he worked on the entirely false assumption that 5,000 ships per week entered and left British ports when, in fact, as Commander Reginald Henderson proved by a study of Ministry of Shipping statistics, it was a mere 120 to 140. Even so, Jellicoe was reluctant to authorise a trial convoy system because he sensed a shortage of escorts. It took an approach by Henderson to the Prime Minister, over Jellicoe's head, to get permission to start trials; a brave defiance of authority in support of the first example of scientific operational research, which instantly reduced sinkings and won a major logistic victory with immense strategic benefits — for the U-boats at once found it more difficult to locate and attack a very few guarded convoys that a host of single vessels. And the Royal Navy discovered that sufficient escorts were available for those few convoys in a war in which the Battle Fleets spent far more time in harbour than out.

Artillery on the Wane

Even before the almost total domination of the battlefield by artillery had begun to wane on the Western Front, educated challenges to its cost effectiveness had been raised. For example, during the planning for the British attack at Arras on 9 April, a logical proposal to simplify and shorten the time needed to prepare the way for the infantry had been discussed. But the advocates of prolonged bombardment, with all its vast expenditure in terms of worn-out gun barrels and huge quantities of ammunition, brought to the gun-sites by prodigies of organisation, transportation and labour, prevailed. True artillery neutralisation, if not destruction, of every-thing in the forward zone, was stunning. At Arras, the German infantry and gunners, who had been deprived of relief, food and ammunition for days, were so demoralised that they collapsed and let the British through on a frontage of five miles. Yet, two days later, the advance was checked. Dead artillery and transport horses, which had been weakened during a bitterly cold and wet winter, were choking the roadside ditches. Yet when, for a few hours, pursuit looked feasible, the cavalry's horses, in that shell-torn quagmire, lacked the energy to break through, in the same way that their riders lacked the nerve and determination. Gunners who hitched men and horses to drag their pieces and waggons across the shattered terrain, floundered to a standstill and looked to wallowing steam-tractors to solve a problem virtually beyond even their cross-country mobility. The 60 tanks available did little better.

Attrition resumed as the French offensive on the Chemin des Dames made no headway at all against a well-forewarned and, consequently, unsubdued enemy. The final condemnation of excessive reliance upon artillery was pronounced by those Frenchmen who mutinied at the futility of it all, leaving it to the British to pursue 1917s offensive operations unsupported.

In Flanders, between June and November, the artillery insanity reached its frenetic peak, at a price of about 380,000 British losses in return for an advance of only a few miles; 200,000 German casualties and no decision except the weakening of both sides. JFC Fuller calculated there were 8,222 British casualties per square mile captured. As Fuller also implies, the 13-day preliminary bombardment, which merely created a swampland barrier to movement, was all the more ridiculous since it destroyed the roads that vehicles depended on. Neither the 2,200 guns deployed in their gun sites, nor the hundreds of 3-ton lorries which alone had delivered four million shells weighing 107,000 tons to the gun sites, would immediately have pushed through the morass, even if the infantry had broken out — and it would have been impassible for horses or a railway. It was painfully obvious that no proper thought had been given to the physical consequences of so heavy and so prolonged a deluge of fire. Much has been written seeking to explain how it was that armies, and even nations, were committed to these vast and seemingly mindless operations which had to be paid for by such a terrible toll of human lives and the expenditure of so great a measure of material resources. Somehow, they seem to have been the by-product of an unthinking process of mathematics and the application of worn out military dogma which overcame all reason. Henderson's operational analysis, which had shown itself to be so successful when applied to the problems of the war at sea, was never employed in relation to the land battle or to the burgeoning air war. One might be forgiven for thinking that too many commanders and staff officers, having got themselves into the rut of contemporary operations, merely sensed and guessed, rather than establishing a firm intellectual basis for their new concepts. Of course there were a number of brilliant exceptions, of whom the Australian General Monash was one — but they were few and far between.

Guerrillas, Aircraft and a New Mobility

To some extent it was the secondary theatres of war where the most innovative, independently conducted operations flourished. In boundless terrain where smaller forces had room to manoeuvre, striking ideas were hatched to augment limited resources. Nowhere was this more apparent and yet so overlooked in post-war years, than in German East Africa and certain Middle East deserts where revolutionary forms of guerrilla war were practised.

In German East Africa the isolated forces of General Paul von Lettow-Vorbeck were outnumbered from start to finish in a largely undeveloped and hostile country with vulnerable communications. When it rained, the roads and tracks became impassible to almost all forms of transport; in the dry weather the ground was arid and extremely inhospitable to concentrations of men and animals. Opposed by British and South African forces, many of whose leaders were experienced Boer commandos, it was a conditioned irony that von Lettow-Vorbeck, using guerrilla tactics, was permitted to stay at large by an opponent handicapped by limitations imposed by his own government. For whereas the British, for political reasons, were at first forbidden to recruit native porters — and therefore were compelled to depend upon the orthodox and often cumbersome means of animal and, in due course, mechanical transport — the Germans possessed unlimited porterage. Through improvised engineering in the crossing of numerous waterways; captures from the enemy and living off the country; and by conscripting native porters on a scale of two per combat soldier, the Germans enjoyed superior mobility and the power to choose when and where to give battle.

Flexible German porter transport was vastly more responsive and reliable than the British system of vulnerable (and frequently cut) railways; enfeebled draught animals (of which, in one strenuous two week period in 1916, no less than 10,000 horses, 10,000 mules, 11,000 oxen and 2,500 donkeys perished); and gradually multiplying lorry columns which, to begin with, faltered in the appalling road conditions. Time and again, thanks to exhaustion and a shortage of supplies, British operations had to be terminated prematurely, allowing the enemy to slip away. In a land with more than its share of pestilence, both sides suffered cruelly and these casualties from disease stretched both the formed and the improvised hospital services beyond capacity.

In olden days, von Lettow-Vorbeck would have struggled on completely out of touch with Berlin. Now wireless rectified this with useful intelligence, broad directives and, most practical of all, a boost to morale created by an attempt at supply by air. In November 1917 the Zeppelin L59 set forth from Bulgaria on a 3,600 mile voyage over the sea and enemy territory in an attempt to deliver 11 tons of ammunition, 3 tons of medical stores, 30 machine-guns and a few miscellaneous items (including mail and radio parts) to the German forces in the field in East Africa.

It might have come off had not von Lettow-Vorbeck suffered a minor defeat while L59 was in transit, prompting a recall radio signal when she was near Khartoum. It was a notable venture, showing a clear pointer to the potential of radio-directed aircraft succouring guerrillas and agents deep in enemy territory — and one which would not be lost sight of post-war. In the meantime, however, the Germans were revived by capturing more supplies from the enemy than L59 had carried — so much so that they eventually outlasted the Armistice of 11 November 1918 by 12 days.

A principal aspect of this campaign, partially obscured in postwar debate about mechanisation, were the combined triumphs of motor transport linked with road construction. After 3-ton lorries failed in the rough forward zones and were relegated to rearward lines of communication, it was several thousand light vehicles travelling along rough-hewn, rapidly constructed tracks (of which, for example, 450 miles were constructed through the bush in a six month period in 1916) which kept the front supplied. Needless to say, workshop capacity frequently failed to keep up with wear and tear as usage increased. But the training of more than a thousand black natives to drive did more than help solve a manpower crisis; it introduced an emancipatory process with very-long term political consquences indeed. And it was another distinct pointer to the military future when the lorries they drove maintained substantial forces up to 500 miles from railhead.

Across the harder, waterless and trackless deserts of the Middle East such feats were made easier through less dependence on road construction and also by the existence of that superb desert carrier, the camel. The impact on major operations will be discussed later, but they contributed mightily to the guerrilla war waged by Arabs against the Turks. Their support of raiding under T E Lawrence, however, underlined certain new aspects in the supply of guerrillas. The Arab Revolt would have been diminished and delayed — perhaps impossible — had it not been for

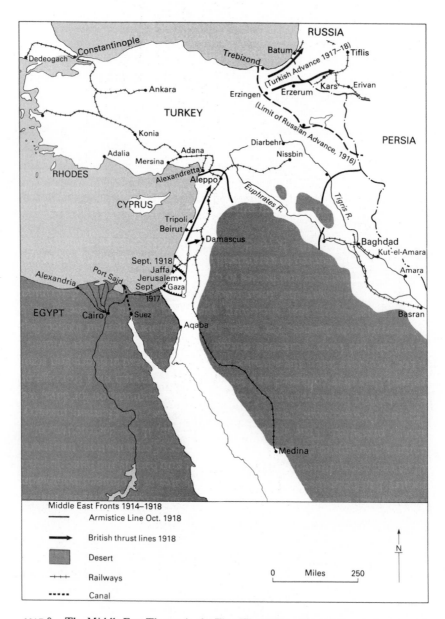

MAP 9.   The Middle East Theatre in the First World War. Note its few vital water and railway arteries and the incompleted Baghdad railway, which hampered the Turks, despite their central position

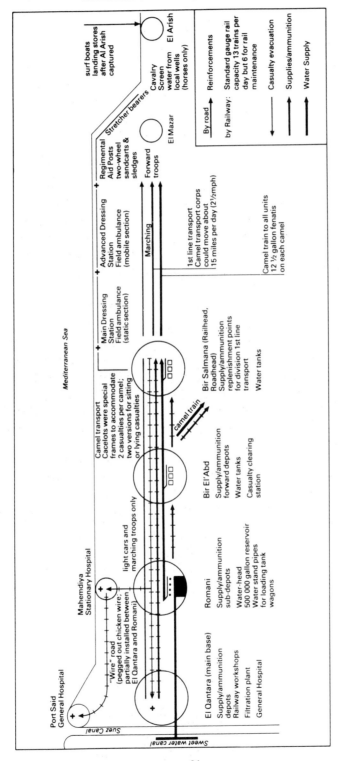

FIG 6.1 The highly developed system of transport across the Sinai Desert from the Suez Canal to El Arish, supplying the front at Gaza in 1917

supply from the sea by the Royal Navy, which established bases along the Red Sea coast as stepping stones to Aqaba. Furthermore, the deployment and stocking of those bases would have been much more inflexible without radio communications in a country without land signal links. But the astute manner in which the British and Feisal's army interrupted the movement of Turkish supplies along the railway from Damascus to Medina, so as to pin down garrisons without completely strangling them, was a masterly application of logistic leverage in indirect pursuit of a strategic aim which did much to weaken the Turkish Army.

Movement by air also played a part when, as the Arab presence on the flank and rear of the Turks in Palestine developed, even big twin-engine bombers delivered men and essential equipment, besides carrying bombs, to desert landing grounds. Thus the techniques of air supply, initiated at Kut, took another step forward just as, on other fronts, including the densely populated Western Front, agents were being inserted by air among the enemy.

As a logistic tool, however, aircraft remained much more a consumer than a provider. In the absence of high capacity transport types, aircraft were confined to the vital realms of reconnaissance, bombing and combat, and were absorbing ever increasing slices of each nation's resources and manpower. Nevertheless, an imaginative proposal by the American, Colonel William Mitchell, that especially trained parachutists should be dropped and supplied by air in the enemy rear, was a revolutionary proposal which only the Armistice of 1918 prevented.

An index of mechanisation's progress among land and air forces may be found in petrol consumption figures. Let us take, as an example, the import of petrol for the British Army in France. In 1915 it amounted to about 1.2 million gallons per month, rising to more than 6.7 million in 1917, a figure which was doubled in 1918, representing increases well in proportional excess often quoted of a feeding strength in 1915 of about 1,048,000 and 2,974,000 in 1918. Similar increases took place in the other theatres of war — notably in Mesopotamia and Palestine where, in 1917, mobility was practised by commanders of outstanding ability who replaced the duffers who had presided over the disasters of 1916. In Mesopotamia there was General Sir Stanley Maude: in Palestine, after his quasi-victory at Arras in April, General Sir Edmund Allenby, two generals whose brilliant strategic and tactical concepts were founded upon a complete grasp of how to apply the latest logistic machinery to the support of operations in under-developed territory.

Maude's capture of Baghdad in March 1917 was the culmination of a masterly concentration against logistically enfeebled Turkish forces. Having put in the right man to improve radically the cargo handling at the port of Basra, he rebuilt the lines of communication to ensure that the assault troops wanted for nothing. Motor vehicles were at the root of most solutions, particularly in support of the pursuit past Kut. Armed river craft not only gave fire support and carried bulk supplies to the front — they actually out-stripped the cavalry and infantry in pace along the Tigris axis of advance. When river craft were unable to meet demand, companies of Ford vans were used in preference to animals whose renowned lack of endurance was compounded by their capacity to consume supplies without return in work. And when the pursuit of a routed enemy got into its stride it was armoured cars, supplied by vans, which spearheaded the advance because the cavalry could not keep up or operate far from the river in wide flanking movements. These motorised, deep penetration manoeuvres contained the germ of the thought behind the armoured divisions of the 1930s.

Allenby's operations against the Turkish defences at Gaza, in similarly inhospitable country, were fought upon much the same lines. Instead of the Tigris he had a railway, a water pipeline and the Royal Navy to supply his forces along the coastal strip from Egypt. But rather less motorised transport than Maude. Crucial to the outflanking of the Turkish coastal position was a 30-mile inland movement to Beersheba — a manoeuvre demanding extensive logistic support (water most of all), the preparations for which had to be concealed in order to retain strategic and tactical surprise. Paradoxically, a principal reason for compounding the supply problem, by allocating no less than two mounted and three infantry divisions to overwhelm this position, lay in the interest of speedy decision. It was vital to prevent the Turks destroying the wells — a point re-emphasised on the day of consummation when the first troops into the town were engineers to ensure a flow of water for so many thousands of men and beasts.

Allenby's celebrated campaigns, the advance to Jerusalem in 1917, the Battle of Megiddo in September 1918, followed by rapid pursuit to Aleppo and beyond, were models of meticulous logistic concept, similar to Mesopotamia in that flexibility of supply, made possible by comprehensive signal communications and sufficient transport, was of paramount importance. When wheeled transport could not cope with the hills to Jerusalem, mule columns were improvised. When infantry advanced into barren land at Megiddo, sufficient carriers of every type were provided. And when the armoured cars shot ahead of the cavalry on the road to Damascus and Aleppo, it was motor transport which kept them rolling — despite horsemen claiming the credit for it in after years.

Techniques such as the above were not, of course, the sole prerogative of the British. Other armies also mechanised extensively — prominently the Italians with Fiat light vehicles. But the pay-off in zones of high military density was only occasionally dramatic. The limited German attack against the Russians at Riga in September 1917, which achieved a breakthrough by the combination of partially unregistered artillery fire (to achieve surprise) and infantry infiltration tactics, did not, in the absence of deep exploitation, overstretch logistics. While similar tactics by the Germans and Austrians, on a much larger scale against the Italians at Caporetto in October, eventually stalled due to an all too familiar logistic breakdown. After a breakthrough on a frontage of 35 miles, which cracked the Italian Army's spirit with an advance of over 40 miles to the River Piave, the logistic equaliser was applied. Concurrent with faltering by German and Austrian infantry, whose endurance was sapped by blockade's deprivations, their transport columns were unable to sustain a momentum which might have been decisive if armoured cars and even a few cavalry, adequately supplied by sufficient motor transport, had been available. As it was, equilibrium was restored by a combination of inspired Italian leadership which stimulated resistance along the Piave in the nick of time — a recovery ensured by their own pouring in of reinforcements, plus the transfer, mainly by rail, of no less than two French and one British army corps from France, over a period of 14 days — after it had taken nearly a fortnight between Allies to settle the movement plan. Once more, the lesson that reinforcement, via efficient lines of communication, would outpace to breaking point the advance of a horse and foot force had been demonstrated — and would be again a few days later at Cambrai.

The Battle of Cambrai — A Flawed Victory

Rightly celebrated though it is, as the occasion of the first employment of tanks in mass, the Battle of Cambrai, fought on 20 November 1917, is far more important as a turning point in history. At last it was possible, by the revolutionary application of unregistered artillery, to achieve complete surprise over the enemy and, at the same time, to achieve logistic economies. This was Haig's last chance of success in a dolorous year of costly failure — an up-scaling on his part of the limited tank raid on firm ground proposed earlier by the Tank Corps under Brigadier Hugh Elles. Haig aimed at cutting the enemy lines of communication to induce the collapse of the entire German North West front — and, but for a lack of reserves, the poor endurance of the cavalry and the logistic flaws of the tank, might have achieved it. But it was Lieutenant Colonel J F C Fuller, Elles' chief staff officer, who formulated the revolutionary plan for close co-operation between all arms and services which broke the enemy on a nine miles frontage and advanced up to five miles in four hours.

Because 376 tanks were able to crush and tow away the vast barbed wire entanglements, and cross wide trenches in a few minutes, there was no need for the artillery to spend days firing thousands of tons of shells for the same purpose. The artillery could concentrate accurately upon counter-battery fire against enemy guns and against nodal points — and did so without warning after the tanks moved off. The latest techniques of survey and meteorology, which made possible this unregistered 'shooting off the map', not only lulled the enemy into a sense of false security (on the assumption that the first blast of fire was only a preliminary), it radically reduced the demand for ammunition and, in consequence, the time required to deliver it to the gun sites along with inevitable disclosure of what was impending. Instead of taking weeks to assemble the assault force with massive supporting services, the concentration of seven infantry and five cavalry divisions, the Tank Corps and 1003 guns with ammunition was achieved by night in about a week without arousing serious suspicion or detection from the air.

Crucial to the assembly of men and stores to their concealed positions was the traffic plan which utilised every road and track for horses and vehicles. Equally important was the single track, full-gauge railway line which ran parallel to the front, and carried ammunition and the tanks close to their assembly areas. An accident or some other hitch blocking this line would have threatened the entire operation since — no railway, no tanks. For because tank track life was only about 20 miles and replacing tracks a lengthy job, the machines had to be delivered on rail flats to within two or three miles of the front. As there were only 144 rail flat cars available the concentration had to be spread over five nights. Moreover, provision had to be made to push forward the railway quickly on the heels of the advance in order to recover those tanks which survived the battle and needed new tracks.

For the first time, large scale replenishment of tanks in battle was envisaged — with 54 supply tanks to lift forward 165,000 gallons of tinned petrol, 40,500 gallons of oil, 55,000 lb of grease, 5 million rounds of small arms ammunition and 54,000 57mm shells. This was the life blood and armament of the modern mechanised army which was replacing the old fodder-fuelled formations — or 'hay burners' as the irreverent sometimes called them. But though these arrangements largely worked, the attack stalled on the five mile mark; partly due to typical battle-field set-backs and local communication problems; but largely because the cavalry which, on this occasion, did reach the front in time to enter an undefended gap, failed to do so. Poor leadership, low animal endurance and lack of urge to co-operate with tanks contributed to the blame. Fundamentally, however, it was the tank's own mechanical shortcomings, compounded by inadequacies of recovery, repair and maintenance which made it impossible to concentrate sufficient machines at the vital spot for a renewed effective advance on the 21st. Another three miles and Haig's aim of cutting the enemy communications would have been achieved.

As it was the German command dithered in panic and nearly ordered withdrawal from their positions to the west of Cambrai. If only the British had taken a few risks on the 21st they would have forced abandonment of prestige fortifications upon which enormous labour and expense had been lavished, in addition to the loss of huge quantities of material and munitions. So stunning might have been the result that the campaigns of 1918 would have followed a very different course. Instead there was a pause, followed by delayed renewal of the attack — a delay which encouraged the Germans to pour in reinforcements from far and wide, one account mentioning trains arriving almost nose to tail in a masterly movements impro-visation at a few hours' notice.

The Ludendorff Offensives of Hopeless Endeavour

Inevitable as was the extensive transfer of German forces to the West after the Bolshevik revolution had taken Russia out of the war at the end of 1917, the concept of defeating the Anglo-French armies before the Americans arrived in overwhelming strength, was extremely suspect. For though it was true that the fighting strength of all the combatants had been worn thin by over three years attrition, it was very much a fact that the Allied blockade had reduced the stamina of the Central Powers in both morale and logistics, almost to breaking point.

There were many factors which gave the German Army a clear tactical superiority over the British Fifth and Third Armies, which were almost overwhelmed by a long-expected German assault, behind a massive bombardment, on 21 March 1918. Inferior British training and morale had something to do with the collapse, imperfections made worse by the length of training time lost by fighting troops who, due to the general labour shortage, had been diverted to constructing defences and shifting stores and equipment. Nevertheless, the Allied logistic services and equipment were in considerably better shape than those of their opponents, as will be seen. The number of vehicles in the transport companies had been increased by pooling arrangements and the elimination of inflexible practices had improved utilisation. No longer would transport units specialise in one type of commodity. Henceforward vehicles could be switched from ammunition, to food or anything else as required. A complete formation could be moved with all its equipment to reinforce a threatened sector at little more than an hour's notice. In one brief period the French used 11,200 lorries in 18,000 trips to help move 100,000 men, plus three divisional artilleries and their horses, a distance of 190 miles. So big was the available Allied transport lift that dependence on the railways was vastly reduced. As a result, when the German advance threatened the vital route centre of Amiens, British supplies were only marginally in jeopardy. Indeed, when railheads close to the front were abandoned, lorries took over their task, some drivers staying at the wheel for 60 hours at a stretch.

This performance the Germans could not match. All manner of excuses have been offered for the failure of their drive towards Amiens — which managed only 40 miles in eight days; but it was logistic collapse which lay at the root. There were insufficient motor vehicles as substitutes for emaciated horse transport. For what few sound horses there were had been purloined by the infantry from both the cavalry and the logistic services: and a dire shortage of winter fodder weakened them all. Engineers were hard pressed to repair damaged bridges and roads. The railway troops could not even keep up with the infantry, who advanced at barely five miles a day. Meanwhile soldiers, whose rations were poor and who had forgotten about luxuries, were diverted from their tasks (as had so many armies in the past) by the temptations of booty. Enemy supply dumps were pillaged as the men gorged themselves instead of pressing on. Valuable booty was consumed as greed eroded discipline. It is said that the looting of some 2 million bottles of whisky helped to retard an advance which was already hampered by shortages of petrol, grease, oil and rubber tyres. Perhaps most demoralising of all was the discovery by the Germans of how much better equipped was their enemy than themselves. So, when each successive offensive was launched and, in due course, with ever-diminishing gains halted, it was thrust upon Ludendorff's frustrated followers, long before the Allied backlash the Battle of Amiens on 8 August

(Ludendorff's 'Black Day of the German Army'), that there was little sense in prolonging a war which blockade had settled.

In one respect, at least, Ludendorff had grasped the futility of persisting in attacks once momentum had been lost. His determination to 'not get drawn into a battle of exhaustion' was an acknowledgement of his inability to overcome an enemy whose 'resistance was beyond our strength'. He was defeated by a logistic imbalance made all the worse by swarms of Allied aircraft introducing a new and deadly threat to his lines of communication. For as the German Army emerged from cover to march in pursuit, it was repeatedly delayed by the need to take refuge from low flying attacks, which further weakened it by the destruction of vehicles and stores. These were lessons which the Germans could not ignore as they were fought to a standstill in mid-July and found themselves stranded in weak defensive positions. Without the resources to establish either a strong fortified zone or the mobile forces to cope with abrupt incursions of the Cambrai kind, they awaited their fate in a state of semi-exhaustion.

The Allied Counter-offensive

If the defeats in Italy and France did nothing else, they concentrated the Allied minds upon the necessity for a unified Command — which led to the appointment on 26 March 1918 of Marshal Ferdinand Foch as Supreme Commander of what he called 'a great military orchestra'. From an operational standpoint, he saved the day by his co-ordination of the Allied armies, which were drifting apart under German pressure. It was Foch who allocated sufficient resources to counter each new threat, redistrubution which was made all the easier by the flexibility of the road transport at his disposal. Foch, who started the German rot with a limited counter-stroke at Villers Cotteret on 18 July, and he whose thrust lines in the months to come would be determined more by a desire to eliminate German lateral rail communications (to prevent troop transfers), than the need any longer to develop rail arteries to supply his own armies. Yet, on the other hand, it was Foch, after the great, tank-heavy Allied punch, which burst through at Amiens and Montdidier on 8 August, and struck hardened resistance on the 10th, who wanted to keep pounding in the same place, with inevitably diminishing returns. And Haig, among others, who declined, insisting instead that the initial breakthrough should be expanded through weaker neighbouring sectors in order to exert flank leverage against the enemy's reinforced strong points. Before Cambrai it would have been impossible, for logistic reasons, to launch a series of major attacks at different sectors at shorter notice than seven days. After Haig stopped the Amiens stroke on 11 August and persuaded Foch on the 15th to accept his strategy, the next blow fell at Soissons on the 18th, followed by another at Albert on the 21st which was pressed only until the 25th. Thereupon a fresh attack was launched at Arras on the 26th, so loosening the German resistance that they were forced into a general retreat to the Siegfried Line which, on 26 September, was breached a few days after the Americans pinched out the enemy salient at St Mihiel. It was one of the logistic feats of the land war that Americans who had fought at St Mihiel could be in action again in the Argonne ten days later as part of a force of 500,000, three-quarters of whom were moved 50 miles in French lorries. The end of the war came into sight when, two days later, the British drove forward in Flanders — a thrust which prompted the Germans to pull back everywhere, forfeiting their lateral communications and immense dumps, which could not be saved in time.

United strategy was not wholly reflected in logistic collaboration. When General John Pershing, the American Commander-in-Chief, advocated pooling of all Allied resources, only the French took him up with enthusiasm. The British were not prepared to change their effective working practices or to lose control of their own services. Conflicts between national pride and practical realities naturally impinged upon such a radical proposition. The French tried to use it as an excuse for placing material at the exclusive disposal of Foch. The British demurred. Standardisation entered into the debate. Because the Americans had failed miserably to produce enough guns of their own, they were compelled to adopt French field and medium and British heavy pieces, for which there was less ammunition than desired. It was thus much easier for the Americans to combine with the French than the British. In practice, collaborations were achieved. The American ration scale was reduced in line with the British. An inter-Allied reserve of transport was formed. French and American ammunition was pooled.[1]

The Central Powers, who suffered far less from such anomalies, were nevertheless at their last gasp as they fell back before a tattoo of blows. For them it was no longer a matter of stabilising the front as the logistic equaliser was applied. The morale and discipline of deprived soldiers had collapsed in disillusionment. The Allies, superbly supplied by their fleets of lorries, could retain the initiative of a fluent mobility. Even cavalry, aided by tanks and armoured cars, enjoyed a few brief moments of old-fashioned freedom of action, by courtesy of lorries and captured enemy fodder. It is arguable that, when the Germans did manage to slow the Allied offensive in the last few days before the Armistice, one important factor was the shortage of tanks in the forward area, a scarcity stemming as much from the inability of broken railways to carry them to within striking distance of the Front, as from inroads caused by battle casualties and mechnical breakdown.

Eight months of practice in mobility on all fronts worked miracles in challenging systems which had fallen into a trench warfare rut. To the credit of the Allies, their logistic services had reacted with commendable flexibility, their systems taking the strain rather better than those of the enemy. Which was all the more remarkable in the light of basic signal communication failures due, in large part, to absence of a doctrine for retreat. During the March retreat in France there was, on the British front, an almost total disruption of land line communication; a collapse which hurt the teeth arms far more than the tail services since the latter functioned through routine procedures which were almost automatic — and, paradoxically, considerably more extensively mechanised. Increasingly it was radio, despite the shortcom-

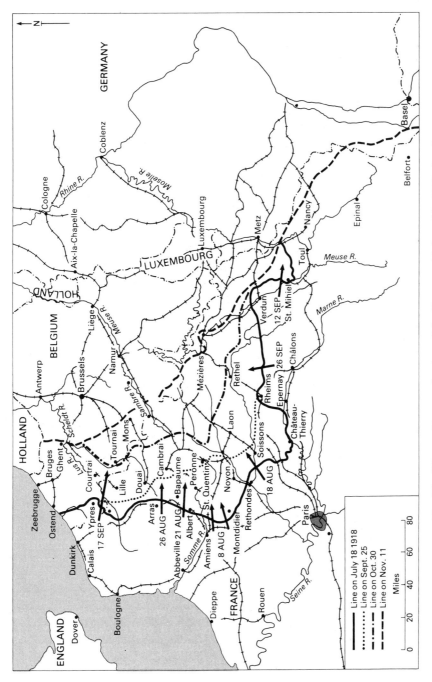

MAP 10. The Western Front at the time of the German withdrawal in 1918, showing that their lines of communication were never seriously threatened

ings of insecure spark sets, which filled the communication gaps. No longer was it just a 'stand-by' facility, but highly desirable.

Radio, despite its low traffic capacity and its liability to disclosing intentions, became as vital to the Allied advance as the Germans had hoped might be the case for them in 1914. Not only did operational transmissions maintain contact with spearhead units when line laying detachments could not keep up, they provided the logistic organisations with guidelines upon which to plan resupply. Furthermore, battery-powered sets imposed a somewhat smaller logistic overhead than land line with its demands upon miles of buried, but still vulnerable, cable, relays, exchanges and maintenance detachments.

As was invariably the case with big 20th-century conflicts, the First World War's end came on the eve of impending innovations in technology which left many questions for the future unanswered. With the promise of greatly improved radio sets; even more lorries; tanks of longer range and endurance; and large transport aircraft in the offing, a person was blind who could not grasp in 1919, in the aftermath of changes since 1914, that nothing would be the same again at war.

Note

1. The parlous state of the American Expeditionary Force (AEF) when it first arrived in France is not well known. Not only did the French and British have to provide artillery pieces for them but horses also. The British gun teams were reducd from six horses to four to make this possible — a heavy sacrifice in the apalling conditions under which the batteries had to redeploy. The AEF was sadly lacking in administrative experience and, in the early days, some of their troops were on the verge of starvation in the trenches. Fortunately, Brigadier General George Marshall, who was to rise to such fame as Chairman of the Joint Chiefs of Staff in the Second World War, became Pershing's principal administrative officer and, thanks to his untiring efforts, the situation was gradually put to rights.

Chapter 7

Upheaval: The Aftermath of War

IT HAS become something of a myth that, during the essential rounds of retrenchment in the aftermath of the First World War, there were fanatical attempts by reactionaries to reverse the all-embracing changes which had taken place since 1914. In point of fact experiment and innovation to a varying degree continued in all branches of the Arms and Services of most major nations with particular emphasis placed on mechanisation, flight and communications — the leaders in most fields being the Japanese, the French, the British and the Italians, with the Germans secretly managing whatever was possible within the severe limitations imposed by the Versailles Treaty.

The variety of political, economic, social and technical changes stimulated by the war were far too strong to be stifled even by influential minorities. If it had been possible to curb the expansionist ambitions of Japan, France, Britain and Italy, and prevent Germany from reasserting herself, commercial entrepreneurs would have persisted in seeking a profit through inventions and techniques designed to cut costs and raise profits. For example, the already well established civilian desire for cleaner, more easily handled oil fuel, in lieu of coal, was as irresistible as the call for machines to replace animal and human labour. Furthermore, the advantages of vastly extended and improved transport, as well as signal communications, were deemed as vital by civilians as by far-sighted military planners, all of whom recognised a 'shrinking globe' when they saw one. Without exception each and every one of these influences were so fundamentally important to logisticians that strategists ignored them (as often they did) at their peril.

Oil and New Aspects of Sea Power

Central to the development of Sea Power and Trade were the sources of oil and the sea and land routes along which it was carried. As oil replaced coal as the fuel upon which all modernised armed forces depended, control of its production zones, in North America, in Romania, in the Middle East, in Burma and the Dutch East Indies, assumed vital importance. Soon, the old coaling bases were being run down in favour of oil tank farms. Pipelines were constructed at sea; larger oil tankers took over from colliers at a time when the nearest thing to a super-tanker weighed a mere 30,000 tons. The size of such ships was limited by the size of the main canals and principal ports — restrictions which, to meet demand, promoted the construction of a great many smaller tankers instead of fewer, very large ones — a proliferation which created far more targets for predators (submarines in the main) and imposed a much harder task upon those whose business it would be to protect them on passage.

However, before 1940, there was not much faith in the efficacy of the submarine as a weapon of blockade. Even amongst the Germans, who pinned some hopes on this type of blockade, there was a feeling that the latest sonar detection methods, the depth charge and the convoy had secured lines of sea communication. It had not been realised that, in collaboration with air power and with the help of centralised radio control, submarine packs would now be able to find, concentrate against and penetrate the defensive arrangements of convoys more easily. One result of this misappreciation was that Britain, France, Italy and America were provoked into a naval race after Japan had disclosed her intention in 1920 to build 12 capital ships of over 40,000 tons.

Japanese fear of blockade, the result of their expansionist policy in the Far East and the Pacific, had prompted the building programme. However, it was demonstrations of naval air striking power by the British during the war, when aircraft had bombed all manner of targets; had torpedoed ships and had been brought to within striking distance of their targets by aircraft carriers, which had alerted the Japanese to a peril which was underlined in 1921 when General Mitchell demonstrated (in admittedly spurious conditions) that well-armoured warships could be sunk by bombs. When K Nakamura pointed out that 'It would be within the power of a superior naval opponent to strangle our commerce and cut off our supplies without sending a single ship into the Sea of Japan', he envisaged the possibility of the nation's economy, let alone the navy, being crippled within only a few months. For Japan depended entirely upon the import of fuel oil, besides many other raw materials. It would even have been possible to bring her to her knees by the threat of sanctions designed to wreck both policy and strategy. In a way, therefore, the Washington Treaty of 1922 (which, for the time being limited battleship construction to Japan's disadvantage) created a loophole for her by permitting aircraft carrier construction — which was a victory for Japan. It was these ships, in harmony with the development of bombing and torpedo dropping techniques, and in association with the building of specially designed amphibious landing ships and craft, which not only strengthened the Japanese defences against blockade but further stimulated her acquisitive intentions.

Yet aircraft carriers which, with submarines, would assume from battleships the role of the capital ship, were not fighting ships. Simply, they were floating airfields and control centres within a very mobile, though limited forward base which, demanded intense close defence and a wide separation from hostile forces in order to carry out their tasks unhindered.

Behind the story of Japan's expansion into Manchuria, into China and, in 1942, deep into the Pacific, the East Indies and to the frontier of India, lies her militaristic government's realisation that without possession of oil supplies, her ambitions were doomed. Therefore, at the heart of her eventual decision to challenge America and the European powers for domination of the Far East, lay a basic logistic problem. It was insufficient merely to cripple the enemy fleets and seize outlying island and territorial bulwarks against counter-offensives. It was far more important not only to seize main sources of oil supply, and other materials, but also to be able to transport them by sea to the homeland. When the Americans stopped oil deliveries in 1941 and Admiral Yamamoto advised the government that, although he might 'raise Hell' for eighteen months among the enemy, he could not guarantee what might happen after that, he was not describing a calculated strategic risk. He was implying a logistic gamble. For it is extremely dangerous to assume the capture of vital supplies from any enemy — least of all those so immense as the Japanese were challenging. It was a fundamental error on the Japanese part that they diminished the weighting of the logistic factor and exalted their faith in mere success at arms as a means to destroy the morale and determination of foes they arrogantly had deluded themselves to despise.

The Air Power Bogey

The shadow of air power which loomed darkly over images of future war tended as much to cloud as illuminate what might happen. The theories of the Italian General Giulio Douhet in his 1921 book *Command of the Air*, were undeniably too far in advance of technical feasibility when they prophesied that a nation's will could be subdued by terror and destruction of cities. Although *Command of the Air* did not win wide support, except in Britain, it did obscure visions of what might be achieved by developing what had proved feasible in 1918. Hero worshippers (including some among the militarily educated) who revelled in the escapades of air aces and spoke earnestly about winning air superiority, usually overlooked how impractical damaging attacks upon lines of communication would have been without air superiority. The enormously expensive logistic cost of strategic bombing in relation to a nation's entire war effort was only scantily considered. Little was heard of such cost-effective operations mounted by the RAF to 'pacify' such wild desert regions as Iraq (Mesopotamia) with a combination of air attacks and armoured car patrols which struck at dissident tribesmen and, as often as not, curbed their depredations by destruction or denial of food, as well as by inflicting casualties. Indeed, in that country where military air supply had first been practised in 1916 at Kut, the air supply of mechanised troops with spare parts and other necessities and the evacuation of wounded was by no means uncommon.

Rather than as a deliberate measure, air transport support evolved from sheer necessity and through the gradual introduction into service of suitable aircraft. Since civil air lines were tardy to start business, such large transport aircraft as at first were available were converted bombers of inferior payload. For example, in the first ever evacuation of populace by air (from Sulaimaniya to Kirkuk in Iraq in September 1925) no less than 29 assorted machines were required to lift 67 people — before the aircraft concerned went over to supplying the army's operations in difficult terrain. At some time or another, all the colonial powers engaged on operations used aircraft to take in men or material and bring out wounded, but it was to the Americans, flying small, single engined bombers, that the distinction went of running a regular casualty evacuation service during a fifteen-year campaign in Haiti.

Loud were those enthusiasts who praised air power's potential mobility. It was, they claimed, impressive how squadrons could be transferred rapidly from one trouble spot to another in a matter of hours. Yet not only was it a delusion that independent air forces were merely complementary to ground forces, it was a deceit to ignore their relative immobility due to dependence upon the prepositioning of adequate and quite complex ground and logistic facilities before a mission was flown. Rarely, during the fighting in dense European environments, had air forces been called upon to practise logistic mobility. Mostly squadrons simply flew from one developed airfield to another. It was a very different matter in under-developed theatres of war where airfields did not yet exist and where everything had to be constructed and supplied; sometimes in terrain which had, first, to be seized by conventional ground forces. Yet in the gradual creation of a military aviation presence throughout and at the peripheries of their empires, the colonial powers laid the foundations of future global, transport systems.

Whether the requirement for military or for civil transport was instrumental in fostering large, multi-engined passenger and cargo aircraft is a moot point. Short-range passenger services started with single engine machines before the air forces, somewhat against their combat orientated instincts, were compelled to devote funds and effort to the provision of operational air trooping on a small scale. Seeking prestige for political reasons in the pursuit of independence, airman preferred combat machines for show. Few airliners of the 1920s carried more than 20 people further than a few hundred miles — and still fewer fully equipped soldiers with their ammunition and supplies. Scarcity of airfields in distant active service regions inevitably restricted air power. It was expensive and commercially hazardous to pioneer and set up commercial bases in thinly populated places — and few were the governments or companies prepared to spend heavily upon well-equipped airports anywhere. Similarly, few were the opportunities to demonstrate air transport's ability to span the gap between rail or road heads in desolate country. Nevertheless, it was done — notably by the British in India — and in a manner to concentrate minds upon the potential of expanding civil air transport as the world drifted towards war in the 1930s.

It was no coincidence that, the German air force, which first saw action in Spain in 1936, was, arguably, not only the best in the world but also the most logistically minded, because it was founded upon commercial lines. To begin with, as a means of getting round the Versailles Treaty, the Germans collaborated with the Russians in the construction of metal aircraft and advanced diesel air engines. Then when the Treaty was relaxed in 1926 to allow civil aviation, a burgeoning aircraft industry produced many different types with dual civil and military potential. Among these the tri-motor Junkers Ju 52, with its 1 ton payload (or 18 passengers) over a range of 800 miles, was pre-eminent. For although the Ju 52, like the Junker-inspired Tupolev transports built in Russia, would prove inadequate as a bomber, or as a cargo, passenger and parachutist aircraft it would be vital to air logistic organisation. Soon the Germans were far ahead in the practice of air mobility. From its early days, each Luftwaffe squadron had one or two Ju 52s on strength. Whenever a quick transfer of combat strength from one front to another was ordered, hundreds of Ju 52s would be employed in a shuttle service ahead of ground transport, to pre-position munitions, fuel, ground staff, spares and airfield and signals equipment. And on special occasions, those same Ju 52s could be utilised by parachutists air landed troops to seize bridgeheads in advance of ground troops and then bring in supplies.

The limitations of air logistic support were, of course, well recognised. The early twin and tri-motor machines were of such short range and low payload as to deny adequate support to any other than light ground forces for limited periods of time and against only light opposition. The four-motor air liners entering service just prior to 1939 showed the way to a transport revolution — although these machines were few in number, since civil airlines were still in their teething stages, catering mainly for the rich, while combat aircraft continued to have first call on resources and finance. Nevertheless, when war broke out in Europe, the basic techniques and strategic value had been established. For example, it was the shuttle airlift of 13,523 troops and 500 tons of supplies, from Morocco to Spain by Ju 52s, which enabled General Franco to establish a firm base in July 1936 for the rebellion which started the Spanish Civil War.

The Mechanisation of Land Forces

If for no other reason than that a rapid diminution of the horse population was making it impossible to envisage sufficient draught (let alone combat) animals for a future major war, military planners were compelled to tackle the problems of wholesale mechanisation. Business men (ex-soldiers among them) for whom survival depended upon the need to cut costs, took priority over romantic horse worshippers and were quick to learn the transport lessons of war and to adopt motor lorries in place of horse-drawn waggons. Pressure upon governments to improve or build better roads was unremitting — to the eventual erosion also of the railway's position of dominance. While a lot of fuss was being made by cavalrymen, horse gunners and the equestrian world against proposals to mechanise the combat arms, the logistic services (who also had their regrets about horses) were becoming wholly mechanised. Moreover, and as an example, the British who in 1912 had paid subsidies to motor manufacturers to instal standardised controls in *all* lorries, to enable quick adaption of drivers to man impressed vehicles in war, extended this practice into the 1940s. They also carried out considerable research and develop-ment into new designs, developing multi-wheeled drive, half and full track supply vehicles against the time when tanks might become a dominant weapon system which had to be resupplied, cross-country.

Not all the new ideas bore fruit at once. For example, because four-wheeled drive and tracked vehicles were more expensive, and did not commend themselves at once to commercial firms, nearly all military logistic vehicles were originally only two wheel drive and all too easily bogged once off the road — despite the introduction of balloon tyres in place of the old narrow treads. As a result, road construction in undeveloped theatres of war remained a pre-requisite of operations by modern mechanised forces. The troops who, for example, penetrated mountain-ous territory (as on the North West Frontier of India) to pacify tribesmen who, for generations under the goad of utter deprivation, had raided in order to survive, now had to build roads for lorries (instead of tracks for animals) to supply their outposts and airfields. Soon those same roads, which opened up previously inaccessible regions, were being traversed by lorries driven by ex-predators who had shrewdly concluded that trading was better than raiding[1]. They demonstrated again what had been learnt in East Africa (and would be re-learned over and over again in all the countries of the world) how easy it was for people of all kinds to master mechanical vehicles, showing that it was unnecessary to be the member of some social élite to drive and maintain a lorry.

All the above had, in fact, been made apparent before the 1920s. Yet when experiments with highly mobile, full tracked cross-country vehicles were started by the British in the 1920s, and espoused as a revolutionary way of winning strategic victories by deep penetration of enemy countries with tank armies, one objection raised was the impossibility of supplying such forces. Many of the early trials used only improvised transport echelons comprised of unsuitable vehicles. Indeed, none of the armies which went to war in 1939 possessed four wheel drive vehicles because financial constraints as well as a lack of developed four wheel drive models, forced two wheel drive types on them. Nevertheless the studies and experiments of the late 1920s and the 1930s did establish systems which, to a large extent,with-stood the tests of war. The principle of mechanised, armoured divisions being self-contained with food, fuel and ammunition was deemed essential during mobile operations. Apart from what was carried in the fighting vehicles, as much as three days supplies were kept on wheels and were replaced as and when required (mostly at night) by successive, echeloned groups of lorries which were controlled by radio as they were shifted from hide to hide on their way to and from the front. Food, to a large extent, was dried or canned. Ammunition came in protective packing which was usually stripped off by the crews of the combat echelon. Lorries were multi-purpose to enable them to carry men or any kind of load, including fuel. But it was the way to supply fuel which caused the most concern and controversy.

Bulk oil continued to move by pipeline, marine tankers and by rail and road tankers to refineries and storage areas where the civil companies distributed it to customers — usually also by road tanker. During the First World War it had been the practice to supply petrol, oil and lubricants (POL in British terminology) to front line units, including aircraft, in cans and drums. With fully mechanised warfare and enormous consumption, it was foreseen that this would not work. For one thing large tankers in the forward areas would be vulnerable as well as useless for other purposes. Eventually it was decided to use cans in the field, employing tankers in rearward areas and on airfields where their quicker delivery rates were an advantage. It was then a question of what type of can: an expensing, robust re-usable 20 litre type, such as the Germans adopted (and which naturally came to be known as a 'jerrican'); or the one trip British 4-gallon 'flimsy' which required protective crating when in transit and which, by its very nature, was easily punctured and therefore horribly wasteful, besides being a deadly fire risk. It was a great relief to all concerned when the flimsy, with a 30 per cent wastage or more, was abandoned in mid-war in favour of the jerrican (many from captured stocks).

A transport problem of considerable importance which was no nearer solution in the 1920s than it had been in 1917 at Cambrai, remained the delivery of tanks to the front. Track mileage was still low and would remain so with most tanks of all nations until the early 1940s when new metallurgy came to the rescue. Rail transport was therefore essential, with its usual vulnerability and inflexibility; and additionally its impositions of limitations on vehicle dimensions to satisfy the rail gauge. Narrower tanks denied essential increases in the size of armament as battle experience established a need for thicker and thicker armour and bigger and more powerful guns to defeat it — so the only way forward lay in an increase in the size of the turret ring and so in the overall width of the tank. In consequence, only road transporters would provide the answer to the strategic movement of tanks, as their weight rose to 40 tons and more. Furthermore, it became essential to increase the load-bearing capacity of bridges on military routes. As the tanks grew in size, so did the dimensions and power of their transporters and so did the scale of logistic complication. Before the outbreak of war in 1939, few tank transporters existed — they were essentially a means of recovering broken down or damaged tanks to field workshops or to railhead for evacuation to more static workshops at the base. Now, within a matter of months, an urgent requirement sprang up for transporters in their hundreds and transporter companies and columns came onto the order of battle. Let it not be supposed, however, that every army was wholly mechanised before 1939. Far from it. Only the British had gone almost the whole hog. The Germans, despite their much vaunted, fast-moving mechanised and armoured (panzer) divisions, continued to be reliant, to a considerable extent, upon rail and horse-drawn transport (as we have already seen). Their lack of mechanised transport was due in no small part to Hitler's insistence upon giving priority to the production of armoured vehicles and lorry production suffered accordingly (see also Chapter 8 page 117). Since this was so, the German failure to realise that the Russian railways had a narrower guage than their own was an almost incredible oversight for which they were to pay a heavy penalty in 1941, as their lines of communication in Russia grew longer and longer.

Radio in the Ascendant

Barely noticed, except by a handful in the know, the communications revolution at the turn of the 20th century had itself been in process of revolution since 1902 when John Fleming, who coined the word 'electronics', invented the vacuum diode valve. Throughout the First World War marginally improved 'spark' 'unquenched' radio, working in the low frequencies, had been in use and of vital assistance to the logistic services in such theatres of war as Russia, Mesopotamia, Palestine and East Africa. Post 1918, 'quenched' sets transmitting continuous carrier waves in the high and very high frequency bands ousted 'spark' sets. And soon, through newly acquired knowledge of the effects of the ionised layers, the latest sets were reflecting and 'beaming' long distance signals with greatly reduced interference. As world-wide radio networks burgeoned, great advances, too, were made with small, rugged sets urgently required by aircraft and mobile land forces. The diode valve, which like quartz crystals, gave accurate, simplified tuning, was the key to these vital improvements, also making possible the transmission and reception of speech in vehicles on the move — at the same time as great advances in land line communications were in the offing. Not only did cable and radio teleprinters (machine fed and working at far higher speeds than hand-operated morse key), using punched tape, achieve immensely higher volumes of signal traffic but the Germans developed a means of laying field cable at the rate of 100 kilometres a day — thus reducing the need for insecure radio networks.

In attendance with this revolution were masses of technical complications with their calls for trained technologists; security hazards, with the need for cyphers; and extra logistic loads, such as the provision of more machines, exchanges, spare parts, millions of miles of cable, together with extra poles, thousands of relays and the like. Having created an appetite for such refinements, it became increasingly necessary to protect the security of diplomatic, commercial and military messages by the use of electro-mechanical cypher machines, of which the German Enigma system represented the peak — until 'cracked' by the British cryptoanalysts of Bletchley Park.

As had always been the case, the vast majority of signals traffic, orders for replenishment, appreciations, planning detail, movement instructions, strength and stock returns and similar material had been of a logistic nature. The romance and drama of sweeping strategic and tactical orders were often the bright facade screening a solid administrative structure to which everything was attached. But whatever the nature of each message there lay within it information of vital intelligence to friend and foe alike — and it should be no surprise to learn that those who tried to break enemy cyphers and codes were looking as hard as they were for operational instructions. For it was knowledge of *actual* enemy movements and stockpiling which confirmed or refuted the credibility of operational instructions. The latter might well be deliberately misleading — part of a deception plan; the former were real.[2] So it was not only against a torrent of words being transmitted by radio (with their give-away through Direction Finding) that an enemy directed his intercept and decyphering attack, but also by agents wire-tapping the cables carrying shipping, rail, road and air traffic to and from headquarters, depots and transit points.

From 1930 onwards, electronic signal communications governed the conduct of war. Radio was no longer regarded merely as a back-up for either means but as the instrument of progress. Whether categorised as an Arm (as by the British) or as a Service (as by the Americans), Signals branches everywhere were prominent in all considerations, wielding real power. The Germans no longer, as pre-1914, excluded their Signals Branch from campaign planning, but consulted it from the outset. Military communication networks were invariably integrated with their civilian counterparts and, in the case of such totalitarian, militaristic states as Russia and Germany, the military steered major construction and routing. Everyone of the major campaigns to come hinged upon or revolved around signal communications and their connection with logistics.

At sea, where radio was almost the sole means of quick, clear communication, the latest technology and techniques were as essential to the development of long-range amphibious operations supported by aircraft carrier task forces (such as the Japanese and Americans were competitively planning for the vast watery expanses of the Pacific), as were the practice of refuelling at sea (first tried by the Americans in 1924) and the construction of island bases supplied by sea and air. It was simply one of those classic oversights by the conventionally minded that when the Japanese displayed their landing vessels and carriers, and their prowess in successive China 'incidents' in the 1930s, their significance was underrated. The future command and control of German U-boat packs, acting in concert at long range in the Atlantic, would also prove to be as dependent upon a well-founded, economic system of maritime replenishment (by supply U-boats among other measures) as it was upon radio — the inadequacies of which, as will be seen, were of crucial significance.

It went without saying that air operations over land or sea now depended upon highly sophisticated radio communication networks as well as navigation aids and electronic early warning systems and other aids. The price of these equipments and their absorption of highly trained personnel (who might have found employment elsewhere in a war of perennial labour shortage) was not to be forgotten in consideration of cost effectiveness. They placed a heavy load on logistic resources, as well as being quite often the subject of contention during consideration of operational priorities. Older sailors and soldiers, for whom the latest technology and techniques were only dimly perceived, tended, occasionally, to misconstrue the demands of airmen; just as politico-military leaders, such as Winston Churchill, were known to protest at the length of the tail by comparison with the number of teeth.

Against a background of competing requirements by the old and the new, land forces negotiated among themselves to achieve a reasonable balance of available resources. As will be seen, apart from the Russians, most armies in 1939 were, arguably, excessively infantry heavy. Italian experience against Abyssinian tribesmen in difficult terrain (where road building to carry motor transport was a prominent feature in achieving mobility) had done nothing to advance the cause of the tank. In Spain, misuse of tanks (few of which had radio) and a failure to use them as part of an all arms team had placed little strain upon logistic support since deep penetrations never took place. Yet when, in the aftermath of the German tank triumphs of 1939 and 1940, attempts were made to shift the balance in favour of tank forces, the proportion of combat soldiers to total personnel dedicated to logistic and administrative tasks — the so-called 'divisional slice', changed but little. Including civilians at bases, personnel involved with air support of armies and the non-combatant elements of fighting divisions (whose strengths generally were about 15,000 men) the 'divisional slice', which had been in the neighbourhood of 40,000 in the First World War, remained around 50,000 throughout the Second. In other words, this substantial number of men and women was needed to supply approximately 6,000 fighting men, only a minority of whom was in contact with the enemy at any one time.

Notes

1. History has shown, time and again, how quickly simple but immensely valuable lessons are forgotten. Had the British remembered this one and built more roads and wells in South Arabia between the wars and after, it is certainly arguable that South Yemen would not be in Communist hands today.
2. During the preparation and concentration for the Battle of El Alamein in 1942, an elaborate deception plan involved the creation of a network of dummy administrative installations, such as pipelines and dumps of all sorts, principally to deceive the enemy over the timing of the attack and to confuse his analysis of photographic reconnaissance reports.

Chapter 8

An Unprecedented Complexity

IN TERMS of strategic and logistic concepts and the conduct of operations, the Second World War bore little resemblance to its predecessor. Unlike the First World War, combat for combat's sake, and head-on attritional blood-baths, were more the exception than the rule. With such recent experience of the pernicious effects of attrition upon morale, national leaders (with notable exceptions, like the 'mad dog' Hitler) tried hard to aim blows at the weak spots in the enemy's most sensitive and vulnerable points and joints. Important though territorial possession often remained both at sea and in land warfare, attacks were more likely to be thrust against lines of communication and vital sources of supply. Few were the offensives which were not eventually decided by the outcome of a contest between the efficacy of attacks upon and defence of logistic installations and their supply routes.

In the back of political and military minds resided memories of how the eventual collapse of navies, armies and states had been due to callous leaders who not only squandered lives but denied their men apparent humanitarian consideration through rest, adequate shelter and sustenance, and reasonable hope of survival. The revolutions of 1917 and 1918 were as much the product of heartless administration as of inept generalship and unresponsive government.

In the Second World War, those memories stimulated a new and much more enlightened approach to the human factor. Soldiers were brought to realise that their lives would not be wantonly wasted and measures taken to boost their morale under even the grimmest circumstances. They were much better fed, clothed and cared for medically and in terms of their personal welfare. Thanks to this new enlightenment, revolutions and mutinies were almost unknown between 1939 and 1945.

Blockade, of course, was imposed by both sides from the outset. As usual, its effects were long-term and fundamental — as will be seen. But in a war which many

101

guessed might become prolonged and world-wide, efforts to make best use of all resources were far better thought through and controlled than ever before. To a greater or lesser degree, attempts to co-ordinate at top level the work of the various logistic directors, in harmony with operational requirements, were central to economic performance. The pre-war evolution of joint planning staffs as the highest levels in conjunction with the emergence of such tri-Service organisations as the German *Oberkommando der Wehrmacht* (OKW) were essential to minimise waste as well as for combining operations. Some loss of the jealously guarded autonomy of Commanders-in-Chief was an automatic consequences, but virtually unavoidable in conditions of ever increasing complexity and greatly enhanced direct communications.

First Campaign: Poland

Resistance to the long expected attack upon Poland, which everybody realised could have but one conclusion, might have been prolonged had the Polish mobilisation not been postponed for political reasons, at the request of France and Britain. Because neither the combat echelons nor their logistic facilities were fully in place before the blow fell on September 1939, the Germans were granted an easier task. Although, of course, if Hitler had not felt bound to postpone the attack from 25 August, as the result of Allied diplomacy, the outcome might have been even swifter. One thing is certain — the air attacks launched against Polish mobilisation centres, lines of communication and depots seriously undermined the fanatic resistance of immobile Poles who fought to the end where they stood.

In that campaign, mobility was almost wholly the prerogative of the Germans who launched their long-prepared attacks from well-provided bases in the assurance that their lines of communication could never be extended by much more than 150 miles. Even a 1914 army would not have been strained logistically, let alone one which had recently practised deep, though admittedly unopposed, invasions of Austria and Czechoslovakia. Those operations had laid bare the administrative weaknesses of the mechanised corps' arrangements, in ways that exercises could never have done. The panzer and motorised divisions which spearheaded the swift drives across the Polish Corridor, to Warsaw and, in the latter stages, from East Prussia to Brest Litovsk, suffered little from the short supply, inept traffic control and inadequate recovery and repair of broken down vehicles which had afflicted the earlier forays. Similarly, the *Luftwaffe*, in stretching itself to a maximum operational effort enjoyed, for the most part, the benefit of flying from well-stocked home airfields within easy striking distance of its principal targets. Such forward deployment of shorter range aircraft as was felt desirable was easily within its capabilities to supply — especially since, like the Army, the ground movement of bulk commodities (fuel and bombs) was relatively unhindered by any extensive enemy demolition of bridges — the *Luftwaffe*'s bombers, like the Army, avoiding damage to these as much as possible.

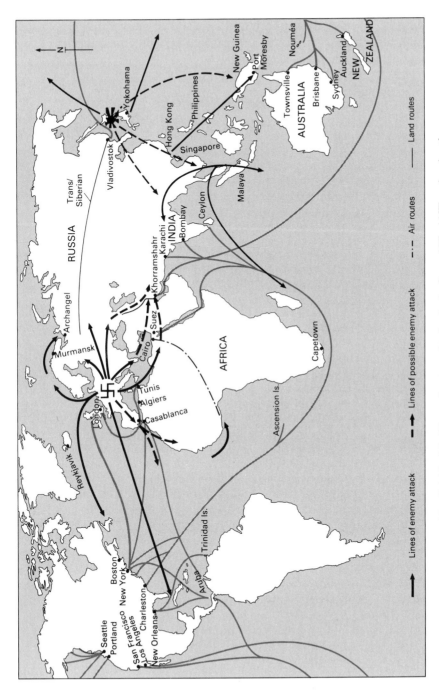

MAP 11.   British global lines of communication in the Second World War, showing the threatened and actual enemy attempts at interdiction

For the *Wehrmacht* the Polish campaign was a useful, practical confirmation of operational and logistic practices which, on familiar ground, struck their roots in past experience. Its next invasion by joint sea, air and land forces into strange terrain in most unusual circumstances would be a very different matter — a trend setting adventure in almost every respect.

Chance and Incompetence in Norway

The reasons behind the struggle in Norway in April 1940 were basically logistic. The Allies sought to stop the movement of naval and commercial vessels to and from Germany and the North Atlantic and to prevent the shipping of Swedish iron ore from the ice-free port of Narvik, while the Germans not only desired to expand traffic, and develop access for sea raiders into open waters, but also to deny the Allies access to Scandinavia threaten Germany's north flank and vital lines of communication through the Baltic. The British decision to begin sea mining of the Norwegian west coast on 7 April was a not unexpected culmination of tensions and incidents over preceeding months. The German plan of invasion, which opened on 9 April, on the other hand was an anticipated and premeditated attempt to conquer the country; of marked originality in execution; very much hostage to chance; and dependent on the slimmest of supply lines.

The German plan hinged upon entering Norway by surprise, unopposed if possible, and setting up a logistic base to pre-empt any subsequent Allied intervention. Through political subversion, which neutralised the Norwegian Government and many elements of the armed forces; and by infiltrating supply vessels amongst the naval ships and transport aircraft carrying *coup de main* units to such vital centres as Oslo, Stavanger, Bergen, Trondheim and Narvik, the Germans had brought off a brilliant stroke, within a couple of hours. Few were their losses *en route*. Even if the Allies had managed later to cut the sea lanes, the Germans already in Norway were strong enough ashore to live off what they had brought, as well as off the country, topped up by almost unopposed air supply. Within hours this position was almost unassailable and made doubly secure by the sheer incompetence of the counter-measures under way in Britain.

It was not as if the Allies had not expected a German descent. When Winston Churchill promoted the sea mining it was with the hope that something of the sort would occur and, for that reason, that a counter-intervention force had been assembled. Amazingly, therefore, the Allies played down as 'too incredible' warnings of German intent, interpreting unusual maritime activity as a possible naval break out to raid the Atlantic shipping lanes. In consequence, attacks against the invaders at sea were tardy, misdirected and few. It was the Allies who were pre-empted, their contingency plan (founded upon the hope of landing ahead of the Germans) invalidated by enemy audacity and subterfuge.

The hasty improvisation which emerged never had much chance, even setting aside that the lodgements projected at Harstad, near Narvik, on 15 April; at

Namsos on the 16th; and Andalasnes on the 18th were strictly second best in terms of strategic selection. Pathetically, the British administrative plan to land troops on a largely inhospitable shore had an almost Crimean look about it; dismissing, as it seemed to do, the many lessons learnt at such cost during the First World War and subsequently refined in post-war studies.

From the start, the administrative staffs were mainly 'unemployed' officers, few of whom were properly qualified for their tasks, banded together, as they had been, at short notice, to tackle problems about which they were ill-informed. In addition to a dire shortage of intelligence about the enemy, very little was known of the situation or facilities ashore. The composition of forces was seriously wanting and the order of loading in ships, hastily gathered for the task, unrelated to tactical requirements. Hence the reason, incredible though it may seem, for the impossibility of producing an administrative plan, as the Narvik force actually was told in writing.[1] Nevertheless, the immediate announcement of the enemy's presence through damaging air attacks acted as a laxative to ship's masters. Their primary intention was to unload as quickly as possible in order to escape from quays and anchorages which were usually quite inadequate in number or capacity. Most unloading was haphazard, attended by utter confusion during ferrying between ship and shore in small local craft. Labour was in short supply; communications sporadic; confidence shaky.

Orders for the Namsos force were almost entirely verbal, formulated at staff conferences on the spot as the situation developed. Cheerfully liberated from paper work, the staff coped with remarkable flexibility in a fluid situation, despite signal communications being sparse and unreliable. At Narvik, where the railway to Sweden was of only marginal potential but where water transport in the fjords was all too obviously vital, the force commander had been given a railway company and no water transport. So the railwaymen found themselves afloat in locally hired fishing boats (called 'puffers' by the sound their engines made) tasked to see that the crews did their duty instead of disappearing up nearby creeks for hours or even days on end whenever the *Luftwaffe* struck.

Everywhere resort had to be made to what little civilian labour, transport and supplies (including fuel) were to be had. Civilian morale was low, made worse by the frequent air attacks which sank ships at anchor and destroyed stores and vehicles ashore. From the beginning the fighting troops were on short commons. Weapons lost were sometimes impossible to replace, often because nobody knew what was ashore or afloat. Medical attention at Namsos was very basic due to the late arrival of the Field Ambulance shortly before the eventual evacuation. Namsos base installations were permanently without protection and hardly ever shielded by anti-aircraft guns. Yet it was noteworthy that although, for example, the roads out of Andalsnes were frequently bombed, they were never wholly unusable. Despite an almost total absence of air cover, the British were to discover that, in broken country, by day as well as by night, road movement in the face of determined enemy straffing was possible — a lesson which tended to be overlooked at a time when dread of air attack grew obsessional. Although the importance of dispersion had been recognised, its implementation at Andalsnes might have been better if administrative parties had been sent on ahead, obviating the need to extract staffs and labour from combat units to organise clearance of the port by sending stores to forward depots, as they arrived, in an endeavour to avoid their destruction at the port.

The Germans had it all their own way, controlling as they did the most populous areas, the best ports, airfields, road and railways — none of which could be seriously threatened by the Allies. With their offensive powers well sustained, it might have been expected that they could prevent the Allies from escaping with anything more than what they stood up in. It was therefore very much to the credit of the ramshackle logistic services and the navies that so much equipment was taken off and so little left to the enemy. At Narvik where the evacuation was made easier by a last minute capture of the port from the Germans, the operation, spread in secrecy over six days, left in German hands a remarkably small percentage of transport (and no AFVs); virtually no supplies, petrol or explosives and very little ammunition. That so many valuable items, in addition to tens of thousands of men so essential to the defence of Britain, were removed, reflected too upon the German Navy for failing to achieve what was at one moment within the grasp of its capital ships — the interception of almost undefended convoys on their way home.

In the circumstances, the Allied operational disaster in Norway was probably, unavoidable. Yet the largely unnecessary logistic chaos was arguably the result of a rosy state of mind within the General Staff which, as General Bernard Paget wrote, '. . . assumes that what . . . is politically or operationally desirable is administratively possible'. It epitomised in fact, yet another example of the teeth getting the better of the tail — teaching again the lesson, as time would show (and continues to show to this day), that easy as cutting the tail is, it is extremely difficult to rectify deficiencies when the harsh realities of adversity are encountered.

The Invasion of Western Europe

The logistic debacles which shattered the French, British, Dutch and Belgians in May were by no means the result of fundamental errors such as deprived administration in Norway. Notwithstanding the handicap imposed by the Dutch and Belgians in their diplomatic refusal to make contingency plans with the Allies for mutual defence against the probability of a German invasion, the forward deployment and logistic support of the large Allied mechanised force which moved north on 10 May was accomplished with commendable efficiency. An ease, hardly remarked upon at the time, in the building up of advanced bases, was due to absence of any real enemy attempt to prevent it by cutting vital rail and road links. Too late did the Allied High Command grasp the significance of the Germans' genius in scrapping their original plan to repeat the old 1914 wheel, replacing it with the rapid and highly effective stroke through the Ardennes to the Channel coast. This was due as much to logistic inspiration as to the desire simply to out-manoeuvre by the achievement of tactical surprise made feasible by mechanisation.

It is by no means certain that the Germans would have succeeded if they had persisted with their initial plan, even though it had included a subsidiary thrust through the Ardennes. Had it been attempted, as conceived, in winter along an obvious axis across sodden ground, it would have proved unimaginative and lacking in surprise. It would have pushed the Allies back onto their bases, inviting a stalemate amounting to failure as the logistic equaliser came into operation. The second plan's deadliness, as conceived by General Eric von Manstein, lay as much in the elegance with which it isolated the best of the Allied troops in the north from their bases to the south, as in the way it struck at the enemy brain by suggesting a variety of indirect approaches against numerous strategic objectives.

The German scythe, sweeping smoothly to the Channel, has sometimes been compared to Sherman's drive to the sea in 1864. Certainly it benefitted by capturing stores and that modern equivalent of fodder — petrol. But, although the railway system was as badly disrupted as in 1914, and the Germans, at some inconvenience, had to divert civil transport to stock up an advanced base in Belgium and northern France, there any similarity disappeared. Far from cutting themselves off from their base, as had Sherman, they depended upon the maintenance of a flow of supplies by road to keep the fast mechanised formations, as well as the slow hoof and foot columns, moving. Unlike Sherman they had to devise march tables which prevented the slow troops from holding up the fast. Such was the initiative of logistic and traffic control staffs in making full use of the considerable latitude they were trained to enjoy, that the march hardly faltered. Blessed by excellently, pre-planned signal communications, which kept pace as well as security, and rarely suffering enemy interference, there was only one bad moment when a corps fuel depot was misreported as 'burnt out' (*ausgebrannt*) instead of 'ready for distribution' (*ausgabeberveit*). The mechanised troops advanced about 200 miles in twelve days — starting off, of course, with fuel for 150 miles and supplies for nine days. Indeed only repair and maintenance of vehicles, with 50% mainly temporary losses in some formations, gave cause for serious concern and induced a celebrated infirmity in Hitler's decision to press on to Dunkirk.

Air power also played its significant part in easing past logistic difficulties. Transport aircraft which deposited airborne troops deep into Holland or in the capture of key bridges crossing vital routes, earned a logistic bonus by continuing to supply those isolated invaders up to the moment of their relief by overland columns. And the use of bombers, instead of heavy artillery, notably to blast enemy opposition during the crucial seizure of crossings across the River Meuse, represented an immense saving in time, effort and traffic congestion by eliminating the positioning of guns and ammunition such as would have been needed, in days gone by. It comforted the Germans to have on call, for emergencies, a fleet of transport aircraft to supplement their land vehicles. Their Army certainly would have preferred better fighter protection as it approached the Channel ports and, for the first time, came under heavy air attack . . . Instead it was stalled by Göring's offer to bomb Dunkirk into submission when Hitler endorsed the order halting the advance on that port. For Göring's ill-considered offer, while paying scant attention to the difficulties of bombing ships at sea by day and the impossibility of doing so at night, also overlooked the logistic plight of the *Luftwaffe*. With the majority of its bombers held back on their German bases, for logistic reasons and for want of captured airfields, it could not mount the long-range effort required as bomber serviceability declined to less than 50 per cent.

It was at this moment, in fact, when Hitler, the amateur strategist and logistician, began to override the advice of his military professionals, that Germany began to forfeit her current operational superiority. As time would show, Hitler never could come to terms with the logistics of sea power — though that also went for many another 'land animal'. It was both amazing and frustrating for the soldiers to watch the Allies escaping from Dunkirk. None could have envisaged the British administrative masterpiece of Operation *Dynamo*, with its incredible improvised assembly of ships and craft to carry supplies to the besieged and bring out 336,425 men (less their equipment) in 16 days, from under the enemy's nose — and to do so almost without air transport, since the Allies could call only on a few dozen airliners, which were soon used up.

Dynamo, however, achieved a lot more than save men. It staunched British resolve, gave hope to the people and, by depriving Germany of the essential quick victory, (bearing in mind the slender state of a war economy fit for only eight weeks of intensive operations) posed her a long-term logistic problem of dire consequences. Although there were German officers who believed that a successful invasion of Britain was possible (and a British Admiralty which felt that a sizeable surprise lodgement might be made from air and sea,) all agreed that the continued supply of those invaders would be hazardous if the weather deteriorated or air supremacy was not won. It was one of history's turning points that the *Luftwaffe's* misdirected efforts failed to achieve the aim as an already luke-warm Hitler chose to invade Russia rather more for ideological, politico-emotional reasons than strategic or logistic considerations.

The Crux: Russia or the Middle East?

Germany's defeat of the Western Allies in 1940 was to have global repercussions which had fateful consequences.

The easy victory encouraged Hitler to strike next at Russia, spurred Italy into joining in a war for which she was by no means prepared and persuaded Japan that the moment was ripe to conquer South East Asia and dominate the South Pacific. They all gambled, since none possessed sufficient logistic resources to overcome, the combined resources of the British Empire, Russia and the USA without a considerable element of luck. For no matter how well the armed forces of the so-called Axis powers prevailed in battle, or the extent to which they combined as an alliance (which was never too well), each was logistically vulnerable because of dire shortages or non-availability of the two most vital elements of supply — oil and transport.

Loot from the West was immense, though the 600,000 tons of oil captured (against an annual consumption of $12\frac{1}{2}$ million tons) would not go far; and the enormous quantities of vehicles captured were not all compatible with German military requirements. Nevertheless, both the large sources of supply and production and the means of transport from the conquered territories which they had acquired, resolved many of Germany's economic worries. Far more important, the British blockade was loosened and, at the same time, the Germans were offered a marvellous opportunity to fix a tighter stranglehold on the British with surface vessels, submarines and aircraft preying on the sea lanes. Although Hitler's postponement of the invasion of Britain was a fundamental error, it might have been redeemable had he listened to Raeder when the Grand Admiral urged the indirect severance of Britain's life line by eliminating her vital strategic positions in the Mediterranean, West Africa, Egypt and the Middle East. In truth, Hitler's proposal to invade Russia created a logistic risk which Germany could ill afford, including, as it did, an exorbitant consumption of materials and fuel, with only distant prospects of recuperation from Cuacasian oilfields; the danger of Allied bombing of the Romanian oilfields; and no immediate imposition of pressure upon Britain. Raeder's scheme offered far quicker strategic and logistic results. With Italian, Spanish and French collaboration, he argued, Britain could be strangled before Russia was invaded from the Middle East as well as Europe.

The map on page 103 indicates the subtlety of Raeder's strategy, showing how the combination of threats to enemy sources also enhanced Axis supply. Taken in conjunction with known Japanese intentions to seize the bountiful resources, including oil, of South East Asia, ahead of preventative measures by the Americans, Dutch and British, the global nature of this joint strategy was stunning. Indeed, from the Japanese point of view, with the need to import 88 per cent of their oil, it was essential to strike without delay before the provocations of their current belligerency provoked crippling sanctions. Fortunately for the Allies and the rest of the world, the Japanese held their hand while the Germans and Italians attempted too much with too few resources.

Making use of the long coastline won by their recent conquests, the Germans could more easily send raiders into the Atlantic while the Italians, after entering the war in June, could almost dominate the central Mediterranean and, in theory, maintain a sufficient threat to Suez from their possessions on North Africa. But, in practice, while Malta continued to hamper Italian activities, the Germans' shortage of raiders and their unreadiness to mount a major blockade gave the British breathing space, during which it was found possible to supply Malta as a launching point for attacks on Italian shipping; and also, on special occasions, to pass convoys through the Mediterranean to reinforce the Middle East. Gibraltar had changed hands, the immense savings in shipping and time (against sailing the long route round the Cape) would have been lost and the chances of the British holding the Middle East much reduced. Likewise, if the Germans had not delayed the construction of supply U-boats to carry fuel, stores and torpedoes to their 'wolfpacks', the range and time at sea of the mere 30 larger U-boats then at their disposal would have been increased significantly. Even so sinkings of Allied shipping exceeded construction of new cargo vessels, and the outcome might have been catastrophic had not those German battleships, cruisers and merchant cruisers which did break out not been sunk or forced back into port for lack of supplies, since nearly all their roving supply ships were eliminated. Later, the miracle of Henry Kaiser's 'Liberty' ships, built at unbelieveable speed in America, saved the Allies from disaster.

If the battleship *Bismarck* had not been sunk in May 1941 and, if the *Luftwaffe* had been made to play a much more effective anti-shipping role before Allied counter-measures proved discouraging, British strategy would have been seriously undermined. As it was, the German naval threat to Britain's continuance at war remained a matter of major concern until the U-boats were mastered in the spring of 1943.

Because, despite all, Hitler favoured the Raeder strategy and events beyond his control pushed matters that way, a semblance of the peripheral strategy emerged. Just how hard Hitler really tried to bring Franco's Spain into the war and attempt to seize Gibraltar is debatable; just as is how much pressure might have been put, from the outset, upon a reluctant Mussolini to allow German troops to join with the Italian army for a drive to the Suez Canal. Decisive, however, were the events which left Hitler with no option but to project a German presence in the very places that Raeder had his eye on. Denied the use of the French Fleet, by British pre-emptive action, and realising that the Italian forces, which were short of oil fuel even before the outbreak of war, were shaky allies who might tax Germany's sources embarrassingly without profitable return, Hitler was unavoidably sucked into a whirlpool of diversion away from his Russian venture by the ineptitude of his weakling ally.

Mussolini's impulsive attack upon Greece, which foundered in winter's mud among the mountains before his ill-supported army lost heart and was thrown back into Albania in November; the failure of his navy and airforce to neutralise Malta; the loss of several capital ships at Taranto; the stalling of the army due to the severe logistic restraints, in its advance from Cyrenaica into Egypt and that army's rout in December by the British; and signs of the supine weakness of the forces in East Africa, all pushed Hitler towards the eastern Mediterranean with its wealth of logistic prizes. Fearful of a complete Italian collapse in February, after their army had been wiped out in Cyrenaica, Hitler felt compelled to send mechanised and air forces to defend Tripolitania with a view, in due course, to repelling the British. Dreading the possibility of British bombers based in Greece hitting the vital Romanian oilfield at Ploesti, and threatening the logistics, as well as the southern flank, of the attack upon Russia, he was also drawn into the Balkans. Rebuffed by the Yugoslav rebellion, which overturned his 'diplomatic' takeover of that country (with its important mineral resources) in April, he invaded both Yugoslavia and Greece to eliminate trouble before it festered. And in May, on the same pretext of fear for Ploesti, he permitted the airborne invasion of Crete.

These were relatively cheap operational victories but, with the planned invasion of Russia imminent, wantonly expensive. For not only did they cause a month's delay to Operation *Barbarossa* from May to June, they further drained logistic support which already was on a shoestring. Yet the victories gave Raeder a pretext to make a last plea for postponement of *Barbarossa* and pursuit of his peripheral strategy, which at the end of May was already well advanced. With the Balkans in Axis hands, the British defeated in Cyrenaica and thrown back into Egypt, and nationalist movements in Syria and Iraq making headway, the way to Iran and the backdoor to Russia's oilfields was ajar. Postpone *Barbarossa*, Raeder pleaded. Redirect but a fraction of that immense force to the exploitation of a drive into the Middle East, he urged, and, within a few weeks, the entire strategic and logistic situation would be transformed in Axis favour.

British consternation and reactions to these threats were testimonies to their potency. Their reinforcement of Malta, the risking of valuable ships and their tank and aircraft cargoes in the ferociously disputed passage of convoys through the Mediterranean (until they were made impracticable by *Luftwaffe* intervention in January 1941), and the reinforcement of the Middle East with men and equipment at the expense of the defence of Britain, were moves of desperation. They had to keep the Suez Canal open. It was the jugular vein of operations in North Africa, and the Balkans, the vital link with an expanding Palestine base with its Haifa terminal of the oil pipe line from the Iraq fields, and a lynch pin of the Empire.

Yet the strain placed upon British resources before the Americans came fully to her aid by the expansion of production and ship building, linked to the Lease Lend Act was overbearing. Yet although the wastage of shipping through the long haul round the Cape to the Middle and Far East seriously worsened the situation, it inspired some exceedingly interesting ways and means to economise. For example, by shipping aircraft (some by aircraft carrier) to Takoradi, in West Africa, and flying them to Egypt, via Kano and Khartoum: and by crating trucks for assembly at their destination, immense savings in the movement of ships and space hungry cargoes were made. In addition minimising imports from Britain by expanding overseas production, also contributed immensely. The fact remained, however, that the Germans enjoyed a fundamental advantage because they operated along far shorter, internal lines of communication than the British, needed smaller reserves at theatre bases and could react much more swiftly to unexpected changes in circumstances.

Worried by the menace of Raeder's emerging strategy, the British were compelled to reserve forces against Axis attempts, with French collaboration, to occupy strategic points on the West African coast. At the same time, in their anxiety to reinforce the Middle East, the Chiefs of Staff indulged in the latest (and by no means last) round of the 'teeth versus tail' battle by complaining how, from one of the Mediterranean convoys (WS 6), nearly an entire division 'is frozen out by administrative units'. To which General Wavell, the Commander-in-Chief Middle East had replied by pointing out that, since the outbreak of war, there had been a shortage of such units which he was trying to overcome. In a vast theatre, where climatic and desert conditions posed extraordinary logistic difficulties, the proportion of tail to teeth was bound to be high, as past experience had shown.

Take, as an example, operations in the Western Desert, where mechanisation was total and animals were excluded; where every drop of water and fuel, plus every item of equipment (less captures from the enemy) had to be transported in; where the sea lanes and ports were every bit as important for maintenance as was the coastal railway to Mersa Matruh; and where the roads and tracks were constantly vulnerable to cutting by enemy raids from the open desert flank. Here, in the tacticians' paradise and logisticians' hell, both sides in the first two years of fighting were kept short of supplies. Loss of ships, compounded by endemic shortages, starved the Italians and the Germans of fuel and road transport for their mechanised forces. Insufficient provision for an unexpected diversity of tasks on many fronts, exacerbated in Spring 1941 by vast losses in Greece and Crete as well as the desert, deprived the British of transport. When the British army won its astonishingly complete victory over the Italians in December 1940, its improvised exploitation beyond Benghazi was strictly controlled by the meagreness of transport lift, the day partly being saved by employing captured Italian mechanics to forage for spares and repair and service their own vehicles to make good British deficiencies. Another serious problem, in addition to a chronic ammunition shortage, was created by the 45,000 prisoners caught in the first day of the attack when only 2,000 were expected. Feeding, watering and evacuation was far more difficult than guarding them.

Likewise, when General Rommel, against orders, quite unexpectedly overran the British in April and raced to the defended perimeter of Tobruk, it was to encounter the logistic equaliser when, against an enemy who backed onto a stocked base, supplied by sea, his own failing transport columns were unable to meet the requirements for a strong enough assault. Thus would the pendulum swing in successive offensives and counter-thrusts as each side, in turn, would build up a logistic advantage only to exhaust it without conclusive results. Rommel might airily dismiss supply problems as 'the responsibility of my Quartermaster,' but his rebuff at Tobruk, his inability to exploit local victories in June over the British and his failure in November 1941 to capitalise on a local success, were the direct result of an inability to resolve his own supply problem while living off enemy resources and, at the same time, attacking and depriving the enemy of his own supply. It was just another facet of the desert war that, to some extent, both sides weakened their men's stamina by the issue of unbalanced and unattractive rations which contributed to the attrition of health and morale.

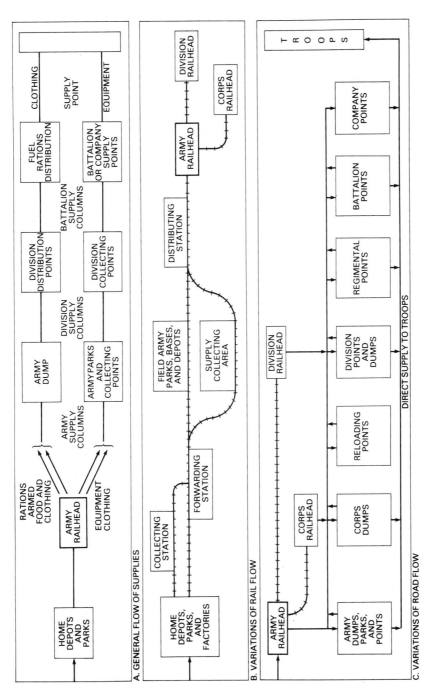

Fɪɢ 8.1 Variations of the German supply system in Europe in the Second World War

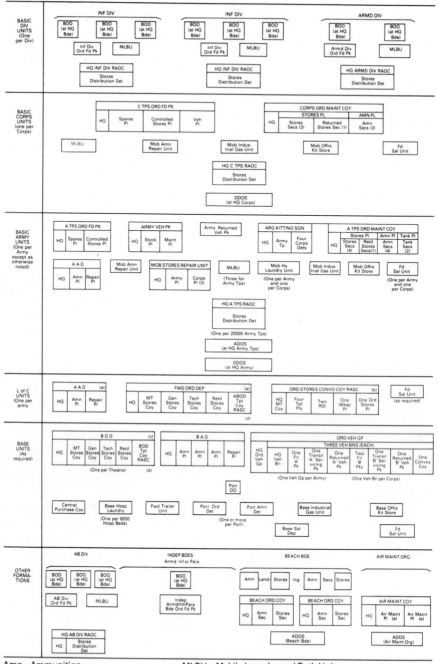

FIG 8.2   British organisation for the supply of ammunition and Ordnance stores in the
Second World War

Amn – Ammunition
OO – Ordnance Officer
BOO – Brigade Ordnance Officer

MLBU – Mobile Laundry and Bath Unit
DDOS – Deputy Director Ordnance Services
ADOS – Assistant Director Ordnance Services

114

The Russian Miscalculation

The trials and tribulations of those in Berlin, battling it out for the Middle East on behalf of Raeder's well conceived strategy, were as nothing compared with the vast miscalculations attendant upon Operation *Barbarossa*. For this was a campaign distinguished by a pernicious German over-confidence which, through inadequate provision due to unwarranted assumptions, condemned the *Wehrmacht* to defeat. Despite the windfalls of western Europe's booty, Germany's underlying economic position was no better founded in 1941 than in 1940. With a mere eight weeks resources for so stupendous an operation, she campaigned on the tentative, rash assumption that Russia would collapse within that period — an assumption flawed, moreover, by inadequate intelligence of Russian strength, deployment or logistic facilities, compounded by an ill-founded reliance upon making up supply and transport shortfalls from captured enemy stocks.

German intentions were telegraphed early, and quite unavoidably, to her prey and her other enemies by the scale of the logistic build-up — which is scarcely surprising when it is recalled that, apart from stockpiling and preparations for army and air force formations (with 4,000 aircraft) and the need to develop communications to the frontier, each of the 145 divisions involved needed not less than 60 trains. Yet there was a world disbelief in its likelihood up to three weeks before the fatal 22 June. For although a strong body of opinion (partly shared by pessimistic Russians) believed that the *Wehrmacht* might overwhelm the Red Army, there seemed little sense in placing in jeopardy the increasing quantity of supplies which Josef Stalin currently was exporting to Germany. To cut off those imports could only weaken German strength, perhaps fatally, if the timetable of invasion was in the slightest upset. Moreover any threat to the Russian Caucasian oilfields (with Russian connivance, as once thought possible) invited British counter-measures against Baku. Of one thing the British were correctly convinced: despite her possession of Romanian oil production and the steady and impressive expansion of synthetic, coal-based petrol production, oil fuel supply was the Axis Achilles heel, when annual consumption stood at about 12 million tons in 1941 and was barely satisfied from all sources. Why the British and their allies did not at once attack German oil production will emerge later.

Before the campaign was launched, the Germans were aware they were entering a sort of logistic and communications wilderness for which maps were hopelessly inaccurate about low grade roads (which soon broke up under heavy traffic, particularly after rain.) Most commendably their Signals troops foresaw and managed to construct an almost totally new radio and cable network, (with extensive bare cable poled across country) where nothing like a modern Russian service existed. A similar feat cannot be credited to the supply and transport troops. They did not allow for the unexpectedly higher petrol consumption that the bad roads would cause or such extra wear on vehicles as to overtax repair and maintenance services, which soon began to run short of spares.[2] They knew, of course, that the Russian railway gauge was still different to theirs, but had diverted their railways troops to other tasks and thus denied training in conversion methods: also they hoped to capture enough enemy stock to keep this vital link running — a prime example of an unwarranted planning assumption unfulfilled. History repeated itself as the Germans became enthralled by the scale and elegance of their thrusts to the detriment of logistic necessity. Determined upon rapid momentum in attempting to seize vital economic and communication centres, and to complete ambitious encirclements, they failed to take immediate measures to utilise what little booty they did lay hands on. In an advance of over 400 miles in 24 days, from Brest-Litovsk to Smolensk, for example, Army Group Centre seem hardly to have noticed the huge piles of valuable equipment left in barracks or at the roadside. These included over 1,000 of the latest T-34 tanks, which were superior to any then in German service and had been abandoned without a fight because of the collapse of the Soviet logistic system.

As was suggested, perhaps Stalin was trying to buy Hitler's goodwill by stepping up supplies to Germany in 1941, against the day in 1942 when Russia would be ready for war. Certainly the state of his own forces in 1941 gave no cause for confidence in their ability to hold off so strong an opponent. For obsolete equipment, notably tanks, was only at that moment being replaced. Training was at a nadir, stocks of tank gun ammunition, with most units, were non-existent. But even if the key Russian tank formations had been fit for their combat role, the instant defeat of their obsolete air force on the first day of war would have denied them the opportunity of victory.

Poor as Russian combat performance was in general, many soldiers fought well. The true causes of this debacle were Stalin's unwillingness to recognise Hitler's intention until the last moment, and a wholesale logistic disintegration due to the lack of any form of administrative plan. With most tank and truck states rarely above 50 per cent and often below 30 per cent, the likelihood of complete units leaving barracks, let alone reaching the front was meagre. If vehicles did roll, their chances of survival were poor because the *Luftwaffe* had decimated the Red Air Force, and so was able to ravage unprotected convoys almost unopposed.

Those trucks not destroyed on the roads frequently took to the open fields where they were lost in undrained ground. Short of ammunition and marooned for want of fuel, spares and trained mechanics, the Red Army disintegrated. So why did not the *Wehrmacht* reach the objectives judged likely to enforce capitulation? How was it the Russians fought on?

Partly, of course, because the Japanese did not join in against Russia, permitting the transfer of troops by rail from the Far East. Largely because the logistic equaliser came into effect as the German motorised forces far outran both the horse and foot infantry formations and the too slowly advancing railheads. After the capture of Smolensk and hordes of Russians with their equipment, the long pause imposed by Hitler, while he vacillated over pursuit of economic targets at Leningrad and Ukraine, or a lunge for Moscow, gave a welcome respite to help make good the mechanical ravages of so exacting an advance and also accumulate fuel and ammunition with the spearhead formations. An opportunity for vehicle maintenance and replacement was essential because field workshop capacity was unequal to major overhauls which in the past, had been carried out in the Reich.

A by-product of the shortage of vehicle spares already mentioned on page 98 was the widespread cannibalisation of broken-down machines instead of the organisation of a proper backloading programme, to be implemented as opportunity allowed. The *Luftwaffe* too fell into this administrative trap. Both were to suffer for it later. Welcome though this period of recuperation was to the Germans, it was to prove a life-saver to the Russians, allowing them to reorganise, re-equip and reinforce their shattered armies.

Stresses within the *Wehrmacht* increased when Hitler felt compelled to press an advance in search of the final decision through autumn rain and mud. Each German pause induced by fuel shortage, quagmires, disrupted roads and inadequate rail supply gave the Russians time to buttress their defences. Nevertheless, early in October, Stalin was told that another rout was in progress, that the door to Moscow was open and likely to remain so due to transport and supply deficiencies. Both sides struggled desperately to sustain mobility and fire power with the Germans denied their last opportunity by a combination of heavy snow, deep freeze and their logistic inability to cope with crisis for which they had made no allowance. Vehicles which foundered in the mud frequently became locked by a sudden freeze. In unheated workshops repairs were hampered by lack of spares. Everything was in short supply, the men at the front in summer clothing were exposed to temperatures down to minus 30°C. Those pathetic stocks of winter clothing available were either taken by rearward echelons for their own protection or held back by a supply organisation in chaos and which gave priority to ammunition and fuel over clothing. And to make matters worse, factory production was down due to a variety of muddles and material shortages. For example, the building of important prime movers was 40 per cent below target and there was a temporary moratorium on the making of spares in order to boost the production of new tanks. In these circumstances, scavenging and the obsessive quest for shelter became the order of the day for desperate soldiers and airmen.

It was a tribute to the Russian commissariat that as the Germans, short of all their main objectives, came to a halt, the Red Army was in a position to follow up enemy withdrawals and also attack with some vigour. Admittedly, it stood comfortably close to vital communication centres and bases, such as Leningrad and Moscow. But credit was due to an organisation and railway system which had saved so many factories from the German grasp and kept the people and the army supplied[3] and the more so since it was oxen and horses which now mainly pulled supplies because so many lorries had been lost without replacement. Indeed, as the two sides reversed direction for the first time since June, both had to cope with the phenomenon of motorisation temporarily eclipsed by old-fashioned, animal and coal-powered prime movers.

Enter the Japanese

Arguably the Japanese let down themselves as well as their Axis allies, by delaying hostilities against the Western Allies until 7 December. If they had co-ordinated their attack with Germany's invasion of Russia in June the result might have been very different. For at that moment the British were in no condition to react strongly, the American mobilisation had barely started and they had not yet imposed the oil and trade embargo. It was the latter measure, from mid-July onwards, which faced the Japanese with a rapid run down of their oil and scrap metal reserves and the choice of either abandoning their aggressive policy or striking out to neutralise America and seize the oil fields and immense resources of south east Asia. In choosing the latter course they gambled, after Admiral Yamamoto (the Naval Commander-in-Chief) stated that '. . . I can promise to give them (the Americans, British and Dutch) hell for a year and a half, but can guarantee nothing as to what will happen after that'.

In the event, Yamamoto was over optimistic by six months because Japan's attack upon and seizure of logistic sources was incomplete. Brilliant in ruthless concept and surprise as was the 'infamous' attempt to win a complete victory over the American Fleet at Pearl Harbor, it failed because not only did the most potent element of that fleet (the aircraft carriers) escape destruction, but the attack left unscathed the oil tank farms and dockyard facilities without which an American recovery would have been significantly delayed. For it was those carriers which, six months later, inflicted decisive defeats in the great battles of the Coral Sea and Midway upon the Japanese carriers as a first step in the denial to Japan of the resources she had captured in her triumphant conquest of the Philippines, Malaya, Burma, Dutch East Indies and numerous South Pacific islands.

The seriousness of the logistic consequences for the Allies of the Japanese eruption will be seen later. The Japanese by acquiring, despite considerable demolition of production and storage installations, ample quantities of oil, nearly 90 per cent of the world's rubber and 40 per cent of its tin, besides boundless food supplies, had, with some ease, demonstrated the immense operational and logistic potency of combined amphibious and carrier-borne air forces for surprise and sustained intervention at long range. But although they had won the resources they so badly needed for self-sufficiency, they had not assured their use. Indeed, they had multiplied difficulties by creating vulnerably extended lines of maritime communications, exposed to interdiction as soon as the enemy was able.

Notes

1. Sixteen years later, the same situation was to arise at Suez (see Chapter 11 page 164)
2. This question of vehicle spares was due very largely to the multiplicity of vehicle types employed (by no means a problem unique to the Germans). Thanks to Hitler's insistence upon giving priority to the production of tanks and self-propelled guns at the expense of lorries, the *Wehrmacht* entered Russia with a motley collection of captured enemy transport and some trucks made in Czechoslovakia or bought from Switzerland. That their mechanics managed to keep

their motorised transport going at all reflects the measure of their ingenuity and high mechanical skills. It must not be forgotten that, even at this stage of the war, the bulk of the infantry divisions remained reliant upon horse-drawn transport — a factor that was to have a dramatic effect upon the pattern of operations. In the advance towards Leningrad, for instance, the badly needed infantry divisions were literally weeks behind the tanks which were spearheading the advance.

3. This factory-saving operation, by which complete production lines were uprooted and moved by train behind the Urals (sometimes with the machines still running on the flats as they travelled) was little short of an administrative miracle. One is forced to ask: what other country would have shown such foresight and imagination? Within weeks, some factories were back in production in their new locations — even aircraft were soon coming off the line.

Chapter 9

At Global War

THE ATTACKS on Pearl Harbor, the Philippines and Malaya which dragged the United States into the war alongside Britain and her allies, set in motion the first full global war; a struggle which could only be won by the Alliance which first managed to think and act operationally and, above all, logistically as a team. It is just possible that if, from the beginning, the Axis had co-ordinated their plans fully and put everything into the common pot, they might have seized even more vital territory with vital resources than they actually did. As it was they managed, by a supreme effort, to frustrate the American juggernaut. For in December 1941, when the British were stretched closer than ever to breaking point and the United States was still only midway through its mobilisation, it was impossible for the Western Allies to produce enough and move what they did produce to the strategically threatened points in time. Many vital weapons had still to be made. There were too few ships. The enemy was cutting the shorter routes while seizing some of the best ports and traffic centres.

The Axis powers would have benefitted significantly if, before the war, they had established joint planning procedures instead of pursuing their own nationalistic dictates; and if, after Pearl Harbor, they had been able to communicate with the same ease and fluency as the Allies. As it was, only through encyphered radio (gleefully intercepted and de-cyphered by the British) was regular communication of a desultory kind possible between Berlin, Rome and Tokyo.

At the heart of the wholehearted collaboration by the Allies, on the other hand, throbbed a superb, mainly secure communication system. Reasonably reliable long distance air travel made possible the series of conferences from which sprang an agreed strategy, joint and combined planning of operations, and allocations of supply and transport. Without the meeting in Washington between Roosevelt and Churchill immediately after Pearl Harbor, there might have been serious misunderstandings and delays in settling first priority for the assault on Germany, along with just sufficient resources to keep the Japanese at bay for the time being. At the same time there emerged the decisions to help keep Russia and China in the war by a swelling volume of supplies, despite enemy opposition. Through the reasonably comprehensive and rarely interrupted international air postal, cable and radio links, a running dialogue enabled fine adjustments, as well as major changes, to be made to evolving schemes, with immense benefit to strategy and the saving of waste. It was the inability to speak person to person by telephone or across the table, or pass documents between themselves, which denied understanding, let alone close collaboration, among the Axis partners.

Confronting the Japanese

Even so, Allied efforts to repair the damage inflicted upon them in the first ten months of 1942 were often within an ace of failure for logistic reasons. Americans who struggled to hold the Philippines never had a hope because it was impossible to reinforce or supply them through waters dominated by the Japanese. Likewise, the British in Malaya were at a disadvantage from the start because the invaders, with complete air and maritime mastery, could outflank the land defences by the threat or reality of landings in rear against lines of communication. When Singapore fell, depriving the Allied fleet of a base from which to defend the Dutch East Indies, it was a grim irony that these ships were handicapped by a fuel oil crisis while within sight of immense sources and plant already in the process of destruction, in the hope of denying them to the enemy. It was salutary for the British and Indian armies in Burma to learn that a Japanese force could function in harmony amid difficult jungle terrain and supply itself while simultaneously threatening enemy supply lines and maintaining momentum with a minimum of fighting.

Not surprisingly the Allied reactions to the unexpected deadly disruption of their own plans produced terrible disorder and mistakes when emergency, improvisations were introduced in ill-considered haste. There was appalling waste, worst of all in the uneconomic use of scarce shipping space, as desperate moves were made to block gaps in a façade ripped open by the enemy. But filled they were if only because, in certain instances, the enemy, who soon reached the objectives of his planned expansion, had neither the strength nor the desire to go farther — or was repulsed. As in Europe, the Allies in the Far East and Pacific had to some extent come to terms with the grim realisation that the enemy had won glittering material prizes, at low cost, while establishing and stocking up strong perimeter defences which might be extremely expensive to reconquer. But which, on the other hand, guarded long lines of communication that were vulnerable to interdiction.

Because the Americans were involved in a Pacific war before they were ready they spent the first twelve months attempting to minimise the enemy damage and rectify their own omissions. There was much duplication and waste as the Navy and Army, working mainly through joint committees, improvised strategic and logistic measures to deal with a deteriorating situation they had not envisaged. Experience from their unopposed occupation of a chain of island bases from Bora

Bora through Samoa, Fiji, New Caledonia to New Zealand and Australia would be invaluable when the day came to strike back with deep penetration of the Japanese island defence system. But in the immediate aftermath of Pearl Harbor, when the Navy had yet to form its own Transport Service; when the Army's Transport Service, dating back to the previous century controlled far more merchant ships than the Navy; and when the 6,000 mile supply 'pipe line' to the West was empty and, because of the shortage of ships and the paucity of Navy organisation, would take months to fill, much was haphazard. General Marshall objected strongly to Admiral King's island base supply line. It was not at all unusual for example, for warships to discover that fuel oil had yet to be delivered to newly constructed bases whose other facilities were also inadequate. Or for ships to be loaded 'commercially' without regard for orderly unloading in the operational zones.

As Vice Admiral George Dyer has pointed out in his admirable biography of the brilliant Admiral Kelly Turner, the commander of the Amphibious Force assigned to the invasion of Guadalcanal (Operation *Watchtower*) in August 1942, '. . . the officers of the Line of the Navy had taken only a cursory interest in logistics in the years before World War II. This occurred because . . . there were few really large difficult logistical problems demanding command decisions'. Not for nothing was *Watchtower*, (hastily improvised to seize the initiative for the Americans after their victories at Coral Sea and Midway) locally known as Operation Shoestring. 'Eighty percent of my time was given to logistics', wrote Turner. 'During the first four months we were living from one logistic crisis to another.' Most cargo had to be manhandled into small landing craft by tired sailors and Marines. Combat loaded ships were the exception rather than the rule.

Nevertheless, *Watchtower* was another turning point of the Pacific war when both sides suffered heavy losses in the five months struggle, but the Japanese failed to dominate the Solomons seaways. This was a struggle which might so easily have swung the other way had not Turner solved his logistic problems and if such organisations as the Naval Construction Battalions (the Seabees) had not built the bases and airfield which were the foundations of combat success.

Plan *Orient*: The Menacing Myth

Lacking substance though it did, the German concept of an Axis exploitation of their twin advances from the Middle East and from the Caucasus, through Persia to link hands with the Japanese in India (Plan *Orient*), was a danger that their enemies always took most seriously. It coloured Allied thinking about almost everything in 1942 when the distinct possibilities of British retreat out of Egypt and of a total Russian collapse threatened irreplaceable resources and the severance of essential lines of communication. It was among Hitler's biggest blunders that he withheld from *Orient* the high priority it warranted. Indeed the confusion in Hitler's mind and his blindness to logistic fundamentals and prospects is well illustrated by his mishandling of the crucial 1942 campaigns when the war hung in balance.

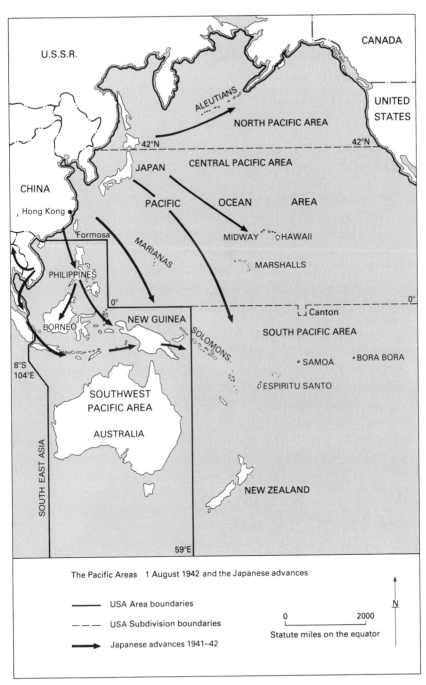

MAP 12. The Pacific and South East Asia Theatres of Operations 1941-45

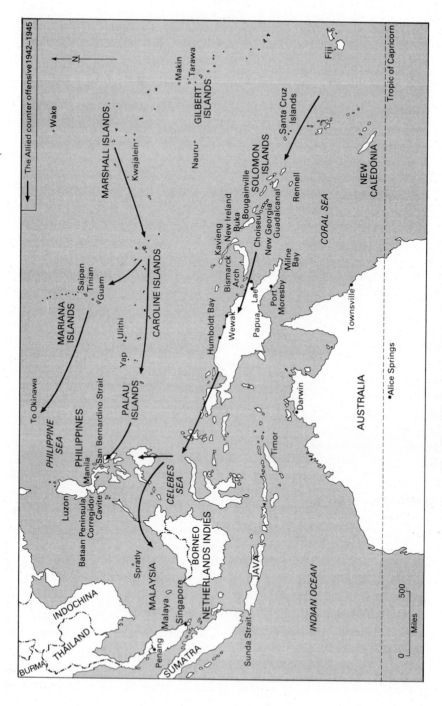

MAP 13.   The Allied counter-offensive in the Pacific 1942-45

Convinced that the Russian winter offensive would be checked and that Germany's offensive power, though diminished, was sufficient for ultimate victory, Hitler backed measures to shake German manufacturing out of its neglected and ramshackle ways. At the same time he concentrated his military attention upon the renewal of the drive for Russian oil in the Caucasus, as the preliminary to another drive against Moscow, via Stalingrad. But also, encouraged by a local success in January by Rommel in Cyrenaica, he gave approval to a case submitted by his Commander-in-Chief South, Field Marshal Kesselring, for the seizure of Malta and the port of Tobruk (in that order) prior to possible invasion of Egypt. A brilliant strategist and administrator, Kesselring knew that until Malta was eliminated as a standing threat to the Axis supply line to north Africa, the security, let alone the offensive power, of the Axis forces stood in jeopardy. Air, surface and submarine attacks from Malta upon convoys (made all the more deadly by the decryption of sailing signals) reduced the Axis advantage of internal communications and condemned a theatre of war, which already was low on the list of priorities, to a chronic hand to mouth existence.

Yet Hitler stood back from an airborne and amphibious invasion on Malta, preferring to have the *Luftwaffe* cut off and neutralise the island by bombing. But bombing, as surely was known, was incapable of imposing a lasting siege. Indeed, although it reduced Malta to desperate straits in April and May and diminished the operational effectiveness of its forces, it also had repercussions upon the Germans' own offensive capability as the enormous expenditure of bombs had to be curtailed at the critical point of the operation because of a threatened shortage for the impending major offensive in Russia. Nevertheless, under cover of the mighty bombardment, Rommel was able to receive sufficient reinforcements and supplies to enable him to launch his attack against Tobruk — an operation which so nearly ended in disaster due not only to tactical setbacks and but also to the Axis striking force becoming cut off from its supply columns. At one moment it was within a few hours of surrender because most of its essential supplies, including water, were almost exhausted. It was simply Rommel's good fortune that a series of blunders by a well supplied but poorly generalled enemy, let him resupply and then strike back to crush the British. Within a few days Tobruk was surrounded, assaulted and taken — an assault, which was fortuitously expedited by the discovery in place of Axis ammunition stocks left untouched by the British in the aftermath of their victory in December 1941.

Overnight an Axis army which had stared defeat in the face and run down its supplies to danger point, acquired from the captured British base a generous supply of fuel, rations and equipment — a bounty which inspired Rommel to obtain from Hitler, despite Kesselring's objection, permission to strike out for Cairo instead of Malta. Like so many of Rommel's projects and Hitler's snap politico-military 'intuitions', the decision was taken without proper assessment of the resources available and the risks involved. It was Rommel's hunch that the British were irredeemably broken, but it was Kesselring's carefully considered view that a 300-mile desert advance with a hotch-potch force, a high proportion of whose logistic equipment was scavenged from the enemy, and whose lines of supply to Europe were very insecure, was impractical. He was proved right when the British, while still considerably demoralised, withdrew to a hastily constructed line at El Alamein (within 100 miles of its base) and let the logistic equaliser settle the issue. Nothing Kesselring could do to provide Rommel with enough fuel to renew the offensive at the end of August would suffice. So difficult was it to transport anything to the front down a single, long road under persistent air attack; so voracious were his mechanised army's demands and so attenuated its transport arrangements (supplemented none too extensively by air supply from Crete), that too high a proportion of petrol was consumed (or lost) on the journey before combat units received a drop.

Similar set-backs and indiscretions, though on a vastly larger scale, characterised Hitler's drive into the Caucasus and towards the Volga. It had certainly abetted the Germans when Stalin exhausted his forces by the prolonged imprudence of his winter counter-offensive, but they later put themselves at terrible risk by projecting nearly 70 divisions into what almost amounted to a logistic void when their principal means of transport, the railway, was still incapable of handling the volume of essential supplies. Track laying beyond Kharkov had not started; there was only one track eastwards and into the Caucasus, via Rostov; lorries and fuel were at their usual premium; animals not in abundance. The Russians, knowing what was coming, duly prepared to give way before an onrush they could not hope to check. When stores could not be consumed or removed they were destroyed. Bridges were demolished. Above all fuel stocks were burnt and, at Maikop, the oil fields were wrecked before the enemy arrived.

Falsely sensing that fading enemy resistance indicated rout, Hitler indulged in the issue of a welter of bewildering operational instructions which confused his commanders and converted ordered supply arrangements into chaos. Frequent changes of direction inevitably created unnecessary movement, misplacement of stores, substantial waste of fuel stocks and reduced vehicle serviceability — let alone exhaustion of men and beasts. It was the 1941 story over again, except that this time the Germans were eventually stopped not by the weather but by physical barriers and enemy resistance which they could not overcome when the logistic equaliser came to bear. In the foothills of the Caucasus, von Kleist's thrust towards Baku's oilfields was brought to a halt by prepared positions. At Stalingrad, where the Russians refused to be thrown out of the city and cross the Volga, and where the German logisticians became hard put to sustain a battle against tough opposition, it was the same. Unusually large tonnages of munitions and ever greater amounts of fuel after an advance of about 300 miles, were consumed by attrition.

The exertions of the Axis forces to crack unyielding enemy opposition at El Alamein at the end of August and at Stalingrad until late November left little for contingencies, let alone to defeat major counter-offensives by carefully husbanded enemy forces. No matter how well Rommel's army held out under a torrent of fire

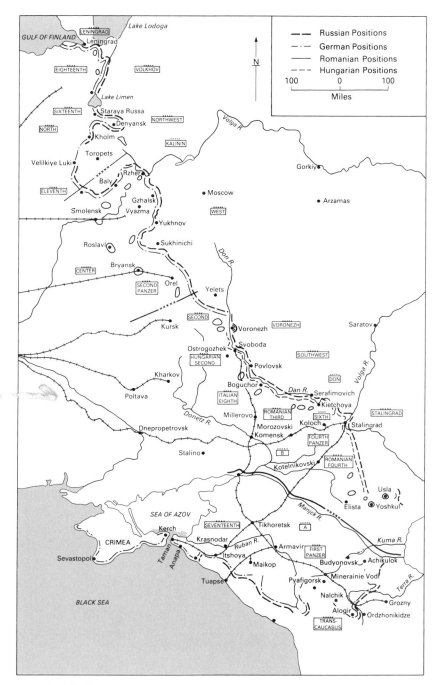

MAP 14.   The Russian Theatre of War in November 1942, showing the fully extended and somewhat attenuated German rail communications which were being cut increasingly by partisans, particularly in the region of Bryansk

for ten days against superbly equipped British forces at the end of October, its collapse had to be absolute after attrition had worn down his infantry, artillery and armour, and the sinking of tankers at sea and the straffing of lorries along the coast road denied his immobile troops of the means of escape. Men and vehicles by the thousand were abandoned in the rout.

Much has been made, very reasonably, of Hitler's insistence that Stalingrad should hold out in expectation of relief when surrounded by a Russian counter-offensive on 23 November. Much credit has been given to the despairing attempts to effect that relief with minimal forces. Insufficient praise, however, had been accorded the Russians for the manner in which they launched their pincer movement, whose horns advanced 70 miles in three days, without disclosing the assembly of their forces to the Germans; and the logistic reorganisation which enabled their mobile forces to be self-sufficient for five days and to travel at least 100 miles without replenishment if necessary. That logistic improvement was what surprised the Germans most; plus the subsequent practical demonstration of the Red Army's way of advancing for days on end at ten miles per day with the help of a fleet of American supplied trucks, supplemented by reviving Russian vehicle production and a vast circus of animal drawn carts. True the rate of advance was inferior to that of the *Wehrmacht* at its prime. But, then, the Red Army was never so sophisticated as that; and, like other armies, tended to put teeth before tail — tanks and guns before trucks — in their willingness to take logistic risks. Paying, also minimal attention to humanitarianism and welfare services, though providing relatively primitive care of the wounded. The Red Army depended on propagandist patriotic fervour, stiffened by fear of summary execution for dereliction of duty, to maintain combat determination — a behaviour often imitated by the Germans in many a barbarous encounter. However rudimentary the Soviet logistic machine may have been, it is one of the marvels of military history how that machine coped with the fluctuations of what must surely have been the most punishing campaign of all time — punishing not only because of the fearful loss of life on both sides but also because of the terrible privations suffered by the soldiers, spread across a landscape of a vastness quite beyond the comprehension of the average European. It remains a mystery to this day how the Russians managed *always* to block each new German threat, somehow finding the troops and the logistic means of doing so, despite the distances to be traversed and the huge tonnages of ammunition and fuel to be moved over the sparse railway system and the primitive road and tracks. Though, as we shall see later, the American lease-lend trucks mentioned above played a critical part in the latter part of the campaign.

Much has been written, too, about the surprise Allied landings in French north west Africa (Operation *Torch*) and their coincidence with the pursuit of Rommel from El Alamein to Tunisia and the subsequent stunning, but by no means astonishing, Russian success at Stalingrad. Taken in conjunction with the Japanese set-backs at Guadalcanal, this series of events suggested that the Axis tide was ebbing, and of them all the logistic turn-about was the most important event. For the deadly menace of Plan *Orient* was killed off as the Mediterranean route was re-opened to the Allies with incalculable savings in shipping.

Germany Stretched to the Limit: 1942-43

Confronted at the end of 1942 with a situation on all fronts almost beyond recall, and despite Hitler's and Göring's lack of realism and joint military ineptitude, the *Wehrmacht* worked logistic miracles on cobbling together a defence, even though its reserves were at a nadir. Both sides gambled. Operation *Torch*, which depended on complete surprise, also relied upon the security of extended maritime routes in the face of an undefeated U-boat and air threat. If the great convoys *en route* from the United States and Britain to the landing places at Casablanca, Oran and Algiers had not got through unopposed, thanks to skilful routeing and deception; had not forces with adequate logistic support not been established ashore at once; and if undamaged ports, worked by the French authorities (once half-hearted resistance had ceased) had not been functioning, the entire project would have been in serious jeopardy. As it was, on 8 November an astonished Axis command had also to gamble by throwing in whatever forces were to hand in the hope the Allies would be slow in taking advantage of their initial success.

It was a nicely balanced struggle. The Allied hope of hastening the seizure of the key ports of Bizerta and Tunis by riskily establishing a forward base at Bone was frustrated only by the heavy shipping losses inflicted in that port by air attacks. Thereafter it was a hand to mouth existence for both sides. The Allied spearheads struggled along inferior roads with a depressingly slow rate of build-up from Algiers, conditioned as it was by the schedule of two initial convoys within five days of each other and thereafter one every fortnight. Yet there was always the possibility of winning since the Axis build-up was also restricted not only by limited shipping and air transport but also by the need to help Rommel escape from El Alamein to Tunisia, and a chronic shortage of supplies of all kinds. Nevertheless, the Axis just held out, converting what the Allied Commander-in-Chief, General Dwight Eisenhower, had hoped would be a sprint into a logistic marathon. Until February 1943 the contest was a close run thing. Thereafter it went the Allied way simply because their reserves were far greater and the Axis was unable to prevent the import of further supplies.

For one thing, the U-boat packs, although enjoying a peak of success in mid-Atlantic (see below) were in trouble elsewhere, and could not deter or destroy the convoys. For another, the *Luftwaffe* had to scour Europe for the 500 transport machines needed for the Tunis airlift, an operation which had to be drastically curtailed when those same machines were called upon to supply besieged Stalingrad. But if the fight for Tunisia, obdurately and expensively insisted upon by Hitler for political reasons, was a running sore in the Axis flank, the struggle to hold Stalingrad bled the *Wehrmacht* white. And nobody contributed more to the demise of the German air transport fleet, reinforced by unsuitable bombers, than Göring himself when he boasted the *Luftwaffe* could keep Stalingrad supplied while the Army arranged its relief. In winter weather against spasmodic Red Air Force attacks, and in the absence of a properly pre-arranged maintenance, despatch and reception organisation, based on well-equipped airfields, this was sheer fantasy. Only 750 transport and 100 bomber aircraft could be assembled where at least 1,000 were needed. Of these, 285 machines were lost in two months. Now, too, for the first time throughout the Reich, fuel shortages imposed severe restrictions on all manner of activities, including flying training, which produced a decline in air crew skills at the very moment that the Reich was coming under heavy air bombardment. Much has been written of the heroism of the German soldiers as they fought grimly on in the appalling winter weather. So great was the cold that, at one point, they were losing 1,000 horses a day. That they kept going as they did, must have been the by-product of blood, guts and brilliant improvisation.

It is unnecessary to dwell further here on the deadly privations afflicting the Axis armies in Russia and Africa post-1942. Win respite as they frequently would by brilliant counterstrokes and seemingly miraculous operational escapes when, due to logistic breakdowns, advancing Allied armies temporarily stalled, the Axis was sinking unpreventably to its doom because of fundamental logistic problems. Ironic savings in fuel consumption because of unremitting retreats which brought the battered formations closer to the sources of supply, coupled with frantic and by no means unrewarded efforts to raise synthetic petrol production — only postponed catastrophe. The Axis was too weak to fight the world and prevent a deluge of men and material being brought to within striking distance of its own vitals: and at a time when those vitals were, for the first time, coming under pulverising air attack, as will be described.

Not until August 1942 did Allied and neutral shipping record a net gain in available tonnage as the result of increased launchings and reduced losses from enemy action. The colossal American ship building programme solving the first part of the equation and defeat of the U-boats the second — after many crises not all of the Axis making. For example, the unwillingness of some Allied air-commanders to commit enough long-range aircraft to patrolling the so-called 'air gap' in mid-Atlantic, where the U-boats had easier pickings; the inability to build enough of the right kind of escort vessels to meet all commitments; the refusal of Admiral King (United States Chief of Naval Staff) to run convoys in American waters, thus presenting the U-boats with their happiest of 'Happy Times' — until General Marshall (Chief of Army Staff) threatened King with responsibility for allowing 'a determining influence on the war'; and the length of time needed to re-open the Mediterranean to through passage, all postponed final victory. Violent were the swings of fortune. In March 1943 sinkings in mid-Atlantic were so dreadfully severe that the British, not for the first time, faced the possibility of crews being unwilling, any longer, to man the ships, and began to wonder if the convoy system should be abandoned. Two months later it was Dönitz, shaken by appalling U-boat losses, who admitted defeat in 'the one battle which could lose the war for the Allies' by temporarily withdrawing from mid-Atlantic.

The Axis defeat at sea was yet another example of the price to be paid for undertaking a major task without whole-hearted commitment or sufficient resources. Dönitz's centralised radio control of his U-boat packs constantly hung by a hair and his campaign never enjoyed adequate production or logistic support. These radio links which, thanks chiefly to Ultra, supplied the Allies with vital electronic intelligence, enabled the skilful re-routeing of convoys, as well as the positioning of hunters to sink attack and supply U-boats alike. Particularly heavy loses of the latter, which, due to low priority, were far too late, into service, and always too few in number, placed yet another handicap on the attack boats by making them return to port through dangerous waters more frequently than desirable. Concurrently, the inability of the Japanese Navy to inflict crippling losses after 1942 created a further guarantee of immense Allied gains of tonnage to help seize the strategic initiative while pouring materials and weapons into Britain, the Mediterranean and also to Russia. Indeed, the latter, sometimes for political reasons, but mostly because she was producing results, was often given priority.

Supplying Russia was a difficult business. Because Vladivostok was closed to American ships when Japan entered the war, Soviet vessels, of which there were too few, had to be employed — although deliveries steadily improved. Arctic convoys to Murmansk and Archangel, since the disastrous losses to Convoy PQ 17 in July 1942, were rated too risky in the short summer nights and hazardous against German opposition at any time. Only the long sea route to Iran with onward transportation by road and rail from the Gulf ports offered a reasonably safe way to the Caucasus. But the diversion of construction, port, ship, rail and road personnel and equipment to this enterprise, aiming at 200,000 tons per month, denied supplies and logistic services for the ambitious American desire to invade western Europe in 1943. The hastily arranged Iran programme inevitably induced errors — among others, too much reliance on road transport (whose drivers were in short supply) and too little on the railway which offered, in the long run, a far greater cargo handling capacity. Set-backs, muddles and failure to meet promised delivery rates there were. Yet this unopposed route continued to be by far the best for supplying Russia with the aircraft and trucks she most needed to offset her worst deficiencies.

After the failure of the last great German offensive, at Kursk in July 1943, the Russians surged westwards once more, benefitting to some extent from their enemy's first serious logistic embarrassment, created by partisans cutting rail and road communications behind the lines. They were also helped by the simultaneous British and American landings in Sicily. These, employing a considerable number of shallow draft landing craft in strength for the first time, managed to supply the assault forces over beaches without immediate access to a port. It was now a question of when rather than how the war would be ended at a speed commensurate with reasonable costs, and whether a dream could be realised by those airmen who wished so ambitiously to demonstrate how bombing could do the trick without the need for fighting every mile of the way to Berlin and Tokyo.

Crippling the Germans

When Italy was invaded and forced out of the war in September 1943 and the Allies went ahead with their preparations for the invasion of France in the following Spring, an important planning factor was the need to restrict German strength in France to about 55 divisions of which, preferably, only 16 would be high grade. If that could be achieved, the Allied build-up after the landing would keep ahead of German reinforcement — provided that the *Wehrmacht* could be diverted to other fronts and its air support and rates of supply could be restricted. High among the demands of the admirals, generals and economic advisors was the need to attack enemy oil sources and transportation.

But the apostles of bombing, who now wielded mighty fleets of complicated bombers built and maintained at enormous cost on scores of airfields constructed with a vast outlay of labour and materials, were determined to demonstrate that air power could win a war independently. They projected a joint offensive with area bombing at night, by the Royal Air Force Bomber Command heavies, and by United States Air Force heavies with pin-point aiming by day. Primarily, they sought a collapse in German morale, viewing the destruction of industrial and logistic resources as a secondary benefit. If all went the bomber barons' way the admittedly hazardous amphibious invasion, supported by the vast fleet of special-ised landing craft (which had been built to the detriment of desperately needed merchant vessels and warships) would be reduced to a safer occupation of surrendered terrain with minimal logistic outlay and risk.

But the attack on morale failed, as such bullying already had failed elsewhere. And the logistic repercussions were disappointing since the Germans managed both to repair the damage and to continue production elsewhere, raising output considerably. Rail and water transportation were almost uninterrupted. Oil continued to flow, even from Rumania in the aftermath of heavy attacks on Ploesti in August 1943. Moreover, the unescorted American heavies often did not hit their targets and suffered such high losses that they were compelled to defer missions of over Germany until, in the winter of 1944, they could be escorted by long-range fighters. Even then, instead of tackling enemy logistic targets, they were directed against fighter aircraft factories to win the battle for air supremacy which both they and the Royal Air Force had to win in order to survive.

Win the Americans did, by out-performing the German fighter force and hitting the factories hard. At the same time the latest electronic navigation aids were giving the Royal Air Force Bomber Command the ability to hit pin-point targets at night. However, by the end of March 1944 when the Allied bombers were better able to attack their preferred industrial targets, General Eisenhower and his senior commanders who were preparing to invade France, insisted that the heavy bombers must supplement the work of the light, tactical bombers by attacking transport targets. Against the wishes of Air Marshal Sir Arthur Harris, Commander-in-Chief, Bomber Command, heavy night attacks were directed against railway yards and repair shops with far greater accuracy than predicted. At the same time General Carl Spaatz, sent his American heavies to precision bomb the much smaller synthetic oil production plants, scattered throughout Germany, in daylight. Argue, as some airmen did, that the Transportation and Oil offensives were less likely to contribute to Allied victory than attacks on centres of population, industry and communications, the fact remains that, prior to the landing in Normandy on 6 June, the Germans were afflicted by dire fuel and transport difficulties all over Europe.

Not that interdiction of the French railway and road network completely isolated the *Wehrmacht* at the front after 6 June. Despite round-the-clock air attacks from heavy, medium and fighter bombers, augmented by the sabotage of rail and cable communications by guerrillas (whose raising and arming since 1940 would have been quite impossible without the use of clandestine radio links to give operational directions and control the delivery to secret reception areas of air and, to a lesser extent, seaborne supplies of arms and munitions) results were not absolute. Air attacks rarely broke bridges; trains continued to run, albeit with extreme difficulty; marching columns continued to filter through by night. But, by mid-July, shortages of fuel were curtailing both flight and manoeuvre when the battle of attrition was on the eve of changing to a wildly mobile phase — for which neither side was completely ready.

The Allied logistic build-up for the invasion, spread over two years and planned with commendable skill to take account of most eventualities, was, despite its revealed defects (as will be seen) a staff and services triumph, and a massive achievement which owed much to the lessons learned in North Africa and Sicily in 1942–43. So massive was it, indeed, that it provoked Winston Churchill, as was his habit, to lean heavily upon General Montgomery in an effort to persuade him, at the last moment, to cut the tail and increase the teeth — an intervention which Montgomery successfully resisted.

Perhaps the most decisive factor of all was the German ignorance of the artificial Mulberry harbours which would be towed into position to make possible full scale maintenance of the invasion force in sheltered waters across open beaches. Their assumption that the Allies would have to capture one of the ports, strongly fortified by three years logistic endeavour, was invalidated at a stroke by technical surprise. Nor had they envisaged the technique of allowing ships to 'dry out' to enable them to unload directly into road vehicles, which drove alongside when the tide receded, or visualised the genius of the Landing Ship Tank (LST), the 4,000 ton prototype of all Roll-on Roll-off (Ro Ro) ferries to come, with their capability of adjusting draught to the angle of beach (by flooding internal tanks) and working through bow doors as well as by ship's derrick. As for Axis anti-shipping operations during the landings, only night mine-laying by E-boats and aircraft had any distinct effect (as minelaying tended to do whenever employed in shipping lanes, rivers or canals). The U-boats, once more, were kept at a distance by counter-measures and suffered heavy losses, due in the main to a massive campaign by the maritime air forces of the Allies.

Nevertheless, although the Allies managed to build up invaluable stocks of supplies and transport during the seven weeks of the bridgehead battle, stocks which were to sustain them during their subsequent and unexpectedly rapid pursuit across France and Belgium, which covered some 300 miles and lasted for four hectic weeks, their overall logistic performance was certainly open to criticism. Of course, their task was made particularly difficult by the devastation of road and rail communications by their own bombing and by the sabotage which had been carried out by the French Resistance before D-Day at their behest, leading to extensive cutting of all telegraphic communications. Nor did the enemy help them by holding tenaciously on to the Channel ports, thereby forcing the Allies to maintain themselves over the beaches for some months to come.

It was a feature of the signal and logistic difficulties of the pursuit that the anticipated flexibility of well-organised administrative staffs and services fell well short of efficiency, since indigenous cable links could not adequately be restored by civil and military engineers, diverting excess traffic to radio links which proved unequal to the task. Since it was sometimes impossible to pass urgent uncorrupted operational messages in less than 48 hours (as was the case at certain crucial moments to the detriment of command and control) it can be imagined what happened to lower priority administrative traffic.

Of a myriad afflictions besetting the logisticians, the need (for political as well as humanitarian reasons) to feed and supply with medical stores a French populace in distress from the complete disruption of their distribution system and from German plundering, was but one of many diversions from the military aim, worsened by the destruction of the railways. Of the 12,000 locomotives available pre-war, 10,000 had been removed by the Germans or were out of action. Only a few bridges over the Seine and Somme rivers were still intact and so the restoration of rail links north and eastwards was a very slow process. By super-human efforts, the shipping in of new locomotives and the repair of about 4,000 damaged or broken down old ones, carrying capacity was gradually increased. But when most needed in September and October, when road transport was stretched to the limit, the rail contribution was meagre and control sketchy. With the telephone system in tatters, managers sometimes were reduced to sending bicycle messengers in search of the few scattered locomotives with directions where to report. After Elbeuf fell on 29 August it was nearly four weeks before the railway bridge over the Seine was repaired. Meanwhile stores from the bridgehead had to be carried by road to make connection with the railway to the northward, with all the time wasting and multi-handling of loads demanded.

By far the most harm to supply was inflicted, however, by General Eisenhower's unwillingness to concentrate all his resources upon a single powerful stroke aimed at the enemy hinterland. This, coupled with his inability to control, by radio alone, from a headquarters 400 miles back from the front led to lost opportunities and waste. Army Group and Army commanders such as Generals Bradley and Hodges, and the over-ambitious Montgomery and Patton, vied for more supplies than could be trucked forward from Cherbourg and the Normandy beaches to fighting formations, whose size was allowed to become inflated in excess of the operational need. Generals who were intolerant of supply shortages and sought the most glory indulged in the most unscrupulous methods. It was commonplace for lower echelon truck companies to be retained in forward zones instead of being off-loaded for First Line transport. Some logistic officers — those of Patton notoriously so — would hijack other armies' supplies and fail to disclose substantial captures of enemy fuel. As a result the logistic system was over-strained, then driven to breaking point, by Eisenhower's selection of a broad-fronted advance into Germany, instead of the narrower (though still 50 mile wide) frontage advocated by Montgomery. Without exploring the well worn controversy of Broad versus Narrow Front strategies, it is pertinent to remark that this was another manifestation of 'Teeth versus Tail' in which leaders were permitted excessive operational scope (as they felt was their right) without sufficient regard to the common cause, let alone being directed in the direction of a goal with pronounced logistic impact upon the enemy's maintenance.

No single episode illustrates this better than Montgomery's commitment, on 17 September, of three airborne divisions to open a corridor via Arnhem into northern Holland as a way of maintaining momentum across the River Rhine into the German plain. So intent became Eisenhower and Montgomery on this operation, in addition to their row over Broad and Narrow Front, that they failed to give due consideration to its logistic implications. Despite clear evidence of a petrol and ammunition crisis in Belgium and also of the Germans being intent upon holding the mouth of the River Scheldt to prevent use of the major port facilities in Antwerp, which had been captured intact on 3 September, they did nothing to clear the approaches to the port, as they could easily have done whilst the enemy's defences were negligible.

That so professional a soldier as Montgomery should have made so unforgiveable an error seems inexplicable. That his highly experienced administrative staff should have let him do it is more inexplicable still. However, it has to be remembered that the euphoria which pervaded the Allied armies after their breathtaking dash across Europe (after seven weeks of very intense fighting, during which Montgomery himself was under enormous personal pressure from all sides) and the prospect of the glittering prize of the defeat of Germany shining in their eyes, could well have swayed even the judgement of so great a commander — though that does not constitute any excuse either for him, his staff or for the Supreme Allied Commander, who had insisted in taking over control of the land battle from Montgomery and therefore must bear the greater responsibility.

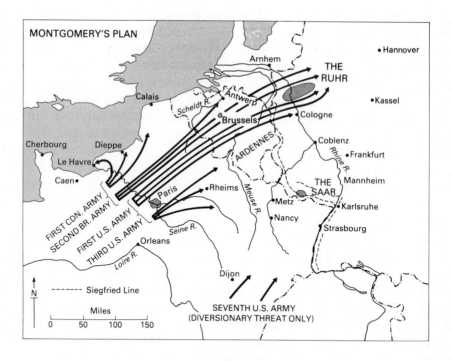

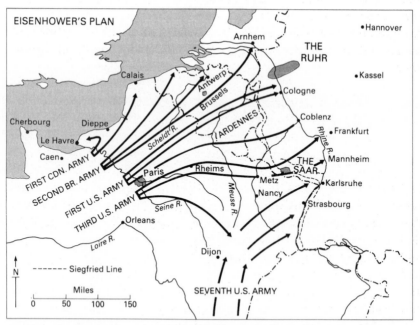

MAP 15. The plans for the Broad and Narrow Front controversy. In both cases the way forward would be hampered by the wreckage of land and signal communications destroyed in the fighting and by German demolitions or pulverised by Allied aerial bombardment

On 10 September, the leading Allied formations were feeling the petrol pinch and detecting the first signs of stiffening enemy resistance as the logistic equaliser came into play. Dropping three vulnerable airborne infantry divisions ahead of the armoured mobile spearheads could only worsen the logistic situation since they would depend largely upon the already over-stretched land transport for supplies. Better by far, it can be argued (as some did at the time), that the 1,545 DC 3 (Dakota) transports diverted to dropping soldiers and equipment should have been employed exclusively with their $2\frac{1}{2}$ ton pay load, to deliver fuel and ammunition near the front. Given the same will and ingenuity as went into the airborne venture, the despatch, reception and onward delivery of at least 3,000 tons per day to the Belgian airfields (which already were handling 3,000 tons per week) was feasible — and without peril. In that way, whether Antwerp was opened or not, and even as part of the Broad Front strategy, the thrust of Hodge's First US Army and Dempsey's Second British (as both desired) could have penetrated the Siegfried Line and driven to the Rhine without pause. In that way too they would have threatened the Ruhr and disrupted Germany's principal water and rail systems, making the immediate recovery which she actually managed impossible. Thus they might have shortened the war by six months, and done so, incidentally, at the very moment when the Russian Army had come to a standstill before Warsaw at the end of August. Here, as almost everywhere else, the perennial shortage of Russian transport (which would have been crippling but for the import of American vehicles) compounded the effect of the wholesale obstructions created by the practiced German route denial measures which were second to none. Indeed the entire apparatus of Russian communications might have collapsed without American Lease Lend if the following items, in addition to tanks and aircraft, had not been provided.

Trucks	376,211
Jeeps	51,503
Locomotives	1,964
Rolling Stock	11,075
Field Telephones	189,000
Signal Cable (miles)	670,000

As it was the battle-worn Russian Army, which struggled westwards through the devastated wastelands of Eastern Europe, found itself hard pressed to advance without pause to recuperate in order to overcome the next enemy stop line, which coalesced as the Germans backed onto their logistic base.

Had it not been for this Lease-Lend logistic assistance, what might have been the political consequences? Would Russia have survived? Might not the Western Allies have conquered Germany before the Russians arrived within sight of Berlin? And what then? Certainly, if Germany had been beaten before Christmas she might have been spared the ultimate devastation of her cities which occurred when the air forces once more indulged in area bombing. Similarly, the wrecking of the transport system could have been avoided. Despite the usual objections by Air Chief Marshal Harris and General Spaatz, this destruction was insisted upon by the High Command. Its thorough application led rapidly to the total collapse of the German economy and means of production. The halting of all military traffic refuted the pleas of the objectors by proving absolutely how crippling such an attack could be.

The War at Sea in the Far East

While the war had been raging in Europe and Russia a deadly struggle was being fought at sea in the Pacific — naval warfare on a scale never before experienced.

Crucial though the development was of mechanised land transport in North West Europe and in the Mediterranean theatre and important though those occasions were when aircraft also played their part — such as with routine German practice; British delivery of fighters from Takoradi to Cairo and a small, similar American trickle from Alaska to Siberia (until Russian shilly shally put a stop to it); Allied strategic air supply to North West Africa and Sicily and Italy; supply of guerrillas on all fronts, and a single tactical delivery of supplies to cut off Polish troops by 13 DC 3s in Normandy — it was in the Pacific and Far East where the greatest progress in supply techniques for sustained periods over long distances was made.

Due to the distances involved and the relatively short range and low payload of transport aircraft, the drives from the South West Pacific and Australian and the subsequent central thrust through the central Pacific towards the Dutch East Indies, and the Philippines and Japan, depended on shipping which carried 98 per cent of cargo needed. Not until 1943, when a trickle of new landing ships and craft (all British inventions including the ubiquitous 4,000 ton Landing Ships Tank (LSTS), 600 ton Landing Craft Tank (LCTs) and 30 ton Landing Craft Mechanised (LCM)) became a flood, did supply meet demand under well planned management. Numerous were the mechanical and electrical teething troubles of these vessels of revolutionary design. Constructed in newly built yards and manned by officers and crews of little or no sea going experience, their maintenance was a problem. Ingenious, as well as hazardous, was their movement across thousands of miles of ocean, some LSTs carrying an LCT on deck on their first voyage on the way out. Marvellous was the training which proceeded in tandem with the construction of new bases and the assembly of the vast 'fleet train' whose cargo ships accompanied the carrier and amphibious task forces as floating warehouses, throughout their deep penetration voyages. As Seabees toiled to construct airfields, safe anchorages, jetties and fuel storage tanks, the crews of the fleet train and their 'customers' — the carriers, battleships, cruisers, destroyers and assault ships practised the techniques of transferring fuel and all manner of munitions and stores at sea which kept the fleet free of a land base for weeks on end. Indeed, as successive assault landings on fiercely defended beaches progressed, and the Japanese air attacks multiplied, bomb and ammunition expenditure, which had never been high in the old days of ship versus ship engagements, became colossal.

Mere figures become tedious and almost meaningless when recited in profusion. Yet it is interesting to note typical support for a relatively minor invasion of the mid-Solomons (Operation *Toenails*) in Spring 1943. A special Operation *Drygoods* shipped, without LST assistance, to the improved Guadalcanal and Russell Islands base, 80,000 barrels of petroleum, 50,000 tons of supplies and munitions besides thousands of tons of equipment. Against such an enormous and ever-expanding weight of effort, the Japanese had little logistic chance. Their own relatively meagre resources could not match the Americans. They fell even further into arrears as their shipping losses rose, their shipbuilding, hit by lack of imported metal, was reduced and as their mobility and imports declined from an oil famine which capture of South East Asia's fields in 1942 had not solved. For while it was relatively easy to restore to production those installations which had been damaged, it was increasingly difficult, in a climate of naval adversity, to move the products to Japan and outlying bases — despite a re-allocation to merchant ship building (mostly tankers) of 80 per cent capacity.

Furthermore, Japanese fighting men, renowned for their fanatical courage in battle, were denied the health care which was their due. In jungle terrain, where diseases such as malaria were rife, they often lacked the latest suppressive compounds, paraquine and mepacrine, and the powerful insecticide DDT, which enabled their enemy to minimise his casualties. Never were they supplied with penicillin which, after 1943, was available in quantity to the Allies as part of the medical service which ensured that more than 90 per cent of wounded who reached hospital survived. Nor had they anything like the chance of air or sea evacuation home by a transport system in tatters.

As the drive towards South East Asia from the Solomons and Australia, and from the mid-Pacific towards the Mariana Islands and Carolines, via the Gilbert Islands and Marshall Islands, towards Japan, gathered momentum in 1943 and 1944, the Japanese were confronted not only by an enemy with an immensely superior logistic strategy and capability, such as they had never contemplated when setting up their perimeter defences, but they were rapidly reduced to impotence by the destruction of their own communication systems. The full irony of this situation became apparent in October 1944 when the Japanese Combined Fleet simply had to be based on Singapore, where there was oil a plenty — but a serious shortage of ammunition; instead of in Japan, as was strategically desirable, and where there was ammunition in plenty but insufficient oil. And the reason for this logistic imbalance? A compounding of signal communication insecurity and inferior anti-submarine equipment and techniques which enabled American underwater craft to play havoc with Japan's mercantile marine.

Before Pearl Harbor, Japan had a call on nearly nine million tons of shipping, and was resigned to losing 8 per cent of it in furtherance of her conquests. In the event it cost rather more. The loss rate would rise to disastrous proportions as the enemy drew closer to her main supply routes. Ships, aircraft, mines and, above all, submarines began to take their toll. Moreover, outlay needed to sustain the perimeter defences, difficult, even in 1942, became quite impossible to provide from 1943 onwards. For by then the Americans were beginning to rectify an initial torpedo failure rate of 37 per cent and were taking advantage of radar for night surveillance to find their prey. Most important of all, intelligence provided by interception and decryption of Japanese radio signals was giving precise information of sailing times and courses. Throughout the remainder of the war, the Japanese believed it was espionage which disclosed the movement of ships and lost them the majority of vessels on passage to Japan. Like the Germans, they never guessed at the power of Ultra to break their machine cyphers. But the eventual loss of eight and a half million tons of shipping, 57 per cent to Allied (mainly American) submarines, was a calamity made all the more certain due to an initial doctrinal reluctance to institute the convoy system (which automatically increased vulnerable signal traffic) and neglect of anti-submarine technology, techniques and tactics. At the same time, their own inability to interupt Allied lines of communication (or to break cyphers) was illustrated by the fact that their submarines sank nothing like the percentage achieved by their enemies.

Chapter 10

Another Transport Revolution

Burma: The Triumph of Air Supply

THE LOSS of Burma in 1942 not only deprived the Allies of an oil source and the British of a valued colony. It placed Japan within striking distance of the vital Indian base and severed the land link from Rangoon via the newly constructed Burma Road to Kunming, so blocking the back door supply route to China. To make matters worse for the Allies, large scale Japanese naval incursions in 1942 into the Bay of Bengal eliminated Calcutta as the main port of entry for the build-up of India as a base and as a transit point for supplies to China.

It was Allied policy to supply and thus keep China in the war, tying down the Japanese Army on the mainland. But while the Americans were intent upon reconquering North Burma and establishing a rail and road link via Ledo and Myitkynia to the Burma Road, the British had additional motives. India was a source of their manpower and material for the war in the Mediterranean and the security of its own North West Frontier where the tribes, sometimes stirred up by Axis propaganda, posed a threat. Additionally, the British were determined to recapture the whole of Burma as a stepping stone to Singapore and the restoration of lost colonies. The Japanese, on the other hand, fostered a long term ambition, in concert with militant nationalists who tried to undermine the Indian base, to invade India. But that would have to wait until construction of the notorious Siam to Burma railway was completed. Virtually all the campaigning in Burma was about logistics. Both sides strained to supply the Burma-India frontier to satisfy their strategic aims and to control access to China. They struggled in the most difficult mountainous, jungle country imaginable. This was a war in which one key to survival was mastery of the medical and health problems and another the combination of engineer effort and air supply to overcome overwhelming logistic and operational difficulties.

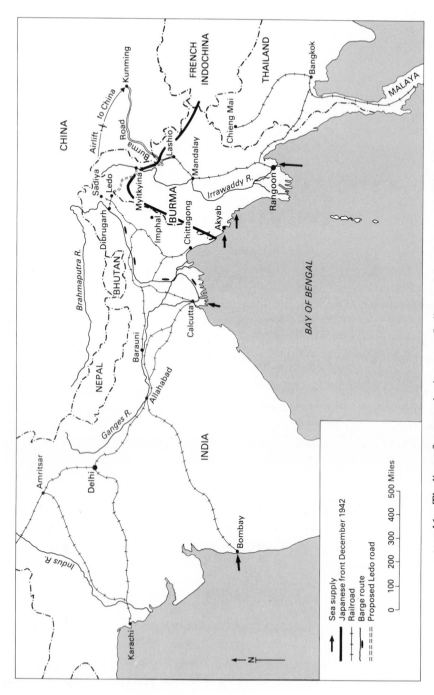

MAP 16.   The lines of communication across India supplying Burma and China. Note also the railways upon which the Japanese were so dependent and which were only occassionally cut

Almost unlimited manpower helped do much of the work, but it was bulldozers, graders and many other types of earth moving machinery which pushed new roads and railways into the hills and through the jungle in the wake of spearheads which, to a large extent, depended upon mule and man porterage. As never before, air transport held the keys to mobility and tactical freedom. Until combined American, Chinese and British operations, delayed at first due to logistic poverty, could clear the enemy from Northern Borneo and reopen the Burma Road, the only way to get supplies to Kunming was in twin and four engine transports over the so-called Hump at heights above 12,000 feet. Construction of the air bases and assembly of what, at first, was a motley collection of aircraft was a prodigious task which was hampered until 1944 by the universal transport aircraft shortage and interception by Japanese fighters. Where political intransigence and haggling on the part of the Chinese was by no means the least of the problems, whatever progress was made had to be won against innumerable frustrations and disappointments. Stores arriving in India during 1943, with China as destination, tended to swell depots because they could not be shifted forward. Though the reinforcement of the air transport fleet in due course achieved something, there were repeated clashes of priorities over transport for the Chinese Army, for the American air units (the Flying Tigers) in China, and support of the forces fighting the Japanese in Burma. And the Burma Road did not reopen until January 1945.

Although the experiment in 1943 of infiltrating Brigadier Orde Wingate's Chindits deep into Burma to harass Japanese lines of communication achieved but little operationally and at high cost, it did prove the feasibility of total logistic support by air drop. When Wingate's forces of divisional size was inserted by gliders and transport aircraft in 1944, the new logistic techniques of control, packing and delivery were those upon which similar operations everywhere were being modelled. Methods which later made it possible to maintain General Sir William Slim's Fourteenth Army even throughout the monsoon and to supply his spearheads in the advance to Rangoon in 1945 with 90 per cent of their requirements.

In terms of logistic surprise, air supply of the British Field Force was, to the Japanese, what the Mulberry harbour was to the Germans. As they discovered when, in February 1944, they encircled a British division in the Arakan and, in March, when they attempted to invade India, the enemy no longer retreated at the mere threat of encirclement. Now he stood, fought and was well supplied by constant deliveries by parachute of fragile items and by free fall drop of everything else. During the siege of Imphal, between 1 April and 23 June, Allied transports delivered 18,300 tons of supplies and over 12,000 men before the road was fully reopened. On the other side of the line, where the Japanese lines of communication were nothing like secure and constantly attacked from the air, there appeared that inescapable logistic and subsequent combat decay which brought their forces to disaster once the British counter-offensive opened. Throughout the remarkable 500 mile retreat to Rangoon, which lasted five months, hardly ever did the logistic

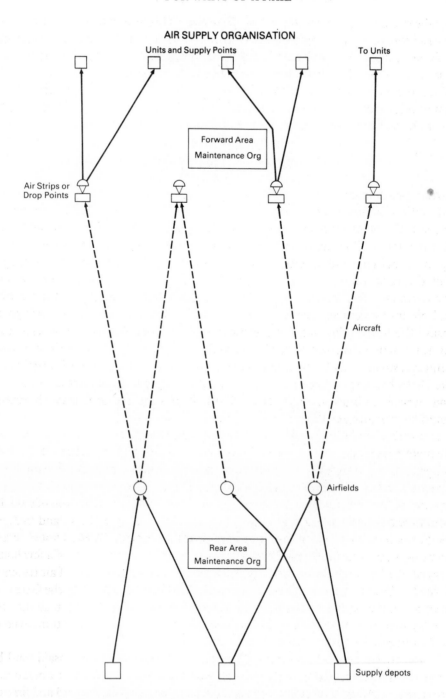

AIR SUPPLY ORGANISATION

FIG 10.1   The basic system of air supply used by most belligerents in the Second
World War but principally in Burma from 1943-45

equaliser come to the rescue of the Japanese. This was partly because of the destruction of their supply routes from air attack, partly because unchecked malaria ravaged their ranks; and very largely because Slim (one of whose mottos was 'God helps those who help themselves') had improvised so well logistically. When the Japanese were starving from being pushed aside from their lines of communications, his men were receiving ample fuel, ammunition and supplies by air, rail, road and mule.

The Heritage of War

Looking back from 1945 to air supply's small beginnings at Kut in 1916, to the first supply of guerrilla operations in the desert in 1917, to the gradual emergence in the 1920s of air transport as a strategic and logistic force of promise, and to its first major contribution as a substantial political factor, when troops were moved by air to Spain in 1936, it could be seen that the fledgling had come mightily of age. There was no anti-climax as in 1918. Not only had the performance of aircraft improved out of all imagination, but the most sophisticated methods of navigation and air traffic control, based upon electronics, had been developed enough to assure the functioning and rapid growth of regular air line services world-wide. Even in many of the remotest places, well-equipped military airfields with hard runways, stood ready for conversion to civil use. Thus air mobility's limitations of the 1930s had largely been resolved. Given the ability to move adequate supplies and control facilities to an existing airfield within the shortest time, air supply could be provided flexibly at very short notice.

It was the flexibility and adaptability of long-range transport aircraft which so frequently demonstrated at the war's end that the role of the ship, though far from eclipsed as a carrier of large, bulk tonnages, was beaten in terms of speed and direction of delivery. Even in 1945 people were coming to understand air transport as a way of life. Emotive movement operations such as the great air drop of food, by British and American heavy bombers, to the starving people of Holland in April 1945, when the Germans refused resupply by other means; the accelerated return home in those same bombers of released prisoners of war in a matter of a few hours instead of what might have been a week or more; the establishment of air trooping to the Far East, to hasten the transfer of troops who had been fighting the Germans to confront the Japanese; and the large scale evacuation of wounded in all theatres of war, were well publicised episodes which caught peoples' imaginations even as civil airlines were getting back on their feet.

In the aftermath of the atomic explosions at Hiroshima and Nagasaki (said by some to pronounce the doom of established logistics as well as of operational methods), it was air transport which assumed a leading role in the cold and limited wars which at once broke out. The clash of ideologies and ambitions between East and West, communism and capitalism; the sometimes related outbreaks of nationalistic rebellions and revolutions — mainly amidst the old colonies and notably in the Middle and Far East — often depended upon or were countered by logistic methods established during the war, and employed the practised operatives and equipment with their experience of clandestine as well as overt reinforcement and delivery. As will be seen, the guerrilla violence which erupted in, for example, Palestine, Malaya, the Dutch East Indies (Indonesia), and French Indo-China (Vietnam) would have been almost inconceivable without the cadres and ideas of the major war.

Berlin Airlift

Few supply operations had greater impact in the Cold War than the air supply of Berlin between June 1948 and September 1949 after Stalin had cut the land routes to the sectors of the Western Allies. With little warning of the siege and only one month's stock of most commodities, the British and Americans, above all the latter who alone possessed a fleet of four engined transports with a ten ton payload, had to fly in enough to feed and keep warm some two million people. By day and night in all weathers, and despite occasional 'buzzing' by Russian fighters and jamming of radio communications, the airlift was operated with steadily mounting efficiency and scope. Tight rationing was imposed upon the inhabitants as the system of shifting the cargoes, marshalling the aircraft through three internationally recognised corridors was improved and as more and more aircraft were acquired. From 1,500 tons daily in July 1948, the lift rose to 12,940 tons on 16 April 1949, by which time stocks had risen above their 1948 level and the people of West Berlin were feeding better than those in the East, whose economy, ironically warped by the blockade of the West, was collapsing. By the time the Russians had been forced to give way and permit land transport to resume, not only had a great political and psychological victory been won over them, but the world had also been shown that, given the machines and bases, air transport was something more than a prop for short-term logistic emergencies. No less than 2,325,809 tons had been carried with great reliability (thanks to high discipline in flight and with maintenance) with fewer than 200 accidents (less than ten serious). The intensive operational techniques developed would be the model for many commercial enterprises, and, if required on the grand scale, a sure alternative to surface transport providing the necessary handling and control facilities were available in the right place.

Above all, the Berlin airlift was one of those rare events in which a shooting war was prevented, without a shot being fired, by the application of logistic power.

Chapter 11

Rewards for the Primitive

A HUNDRED years after steam driven railways and cable telegraph had revolutionised war by pulling communications out of their mediaeval rut, logistic
practice had attained a position from which combat units could be provided with
sufficient supplies to fight and move with almost untrammelled freedom in all but
the most inaccessible parts of the world. With the wide range of transport systems,
base facilities and signal communication networks set up throughout the civilised
world (with tentacles probing even into wild mountainous, jungle and arctic
territories) mounting a large military operation almost anywhere at any time of year
at relatively short notice was feasible — provided that the principals of administration laid down by most General Staffs were adhered to. Lack of foresight,
Economy, Flexibility, Simplicity, Co-operation and Self Sufficiency — crucially in
fuel — when planning an operation, however, was as likely to invite disaster in
1950 as they had done in 1850, as will be seen.

The Nuclear Shadow

To the handful of people who, in 1945, gave profound consideration to the affect
on logistics of nuclear weapons it appeared unlikely at first that anything would be
the same again. Concentrated base installations, such as those created in Normandy and certain Pacific islands — let alone the conglomerates to be found in the
homelands — were so vulnerable to nuclear strikes that their survival (if survival
was possible) had to rely upon widespread dispersal. Similarly, combat formations
would only rarely concentrate, and then only for short periods. When the thermo-
nuclear weapon system was exploded in 1951, it dawned upon even the most
optimistic thinker that such logistic resources which remained intact after an
exchange of these weapons would need to be committed to the survival of the
human race rather than the supply of armed forces.

Nevertheless, studies and exercises were conducted into ways and means of support for nuclear warfare. How to keep stores safe; how to move them from dispersed locations to dispersed combat formations and units; how to care for multitudes of casualties, how to replace or repair masses of weapons vehicles, aircraft and ships; and how to control these complex activities from headquarters which were themselves under threat with their signal communications largely broken and disrupted. The solutions of hard cover or underground storage; more flexible transport by sea, air and improved cross-country vehicles; duplicated headquarters and signal communication systems were all investigated. Lip service was paid and some attempts made to improve chances of survival — but limited to the extent that financial resources permitted. At the back of everybody's mind lay the realisation that foresighted dealing with the incomprehensible was impossible and that if the catastrophe occurred only improvisation of the most incredible kind would prevail.

In the meantime wars of low intensity of a much more comprehensible nature employing the hardware, the technology and the techniques of the past had started before the last shots of the Second World War had been fired. No sooner had the Germans and the Japanese laid down their arms than the cadres of guerrillas and embryo armies which would fight in the cold and limited wars of the next four decades were picking them up by begging, borrowing, purloining and, every now and then, formally purchasing them for money. The partisans of Europe who would wage civil war in Greece, in Palestine and in parts of Africa would, in addition to arms obtained from the Western Allies, be equipped with German and Italian weapons. Likewise the anti-colonial groups of South East Asia and the communist armies of China would acquire much from the Japanese. Subsequently, as will be seen, they managed resupply and maintenance on traditional lines — by clandestine acquisitions, captures from the enemy and subsistence off the country. Logistic techniques learnt the hard way by Chu Teh's Long March of 1934–1935 when 200,000 people covered 6,000 miles in thirteen months (fighting most of the way) had firmly established Communism in China; and the system of supply through village communities linked by a network of communications (mostly messengers) had withstood counter-measures from both Nationalist Chinese and Japanese forces.

Guerrilla Warfare — Palestine and the Dutch East Indies

Like most subversive armed struggles for independence, the tussles between indigenous Arabs and Jews to take control of Palestine, after a unilateral abandonment of the British Mandate, was a long expected event for which all three parties had made logistic preparations. Originally the British had visualised Palestine as an extension of their Middle East base, whose main depots lay in Egypt. Since ejection of the Turks in 1918 the Palestinian Arabs considered it their homeland;

they wanted the British out. The guerrilla war that the Arabs had waged since the 1930s had been supplied clandestinely by neighbouring Arab states. The Zionist Jews, intent upon seizing Palestine as their homeland — Israel — had gradually built up a large underground army. They acquired their arms and munitions by whatever means possible. Some were smuggled in from the sea, paid for by Jews world-wide — mainly those in the United States. Throughout they were hampered by the British who tended to favour the Arabs.

When the British withdrew in 1948 and the long fought underground tussle flared into open warfare between Arab and Israeli, the latter's effective fighting force numbered some 15,000 with only a few thousand small arms and medium machine-guns and hardly any heavy weapons against the theoretically numerically superior armies of Jordan, Iraq, Syria and Egypt. But, in addition to a fanatically higher standard of leadership and motivation, the Israelis had the advantage of fighting when based on short lines of communication with what little ammunition (three days supply and even less at times) they possessed, against an enemy who, in the Egyptian and Iraqi instances, had to travel from afar. The Israeli strategy was to hold their settlements (which harboured a small arms manufacturing industry) while improving their organisation and their training and bringing in more supplies, of which some came by air through two landing strips. At once the Arabs laid siege to the roads. Meanwhile the Israelis fought for time in which to infiltrate supplies to the settlements by night. In particular they struggled to keep open the road to their people in Jerusalem where Jordan's Arab Legion posed extremely tough opposition.

By 1949 the Arab forces were morally and logistically exhausted. Not one Israeli settlement had fallen and they were growing stronger rapidly as supplies, aircraft, tanks and artillery arrived from many sources. Once the lines of communication were freed, mobile warfare began and the poorly administered and led Egyptian Army fell back after defeat. As an exercise in the conversion of a guerrilla force into a field army capable of fighting pitched battles, the Israeli achievement was a classic made all the more remarkable by their improvisation of *ad hoc* logistic services as the fighting went on. Out of chaos, in less than a year and despite the absence of self-sufficiency, organised forces with the semblance of a doctrine had been assembled within the stabilised frontiers of a new nation of immense vitality.

⋆   ⋆   ⋆   ⋆   ⋆

Equally complicated was the struggle which broke out in the Dutch East Indies. In August 1945 the Japanese encouraged Indonesian patriots to proclaim the state in order to pre-empt the return of the Dutch, but a few days later declined to hand over their arms except to the British and a few Dutch, who did not begin to arrive in strength until the end of September. Guerrilla warfare broke out between Japanese and Indonesians when the latter attempted to arm themselves against the Dutch — for there was no other way in which they could provide for the security of their new-found independence.

The civil war, which involved the British as they strove to comply with an earlier undertaking to help the Dutch regain their colony, centred upon a battle for arms and munitions in which the Indonesians barely managed to acquire enough to enable them to hold their own. Yet it was enough to win a political identity, recognised by the United Nations, and to enable their underground forces to fight when they chose. In city and deep hinterland they lived comfortably off an entirely friendly country and built up their strength. Correctly, they calculated that the Dutch, weakened by the catastrophies of 1940 and 1942, wilting at the end of long, slow-moving lines of sea communication, forced by the threat of an almost entirely hostile population to dissipate strength on guarding bases and communications, and under political pressure by the United Nations, would have to give way eventually. Logistically impoverished as the Indonesians remained, and usually defeated whenever they emerged to fight pitched battles, they demonstrated how perseverance in survival could pay off — as it did in 1949, when the Dutch withdrew.

Emergency in Malaya

Many lessons could be drawn from the Indonesian victory of perseverance by a logistically weak and partially isolated guerrilla force. But the answers were far from clear cut and certainly not applicable to all situations. Not one of which would ever be the same as the next. For example, if (as is unlikely) the Malayan Communist Party (MCP) with its Malayan Races Liberation Army (MRLA) and clandestine Min Yuen (which arranged recruiting and supply in addition to propaganda and sabotage), had based their decision, under British counter-terrorist pressure in 1947, to begin guerrilla warfare on the Indonesian experience, they would have done well to reflect longer.

The first great misconception by the MCP, when its escalating campaign of violence (prompted by misgivings over British willingness to transfer power to the people) led to its proscription by the British in July 1947 and subsequent enforced departure to jungle hides, was that the British with their world-wide distractions, were inherently no stronger than the Dutch. Even though the Socialist Government, beset by dire economic problems, was in the act of a precipitate withdrawal from India under pressure of Indian civil disobediance, that was insufficient reason to think they would retreat everywhere. This led to a second false conclusion — an over-estimation of their own strength. Although they had managed the organisation, training and clandestine supply for survival in the jungle against the Japanese, with considerable British assistance, they had not, in fact, caused the Japanese great inconvenience. They had learnt how to live in the jungle but in combat were barely tested. It could hardly be otherwise when it is recalled that air and sea supply had sent in only about 200 agents, 50 radio sets and 76 tons of weapons, munitions and medical stores before the war ended. Thirdly, the somewhat arrogant assumption that a force of 4,000 to 7,000 guerrillas (90 per cent of whom were Chinese) would prevail (nourished, no doubt, by the thought that if the Japanese could beat the British so could they): for they overlooked the fact that the Chinese populace of Malaya, (excluding Singapore) was a mere 20 per cent compared with the rest of whom the Malays compiled some 60 per cent. Their people's crusade, in other words, was not unified in the same way as the nearby Indonesian one. This racial division eventually made it easier for the British to evolve a political solution in a hand over of power which isolated the MCP.

The Communist forces retired into the jungle when their campaign of strikes, terror, sabotage and extortion had won them a reputation for ruthlessness, which coerced some self-interested or fearful citizens to collaborate. They had sizeable financial assets and, in readiness, the underground District Organisations which had covered the country during the war and had not been disbanded. At the start, the first phase of their plan to wear down the Government and Security Forces by guerrilla warfare had credibility provided that their strength could be built up at the same time as the populace was being coerced. Actuating the second phase of cutting lines of communication and occupying important centres was more tentative and dependent on the success of Phase One. But the third phase, of forcing an exhausted enemy to abandon the struggle after being pushed onto the defensive, was far too reliant on speculation to be taken seriously. For it not only tended to despise the opposition but also overrated the feasibility of acting aggressively without, at the same time, being self-sufficient. For although the MCP could count on Chinese and Communist sympathy at a time when Mao Tse Tung's forces were winning great victories on the road to complete power in China, there is little evidence that they expected much material outside help. Unlike the Indonesian rebels, the MCP was not recognised by the United Nations. Rather like the Boers in 1899, they were almost totally isolated from outside supply. Their only semi-reliable source of essential arms and munitions and medical stores — the items of which perennially there was a shortage — was Thailand. Smuggling from there would be ceaseless and the target for many a security operation and diplomatic manoeuvre.

A principal task of any revolutionary movement must be the maintenance of momentum. Usually this is done by political initiative and mobile operations in the field. In neither of these spheres were the MCP able to make the necessary headway. In due course the British appreciated that a political solution, founded on the eventual grant of independence to the Malay state, was essential, and that a predominantly Malay influence in government, with Chinese and other racial groups participating, would lose the MCP support as well as being democratic. Eventually this political initiative would be associated with what the High Commissioner, General Sir Gerald Templer, termed the fight for 'hearts and minds' — a psychological struggle with strong practical, persuasive tones overlain by the need to crush the MRLA and Min Yuen.

Inherently, however, the MCP district organisation was immobile due to its widespread dispersal throughout the country based upon jungle camps. The Boer guerrilla logistics against the British had depended upon mobility across open spaces in order to acquire food; the MCP relied upon being static in deep cover in order either to obtain food from the cowed local populace or to grow it on the spot. Either way was detrimental to operations since offensive power declined in relation to the effort spent on logistics. So long as the MCP kept the initiative, from 1948 until 1952, it was able to replace arms and ammunition from captures during raids on police and army posts and also replenish food stocks through 'contributions' from the village and squatters. It was not a lack of food, however, which limited the forces living in jungle to about 4,000, but the arms shortage. Without manufacturing facilities, in the Israeli manner, the weapons which had been acquired and hidden away from British abandonments in 1942, Japanese surrenders in 1945 and those which had been sent by the British in 1944 and 1945, and which had not been handed in, gradually declined. Damaging to the country and prestige raising as the initial frequent small MRLA raids against economic targets and against unprepared Security Forces were, the crucial contest which would decide the issue was between the Min Yuen and the British administration for control of supplies.

Economy of own force and denial of supplies to the Min Yuen lay at the heart of most British counter-guerrilla measures. They reinforced the number of trained soldiers and police engaged in hunting the MRLA while attempting to reduce the number guarding logistic installations. They specifically attacked the main enemy providers of supply, of whom some half million illegal Chinese 'squatters' who had immigrated since 1945 were the principal culprits. Central to these measures was the Briggs Plan of 1950 named after its innovator, Lieutenant Colonel Sir Harold Briggs, which sought to undermine the Min Yuen by separating it from the squatters and outlying villagers upon whom it preyed. Concentrating mainly, but not wholly successfully, upon improving the flow of intelligence through a more efficient communication network, Briggs also took a leaf out of Kitchener's book by 'resettling', (to use the official term) the squatters and others in camps behind barbed wire, and repatriating some of the Chinese whence they came. Not to be compared in squalor and inhumanity with the Boer War concentration camps, these reasonably well run camps had, within a year, removed some 400,000 people from the Min Yuen's clutches. They had improved, too, the health and living conditions of the detainees, besides seriously disrupting the MCP supply and communication systems. Instructions to guerrilla bands, most of which travelled by hand, were slow. Meanwhile, half-hearted communists for whom the 'hard life' was not to be compared with 'good' Resettlement, took the opportunity to abscond or fade away. It would take several months for the fat upon which the MRLA lived to be eaten up. Indeed, for a while it profited from a bonus of arms stolen from the inexperienced guards of the Resettlement camps.

Nevertheless, the indirect attack upon the Min Yuen, along with the gradual cutting off of supplies, forced the MRLA into the open — as Briggs desired. The Min Yuen fell into decline and any hope the MCP had of staging Phase Two of their plan in 1951 was snuffed out. Once the Min Yuen faltered, the MRLA was compelled to forage for itself. Its number of recruits began to diminish, casualties and desertions increased and, most harmful of all, food and ammunition became scarce. Fortunes were reversed. Always well armed and supplied, the Security Forces' confidence rose as their prowess and successes burgeoned. Armed only with shot guns and small arms, 5,000 or so deprived guerrillas, with about 50 rounds per man, fell into deepening trouble as they were driven away from the vital localities.

The decimation of the MRLA was geared to the rigours of strangulating the MCP's attempts to strengthen its broken supply organisation without further alienating the population and, at the same time, exposing its doctrine and combat troops to undue pressure, a task bordering on the impossible. In October 1951 the MRLA assumed direct responsibility for supply from the Min Yuen, a reorganisation which ordered the formation of a jungle cultivation corps and put logistics before operations. But these ideas were usually overtaken by events before instructions had reached outlying operatives.

At a steady rate, those operatives were being changed from fighters into farmers as the Security Forces increased their pressure. As losses mounted and the withdrawal to deeper jungle continued, contacts with suppliers were broken and morale sank. An attempt in 1952 to improve the MCP's public standing as a Party of the People, coincided with purchasing food, instead of impounding it. The cash balances soon disappeared since neither by robbery nor with the contributions of a declining number of well-wishers could they meet the bills.

No longer could the guerrillas encamp in close proximity to his targets and suppliers. No longer was he kept well informed as the MCP communication system crumbled and, to make matters worse, was further centralised. Life in the camps, previously spartan but relatively safe with sufficient food and medical supplies, became frugal in the extreme, a struggle for survival. By the end of 1952, MRLA numbers were below 4,000 and falling. Since 1948 they had lost nearly 4,500 killed, captured or deserted — many of them hard core. Discipline was ferocious, propaganda relentless — and intensifying — as conditions worsened and the leadership felt bound to make far greater efforts to placate the waverers — who wavered all the more. With every set-back and every indication that the British genuinely were intent upon granting self-government to the Malay people, the MCP cause was eroded.

Meanwhile the Security Forces were improving. Their morale and techniques of jungle fighting, allied to adequate feeding and medical arrangements when operating in dense jungle became somewhat easier as air supply techniques improved. Not that jungle air supply was easy. As with the usually ineffectual bombing of MRLA camps, finding the drop point took much skill. As for the bombing, there was no guarantee, even if a camp was located, that the target would be hit. Casualties and damage were rarely caused to a dug-in enemy or one who, forewarned, had moved out. Logistic inconvenience was the most that could be expected.

Disappointing to begin with also was the contribution from that most potent new transport vehicle, the helicopter. Long desired for its vertical take off and landing capability, it was not until 1946 that the Bell Company of America produced an operationally practical machine. Visualised, at first, as being mainly for reconnaissance and supply, its first ever military use was casualty evacuation. In May 1950, when a Royal Air Force Westland Sikorsky Dragonfly picked up casualties from a jungle clearing, it initiated what would become a regular direct front line to hospital service which, in the years to come in innumerable campaigns, would save countless lives while reducing the suffering of patients who might otherwise be jolted by stretcher and other forms of land transport.

Light, fixed-wing aircraft, indeed, came to be feared more by the guerrillas than the heavy bombers and rocket firing fighters, fast jets among them. It was the slower flying machines which had most chance of detecting camps and directing the Security Forces to them. They also found the cultivation areas and, in company with helicopters, sprayed them with weed-killer as part of the crop-denial campaign which further worsened the MRLA logistic state.

By 1953 the MCP and the MRLA were beginning to suffer systematic elimination, district by district, state by state, band by band. Beaten in the field, as they were in encounter after encounter, defeat stemmed, fundamentally, from the combined loss of popular esteem and the collapse of the logistic system. It would be 1960, after the loss of about 11,000 guerrillas (nearly 7,000 killed) before the so-called Emergency was proclaimed as a victory for the non-Communist Malayan State. That victory might, nevertheless, have been an MCP triumph, had they not antagonised the bulk of the people.

By this time a whole new catalogue of rules relating to modern guerilla warfare and counter-insurgency operations, with emphasis on the predominant logistic factor, had been compiled — a catalogue whose lessons would have only a partial application to what was going on simultaneously in French Indo-China, where guerrilla warfare of a more sophisticated type was being conducted by nationalistic communists against the colonial power.

The French in Indo-China: Ho Chi Minh's Well-supplied Venture

At the end of the Second World War, political events in French Indo-China, where the nationalist communist Vietnamese Republic was proclaimed on 2 September 1945 by Ho Chi Minh, ran roughly parallel to those in the Dutch East Indies. The French colonial power, having recognised the new order then proceeded, with British assistance, to assert its old authority by endeavouring to limit Vietnamese power. From the start, British, Indian, French and Japanese troops were used to keep order by tackling the 10,000 strong Viet Minh forces under Vo Giap, which, with Nationalist Chinese assistance, had already been armed as an anti-Japanese Army and was strong in the north. No sooner had the British and Indians withdrawn in January 1946, than an obvious French determination to govern compelled the Viet Minh in December 1946 to resume guerrilla warfare. At that moment, both operationally and logistically, any parallel with the Dutch East Indies (or for that matter Malaya) ceased.

For the French, though by no means ready for a long war, were much better armed than the Dutch — though still short of equipment and pleased to make use of quite as many surrendered Japanese arms as those they had obtained from the British, the Americans and the Germans. All manner of weapons were in French use — pre 1940 French, Japanese (including ships and fighter aircraft), British, American and even some German Ju 52 transport aircraft. It is possible, indeed, that the Viet Minh was better standardised by its use of mainly Japanese and American equipment; the latter obtained through its wartime contacts with the Chinese and the American Organisation of Strategic Services. But the mere 40,000 troops available to the French under General Henri Leclerc in 1946 were insufficient to stamp out a determined and growing force of 30,000 or more guerrillas whose dedicated support from the people, particularly those in the north, could be reckoned upon. Vo Giap's forecast that the initial French offensive would be contained and be transformed into a war of long duration which 'he has to drag out . . . in order to win it and does not possess, on the other hand, the psychological and political means to fight a long, drawn out war . . .' proved shrewdly correct. By implication it was based upon the presumption that the Viet Minh could live off the country, without loss of the people's loyalty and affection, and that sufficient arms and munitions were obtainable. Also in the hope that weapons could be smuggled in from a variety of sources by land and sea, as well as captures from the enemy.

It was the Viet Minh's justified confidence in the maintenance of goodwill and supply which placed it on a totally different footing to its communist counterparts in Malaya. Even when the fluctuating political struggle sometimes shifted in French favour, and the French forces, after a series of military reverses in 1947, managed in 1948 to tighten their grip over key areas of the hinterland and upon the main entry ports (such as the Red River Delta), the Viet Minh managed to survive. It kept up attacks upon French bases and communications and raised its strength without antagonising the mass of its supporters. Unlike the Malayans, too, but much more in line with the methods of the Chinese communist guerrilla armies under Mao Tse Tung, the Viet Minh made a speciality of encirclement to starve out resisters as a prelude to imposing control on a neighbourhood. Sometimes it worked, sometimes not: and when it failed the besiegers just dispersed to try again elsewhere. The crucial aspect of such tactics lay in the ability of the Viet Minh's steadily improving, yet primitive, supply system, to maintain quite large groups in contact with the enemy without, as for similar forces in days gone by, stripping the country to the point of famine. Controlled by existing public (as well as super-imposed military) telephone and radio links, the Viet Minh far outclassed the MRLA in its ability to react swiftly to changing circumstances, they could direct their well

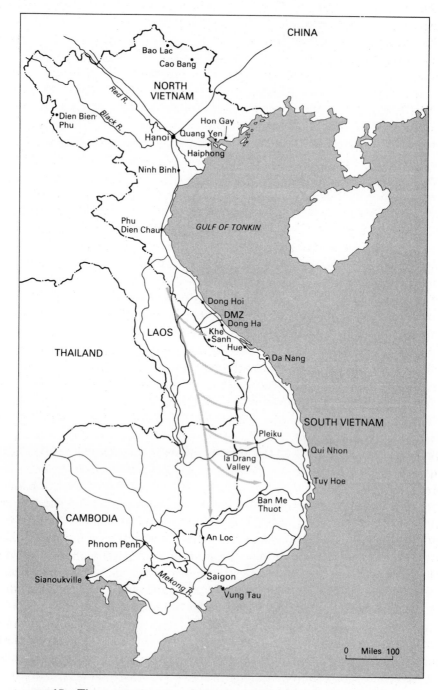

MAP 17.   The communications to and through Vietnam, including the elaborate
Ho Chi Minh Trail

organised, ant-like porterage columns, here and there supplemented by road transport, to concentrate or disperse as required.

The turning point in the Indo-China confrontation was promised in 1949 when China's communist armies overcame their Nationalist enemies, assumed control of the country and closed up to the border with North Indo-China. From the day in January 1950 when both Russian and Communist China recognised the Viet Minh, the logistic problems of Ho Chi Minh and Vo Giap were solved. Henceforward a flow of supplies by land and sea could be infiltrated almost with impunity from bases in China where Viet Minh guerrillas could rest, train and scheme. The French had either to reinforce substantially or admit defeat by patching up a treaty with the Viet Minh. However, in 1950, as the latter fastened an extremely firm grip on the province of Tonkin, the fighting grew much fiercer as the French, now under Marshal de Lattre de Tassigny, retaliated with skill, determination and not a little success. The possibilities of an agreement receded further when the Americans involved from 1950 in a war against the communists in Korea (see below), became committed to confrontation against China.

With hindsight, the French might admit that they never came to understand or calculate the strength of the flexible Viet Minh logistic system. They did not comprehend the thousand upon thousand porters who, ant-like, trudged through jungle paths carrying loads up to 45 lbs per man plus food and equipment: or that, from 1951, thousands of bicycles, made by Peugeot factories, had been adapted to carry 450 lbs, pushed along the trails; or that, towards the campaign's end in 1954, the trails had been improved to take some 600 $2\frac{1}{2}$-ton trucks provided by Russia. In the face of evidence to the contrary, they deluded themselves into imagining that, by retaining control of communication centres, they could strangle a primitive opponent. They had not realised that, primitive as the means of Viet Minh transport were, its labyrinthine organisation and vast scale made it proof against mere interdiction. Indeed, the French programme aimed at the destruction of secret bases, built up throughout a country which was largely hostile, was not decisive. A security task, historically shown to be impossible, faced the French as they attempted to guard their own bases and lines of communication while lacking local sympathy as well as manpower. It rated as only a relatively minor Viet Minh set-back when, for example in January and February 1953, the French seized a secret supply base at Quinhon and destroyed a number of arms factories in South Vietnam's jungle. At such Giap would shrug and set about replacing the losses along a network of sub-standard jungle roads and tracks connecting with China and numerous coastal inlets. As a general rule, even a medium-sized guerrilla movement with a dedicated aim will survive, provided that it is even meagrely supplied from reasonably secure sources. But to win absolutely, it is essential for it to possess uninterruptable sources of supply, connected by strong lines of communication, as with any field army, in order to supply large forces in bulk — a capability that the Viet Minh was to demonstrate in 1954 when it confidently opted for what the

MRLA called Phase Two: i.e. cutting lines of communication and occupying important communication centres.

French political deviousness (which, perniciously, merely encouraged Viet Minh resistance) ran concurrent with logistic miscalculations. In November 1953, when the Government announced it was seeking 'an honourable' settlement without calling for Viet Minh 'unconditional' surrender, they flew some 15,000 men a distance of 180 miles into the Dien Bien Phu valley with the intention of cutting the main supply route to Laos and provoking a decisive pitched battle. It was an indication of General Henri-Eugene Navarre's paucity of information about the Viet Minh that he deluded himself into thinking that, with a mere 100 twin-engine transport aircraft (mostly DC 3 Dakotas) as a supply train, he could win a victory by fire power. For if he had known that the Viet Minh possessed numerous heavy weapons, light anti-aircraft guns, 200 pieces of artillery, all, in due course, well supplied with ammunition, he might have reconsidered the logistic balance. Indeed the French firepower would be niggardly — only 28 artillery pieces, a few light tanks (delivered in pieces and assembled on the spot) and 3,700 close support air sorties of dubious effect. It could not long prevail if Vo Giap really did take up the challenge, bearing in mind the inadequacy of air delivery which, in $5\frac{1}{2}$ months, would deliver 6,410 tons from 6,700 transport sorties.

From the moment they landed on 20 November the French were overstretched. With minimal plant for building fortifications, dumps and the air strips upon which they were logistically utterly dependent, they had to divide man hours between labour and the sending out of columns to seek the Viet Minh in battle and upset their lines of communication in what was, for them, a tight situation. When Giap decided to send 60,000 Chinese-trained troops (80 per cent of his main force) to encircle a French elite which represented only 4 per cent of the French strength in Indo-China, he did so in the confidence that, by simultaneously invading Laos, he could ensure his own adequate and uninterrupted supply for a prolonged siege conducted with superior fire power; and do so, moreover, in the sure knowledge that the French were irrevocably committed to a static fight in an area from which withdrawal was almost impossible. Hence he had ample time to assemble his forces and stock up with ammunition before delivering an assault. Furthermore, while the Viet Minh lines of communication beneath a jungle canopy were rarely threatened by scattered bombing and by raiding French columns, they enjoyed the knowledge, from a glance at Dien Bien Phu's airstrip, of the exact flight paths used by transports landing and taking off and, therefore, where best to emplace the anti-aircraft guns.

It took the Viet Minh nearly four months to concentrate. Months during which enough of a stranglehold was fastened on the French air bridge seriously to reduce the planned rates of delivery. Then it was thrust upon the French that an opponent who lacked aircraft was winning the air war. Transport and combat machines approaching or departing from the air landing zones came under a volume of fire which some veteran air crew described as more deadly than that encountered against Germany in 1944 and 1945. As losses in the air mounted, shelling of the landing zones aimed at parked aircraft and dumps, imposed severe restrictions. Fourteen machines — mostly vital transports — were destroyed on the ground; this out of a punitive total of 48 all types shot down and 167 damaged. No longer could the combat aircraft deliver their attacks with reasonable accuracy from low level. Nor, in due course, could supplies be air landed. Instead they had to be air dropped from above the ceiling of the anti-aircraft fire, with consequent reductions in payload (for weight of packing and parachutes) and declining accuracy of delivery — the Viet Minh being the grateful recipients on more than one occasion. So, when the ban on air landing came into force, the plight of the wounded, who could be evacuated no longer, worsened and morale inevitably suffered.

By the time of the first Viet Minh assault on 13 March 1954, on the heels of a storm of amply supplied artillery concentrations, the besieged had completely lost the initiative and had little hope. In no circumstances could they be reinforced, adequately supplied or rescued by an overland operation far beyond French resources to mount or supply through thick jungle and undeveloped tracks. On 27 March, when the Viet Minh seized the air-landing zones, the garrison was doomed. Even if the Americans (who in 1954 were aiding the French to the tune of $1 billion — 80 per cent of the war's cost) had complied with a further French request of direct military assistance, it would have been too late to prevent the overrunning on 7 May of a starving garrison whose ammunition stocks were fatally depleted. It was a catastrophe which not only put an end to French aspirations as a colonial power, but re-emphasised the logistic importance of a unified race in a struggle for survival.

There was something old-world about the manner of the Viet Minh's victory which drove the French out and returned Indo-China into the separate states of North and South Vietnam, Laos and Cambodia. The mechanised logistic and operational methods which prevailed in Europe had failed against a dedicated opponent whose logistics were indigenous, dependent on muscle power and managing without much call on fuel supplies. Time-honoured supply by men and animals had mastered modern mechanisation in a struggle hardly affected by the logistic equaliser which often conditioned the more complicated, sophisticated European systems. The Viet Minh's superior methods to those of their communist counterparts in Malaya demonstrated that the escalating three phase long drawn-out system *could* produce results — but only, as we have seen, if supplied from a secure source via uninterruptable routes; and if commanded and controlled through a reliable signal communication system. There was much more to learn from them than from the efforts of their comrades of North Korea, who, in 1950, had attempted to conquer South Korea by a campaign modelled on mechanised Russian advances in Europe and Manchuria at the end of the Second World War.

Korean Stalemate

The North Korean Army which, on 25 June 1950, crossed the 38th Parallel in its attempt to conquer South Korea by mechanised 'Blitzkrieg' contained ten well trained divisions and a tank brigade. Some 25,000 men of this army, which was backed by reserves of 100,000, were veterans of Mao Tse Tung's triumphant Chinese communist army. But on top of the 150 tanks, 180 piston engine aircraft and considerable quantities of artillery, mortars, ammunition, signals and medical equipment, along with transport shipped in by the Russians, there was superimposed a much more pronounced leaning towards Russian organisation and doctrine than to Chinese. Indeed, if the North Korean Army was to have any chance of seizing South Korea at the speed necessary to pre-empt intervention by the United States, it was vital to move much faster than the foot and hoof armies usually did. To sustain momentum modern transport of supplies protected from the danger of air interdiction were vital. Thus, as frontier incidents multiplied and political tension increased, the North in March secretly began to concentrate their troops closer to the border in March and to transfer supply dumps from the towns to safer rural areas.

In the absence of naval forces, the North Korean mechanised advance had no alternative but to follow the main road and rail arteries. Its main thrust was along the old double track railway line, with its parallel main road, from Kaesong through Seoul and Taejon to the vital ports of Mokpo and Pusan — final objectives whose swift capture would prevent a large-scale American intervention should that be contemplated. Correctly the North Koreans placed low value on the Republic of Korea's (ROK) meagrely equipped and poorly trained army of 100,000. They expected to overwhelm the South without much loss of momentum — as indeed they did in the first onrush. Incorrectly, they hoped that the Americans would either stand aside or, if they did come to the South's help, would be too late with too little to retain a foothold — it being known that the four American divisions in Japan stood at something like half strength. Within a week, American troops, in accordance with a United Nations motion stating that the invasion was 'a breach of the peace', were in motion by air and sea, and the United States Air Force had shot down several enemy aircraft — the prelude to the fight for air superiority and a steady intensification of attacks on the lines of communication in the traditional manner.

Indeed the whole campaign was traditionally run using, for the most part, the techniques and technology of 1945 and leading to the natural gradual application of the logistic equaliser's brake. Such, however, was the fast pace of the North Korean advance, that it swept ROK resistance aside to seize crossings over the Han River, beyond Seoul. Initially feeble air blows against its transport, imposed no pronounced deceleration for several weeks. Its progress was made the easier by failures on the ROK part fully to demolish some vital bridges. It was of immense importance to the North that, 36 hours after capturing the damaged Han railway

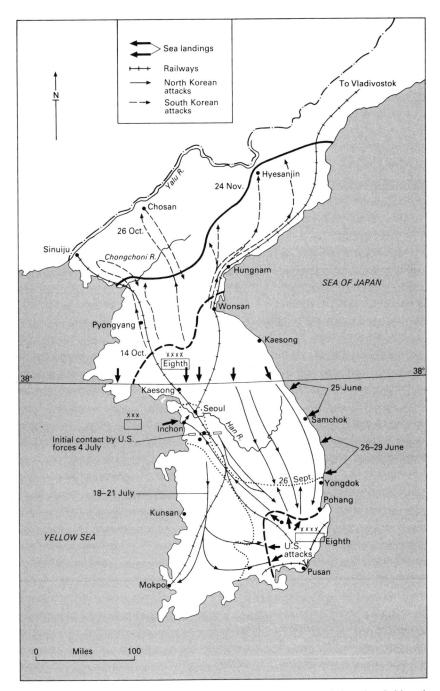

MAP 18. Korea in 1950 – its basic communication structure and the related ebb and
flow of battle

bridge, they had repaired and decked it to take tanks and wheeled vehicles. And that, within a matter of hours, the port of Inchon was in their possession, ready for coastal traffic. The North Korean logistic arrangements worked admirably, maintaining a steady flow of supplies to troops who advanced rapidly against a poorly supplied enemy who now began to melt away. Even if there were reports of delays due to troops stopping for pillage, there was no respite for the ROK and the first Americans on the scene. Though American air strikes against the railway and truck convoys moving through open country intensified, the North Koreans continued to receive what they required at the front because bridges were rarely broken, vehicles were plentiful and the majority of resupply took place at night.

Nevertheless, a compound of vehicle losses, which could not be fully replaced, and extending lines of communication which, within six weeks had lengthened by 200 miles, worked their attritional spell as American strength built up at the phenomenal rate of which that nation is capable when faced with a military crisis. Through to the well-appointed Japanese base and into the port of Pusan — the best in Korea — moved a deluge of men and material. Some came direct from the United States; much from a so-called 'roll-up' plan, conceived in 1948 to reclaim the immense quantities of equipment which littered scores of Pacific islands. Huge numbers were repaired by Japanese industry which also modified fighting vehicles and at very short notice made anti-tank mines. Nearly everything was of World War Two vintage, including the cargo ships and LSTs which plied regularly to Pusan where the harbour's capacity was improved as a matter of priority. Air transport, augmented enormously by the latest four-engine aircraft, played a leading role to begin with when every man and every ton delivered at the front was worth more than ten tons near the rear a week later. Some came straight from America, a distance of 6,000 miles or more via established staging posts.

A principal customer from the start was a pinched ROK army which was deficient of everything; on 28 June, for example, 119 tons of ammunition were urgently flown to within a few miles of the front at Suwon. Within a month, a lift of 200 tons a day was available — yet not always taken up because, by then, large tonnages were arriving by sea and were moving up by rail and road without hindrance from the defeated enemy air force. Improvisation was the order of the day, with its inevitable, attendant waste — as once before in December 1941. But one such improvisation, the rapid invention and manufacture of a special rice and fish based pack ration for the ROK Army, was among the services which made all the difference to the morale of a hard pressed ally. Suffice to say that, as the United Nation's rearguard backed into a bridgehead securing Pusan, it was to occupy a defensive position held by reinforcements supplied with ample food, weapons and ammunition to produce a firepower which the weakening enemy could not match.

Early in August, when the North Koreans were rebuffed with heavy losses at the bridgehead perimeter, their logistics staff understood, even if the operations people would not admit it, that they were in trouble. Although stores continued to move with commendable efficiency, they arrived in nothing like the quantity required to satisfy great fuel and ammunition expenditure. Trucks were too few in number and the supply of food and replacement of all natures of weapons, ammunition and equipment was drying up. Losses from attacks were just part of the trouble, although, as usual, few bridges were out and rail repairs were quickly made. What made matters worse, was the vulnerability of coastal communications to repeated naval attacks as part of the blockade which had been imposed by ROK and Anglo-American ships at the start of hostilities. No longer could ships from Russia or anywhere else sail to North Korean ports or to small ports in occupied South Korea. However, Russian weapons and material of all kinds continued to be sent uninterruptedly from Vladivostock via the port of Rachin and across the Yalu River from Manchuria because the United Nations forces were forbidden, for political reasons, to bomb the docks or the bridges.

When the United Nations forces had received substantial reinforcements, and the logistic equaliser had swung their way towards the end of August, it was arguable that the North's over-extended forces facing the Pusan bridgehead perimeter would have been compelled to withdraw under pressure once the United Nations chose to make a direct operational push. In the event, the North Korean's were cut off when General Douglas MacArthur applied direct logistic pressure by a brilliant amphibious landing of corps strength (laid on after a month's planning) at Inchon on 15 September to sever the North Korean main supply route. Having already failed, not least due to the inability to build up sufficient stocks at the front, to win success in their final desperate attack against the perimeter, there was nothing the North could do but run. For an enemy who had taken a risk in landing across very difficult beaches nearly 200 miles in their rear was almost at once unassailable after seizing Inchon's port and the nearby Kimpo airfield. It was almost a formality when the Americans broke out from the Pusan perimeter and raced northwards to join the pursuit which, amply supplied and, for better or for worse, MacArthur aimed at the Manchurian frontier.

It is unnecessary to dwell upon the saga of the United Nations pursuit to the north of the Yalu River; upon how a provoked China, after due warning, threw back UN forces which, faced by massed manpower infiltrations, suffered a lapse of confidence; and how, in the first five months of 1951, the tide of battle ebbed and flowed on both sides of the 38th Parallel until a line coalesced in a hill-top, entrenched zone reminiscent of the First World War. But it is necessary to comment upon how diligently, yet slowly, the unsophisticated Chinese moved and supplied themselves by labour-intensive, mainly hoof and foot transport in pursuit. Yet how outclassed they were once the United Nations stopped retreating at full mechanised speed and turned to crush with firepower an opponent who was incapable, of prolonged, highly mobile operations in difficult country due to shortage of artillery, ammunition and fuel. Which explains how it was that the American forces managed to conduct quite the most remarkable amphibious operation in reverse when they were compelled, in December 1950, to evacuate the hard-pressed X Corps from the ports of Wonsam and Hungnam. In two weeks no less than 105,000 United Nations troops, 98,000 Korean civilians, 17,500 vehicles and 350,000 tons of stores were extracted, some by air but the vast majority by sea. A logistic feat in freezing weather which paid tribute to the efforts of the Marine rearguard in making it possible to keep casualties to a minimum while leaving hardly anything behind for the enemy which was not in flames.

Except for one piece of new technology — the helicopter — the Korean war disclosed little that was logistically or operationally revolutionary. Nor did the small single piston engine helicopters, committed to reconnaissance and liaison duties close to the front line, make much logistical impact since their payloads were too small to lift more than three men or a handful of light stores. For casualty evacuation (casevac), as the British had already demonstrated in Malaya, they were, however, invaluable. Taking two stretcher cases from front line to treatment in a Mobile Army Surgical Hospital (MASH) was a matter of minutes, instead of painful hours being manhandled by stumbling stretcher parties down steep slopes under enemy fire. The casevac helicopter greatly raised morale by significantly reducing the death rate in transit amongst the seriously wounded and thus improved further upon the existing medical services' record of losing only 2 per cent of those who reached them alive.

1956: Suez and the End of the Second World War Era

When the first low yield nuclear shell from a 280mm gun was fired by the Americans in 1953 the influence of such tactical battlefield weapons initiated a complete reappraisal of warfare, including the logistic consequences of massed destruction and casualties. Until then most attention had been paid to air delivered high yield nuclear weapons aimed at strategic targets in the enemy hinterland, as the ultimate deterrent to global war. The supply of atomic bombs to aircraft posed little that was logistically new, provided that the safety of aircraft and their dispersed bases remained secure. The threat of relatively localised nuclear explosions over the maritime and land battlefields, however, posed far more complex problems of supply and security.

Innovators and planners excelled themselves in grappling with the almost insuperable difficulties of how to fight and supply forces amidst fantastic destruction. They aimed to achieve rapid, flexible responses by developing an operational capacity to concentrate and disperse rapidly and of being either totally self-sufficient or maintained by adequate access to dispersed sources of supply. A host of new organisations were devised, along with a myriad improved means of safe storage, high mobility transportation and reliable communications to cope with the unimaginable. At root, however, lay the traditional demands of survival and how to fuel mechanised or animal-powered transport — the obvious use of nuclear power for ships turning out not to be the prime mover so many people assumed as the answer. But while, as will be seen, many useful inventions appeared to enhance mobility and protection in the event of a nuclear holocaust, the fundamentals of logistic service remained largely unchanged in the face of numerous non-nuclear wars. Nevertheless, the moment when the techniques and technology of the Second World War had to give way to something new could not long be delayed — as the events of November 1956 in the Middle East showed.

An end was put to the British Middle East strategic base when a negotiated withdrawal, under pressure, was made from Egypt in 1955, and the extensive facilities and stocks placed on a care and maintenance basis for British use in certain circumstances. In effect, everything fell into Egyptian hands when a major political confrontation occurred in 1956 between Egypt (under General Nasser supported by Russia) and Britain and France in collusion with Israel. Threatened by the closure by Egypt of the Suez Canal, that vital artery upon which Europe depended for so much, the British and French, in agreement with the Israelis, planned a joint invasion. But whereas the Egyptians, supplied with all manner of weapons from the ex-British base and with tanks and aircraft from Russia, had only to fight where they stood, their opponents had extraordinary logistic problems to overcome.

Least handicapped were the Israelis: supplied with weapons from many sources (chiefly France) they had only to advance down a long, well worn axis across the Sinai desert, to the canal, drawing from depots close to the Sinai border. The British and French, on the other hand, were compelled to launch an airborne/amphibious operation, for which, against the background of their extensive involvements with NATO's European defence and several counter-insurgency campaigns, they were ill-prepared. It was an operation whose lines of communication projected forwards from Britain and France to forward bases in Tripolitania, Algiers, Malta and Cyprus — none of which were entirely satisfactory. The Tripolitanian base was soon neutralised in the cause of Arab solidarity by the veto of the Libyan government. Malta was six days' sailing from the entrance to the Suez Canal (which was the eventual objective of invasion). Cyprus, its garrison absorbed with internal security problems against Greeks and Turks, was anything but an ideal launching pad because the few airfields were overcrowded, it lacked a good port and so was no place from which to despatch a seaborne force.

But the major weaknesses of the amphibious corps, sailing at a mere six knots from Algiers and Malta, were its cumbersome nature and the time it took to assemble. Since most of the conscript British Army was 'anchored', for political reasons, in Germany and the Strategic Reserve in Britain was heavily committed to training the part time Territorial Army, many reservists had to be recalled to fill the ranks of both combat units and logistic services. A confused mobilisation, which began at the beginning of August was incomplete in mid-September, when some units arrived in Malta where they began training and final preparations. Many of the LSTs had been brought out of reserve and were in poor mechanical shape. Several units, particularly the armoured and artillery ones, found themselves at odds with a task bedevilled by fluctuating plans. Day by day the chaos grew as, day after day, postponements were announced. The shipping arrangements were subject to frequent and fundamental changes; one of which loaded the designated leading armoured regiment into civilian manned LSTs, making it necessary to send the follow-up regiment in the van of the assault since they were embarked (unwaterproofed) in naval ones. Soldiers recalled from civil life became angry at the number of administrative mistakes, which lowered morale. In some units, reservists were on the verge of mutiny.

As in Norway in 1940 (see Chapter 8, page 104) the troops were committed to the assault without any form of written administrative plan — due to three major factors. The political shilly-shallying over the launching of the operation led to the force being split during the build-up, with part in the Mediterranean and the rest in England (the Corps headquarters charged with command of the enterprise); the objectives were changed at the last minute; and the excessive security control prevented the headquarters from issuing written orders to units before embarkation. Despite all the experience of amphibious assaults gained in the Second World War, the shipping was loaded in a completely haphazard fashion — so much so that the first vehicle up the beach at Port Said belonged to a unit not even in the order of battle! Ammunition and canned petrol were stowed on top of one another in the same ship — so that when an urgent call from ashore came for fuel, a 'well' had to be made through the ammunition to get at the jerricans in the bottom of the hold!

Miraculously the airborne and amphibious forces which seized Port Said on, respectively, 5 and 6 November did so without much trouble. Largely because the Egyptians had been compelled to thin out against the more immediate threat of victorious Israeli columns nearing the canal in their rear; partly because of an erosive deterioration of logistic support; and partly because the Anglo-French assault looked very menacing (helped immensely by the impressive first major operational and logistic use of cargo helicopters (pay load 900 lbs)) and well able to strike in depth. Yet how well Anglo-French supply would have worked, as they plunged southward towards Cairo, was never tested because external political, economic and logistic pressures, applied by Russia and America, deterred the British and French governments from proceeding. Threats of rocket attacks and the despatch of 'volunteers' by Russia may not have been taken quite so seriously as the run on the pound sterling and the menace to British trade and supply portended by the Americans. The Super Powers had set a unified precedent by snuffing out, within a few hours, an operation which might have succeeded if it had been mounted with lightning speed. A deftly delivered blow in mid-August by a smaller, well-trained, faster-sailing amphibious force, spearheaded and supplied as well from the air, could have achieved the political aim before the storm of world condemnation had gathered.

As it was, the death knell of ponderous Second World War type interventions was sounded, particularly when dealing with so-called 'brush-fire' incidents. Henceforward, it would be a bold non-self-sufficient nation which, lacking the political and logistic support of one or other of the Big Powers, attempted to 'go it alone' in a major military/political operation. From 1957 onwards the old concept of launching major operations at long range with slow moving amphibious forces was out-moded. Rapidity of intervention would depend extensively upon air-delivered men and supplies, backed up by seaborne echelons whose heavy equipment and principal supplies were drawn from pre-positioned stocks held in well chosen and sited strategic bases. The fastest troopships were obsolete, as the British, with their lines of communication to the Far East, had discovered. Not only could they be prevented from using the short cut via the Suez Canal, they cost £120 per person for passage to Singapore (at 1957 prices) against only £45 by contract air trooping. Furthermore, sea travel separated the individual from his proper duties for anything up to three weeks, against a 48 hour flight.

The future of the logistic support overseas, as will be seen, lay in the new generation of fast, roll-on roll-off ocean going ships with heavy lift derrick capability and as shallow a draught as possible. Cargo would be moved chiefly in containers and be mechanically handled to dispense, as much as possible, with temperamental, costly and slow working dock labour organisations. Since the first propeller-jet airliner (the Vickers Viscount) entered service in 1950, to be followed in 1952 by the first turbo-jet liner, the DH Comet, the speed of passenger air transport had been vastly increased at the same time as pay load was raised in specially constructed military cargo aircraft. Of the latter, those with nose or tail (or both) doors to facilitate rapid loading and unloading, including air drop were the most important. They ranged from such monsters as the Short Belfast (lifting 36 tons), the Lockheed Galaxy (lifting 117 tons and capable of carrying a 60 ton Abrams main battle tank; ten of which, it had been suggested, could have coped with the entire Berlin airlift) to the ubiquitous, sturdy, prop jet Lockheed Hercules (lifting 18 tons) with its relatively short landing and take-off capability from rough airfields. All these aircraft were in mind or existence as the new era began and as the latest electronic technology (miniaturised and made more reliable and powerful by the invention of the junction transistor) introduced immeasurably more efficient and flexible computing communication and navigation systems to amplify air power and transport. With longer range aircraft, a plethora of landing grounds available in almost every corner of the globe and flight refuelling to make possible the circumnavigation of the world without landing, a logistic revolution of almost incalculable magnitude occurred in the 1960s and on the eve of two decades or more of deadly confrontations, involving most of the world's nations.

Chapter 12

The Age of Electronics and Rationalisation

THE SHEER intricacy of the logistic demands of modern warfare and the technological developments spawned by two world wars between them generated a complete revolution in both the control of the maintenance of forces deployed on operations and in attitudes towards the science of logistics. Now, even in the most inaccessible parts of the world, whether in desert or arctic wastes, mountain ranges or deepest jungle, it had become accepted that troops would be supplied with their essential needs despite the physical obstacles to movement. As we saw in Chapter 11, even such Third World countries as Vietnam had become capable of sustaining staggeringly efficient logistic systems by the combined use of primitive and modern methods. No longer was the well-being of the troops a matter of secondary importance, its value as an important contribution to success through the maintenance of morale and the prevention of manpower losses from disease and wounds had been amply proved, most particularly in Burma between 1943 and 1945. In consequence, there was a new found diligence to ensure that armed forces were supplied with the tools essential to the complexities of modern warfare. A new range of ingenious equipments became available to the logistic services — heavy lift helicopters, hovercraft, high mobility amphibious load carriers, over-snow vehicles and a wide range of specialised shipping for the support of amphibious operations. In addition, new wonders, such as the true nuclear-powered submarine, which can stay submerged until food or weapons need replenishment, introduced new possibilities of self-sufficiency. To back up all these developments came a comprehensive network of secure and reliable communications using revolutionary techniques, such as the satellite, and keyed to miniaturised and equally reliable data-handling systems for the management and stock control, maintenance and positioning of equipment, materials and supplies. There was, of course, a price to be paid in the tendency for the tail to grow, once more at the expense of the teeth. All these seething centres of logistic activity and of command and control were dedicated to the support in the field of sophisticated units whose combat strengths were ever in decline in proportion to the base support needed to sustain them.

Paradoxically, it had been the advent of the nuclear weapon which had led nations suddenly to take the requirements of conventional warfare so much more seriously, for the realisation of the horror of nuclear war and the need to strike some sort of military balance between East and West also brought home the need to be able to compete right across the defensive spectrum if a successful deterrent policy was to be established. At the same time, it must be said that it was the compelling need to face up to the possible demands of the nuclear battlefield which first provided the impetus behind the search for newer and more effective weapons systems and the logistic machinery to enable the fighting units to survive for more than a few hours, or days at best, on the devastated battlefield which was generally envisaged. Once the time had arrived at which both sides had the resources to inflict utterly unacceptable damage upon one another, so did the emphasis upon winning the opening conventional phase of any future war begin to take pride of place. Most of the collossal outlay already made to prepare the forces of NATO and the Warsaw Pact for nuclear war provided them with the staggering range of new equipment and weapons with which they are now supplied for the conventional phase also and for which new logistic techniques have become necessary — although the principles remain unaltered.

New ways to create, steer and control these emerging techniques by the application of the latest concepts of management and organisation began to be considered in the 1950s. Under the influence of recent experience, highly perceptive war gaming and scientific operational analysis, a tendency towards more functional organisations evolved. Rationalisation in the name of simplification and reduction of waste became the order of the day. For example, in 1966, the United States Navy abolished most of its commodity technical services in favour of logistical services under a staff supervision through computers. And the British Army radically brought nearly all supplies, equipment, fuel and ammunition under Royal Army Ordnance Corps control; thus removing fuel and food from the control of the old Royal Army Service Corps — which then became known as the Royal Corps of Transport, with responsibility for all transportation previously exercised by several other agencies which were abolished. At virtually no cost, dramatic improvements in logistic efficiency had been achieved.

Yet, despite the rationalisations and the almost unlimited transport and resources available at short notice in most parts of the world, campaigns remained as subject to logistic factors as ever they had done. Meanwhile wise operational commanders studied assiduously the ways and means of deflecting or defeating an enemy with threats or by attacks upon his logistic facilities. Take for example:

The Arab-Israeli Wars of the 1960s and 70s

In the aftermath of the formation of the State of Israel and the armistices arranged with its neighbours in 1949, the major contenders in the Middle East imbroglio —

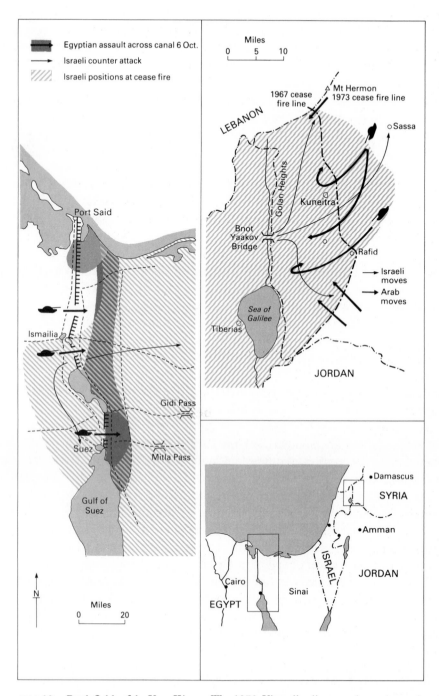

MAP 19.   Battlefields of the Yom Kippur War 1973. Virtually all re-supply was by road

Egypt, Iraq, Syria and Jordan and, of course, Israel herself, entered a period of consolidation while developing their armed forces. Against a background of tension and hostility which rose to a peak during the war of 1956, each side came to study with great care the lessons of that Arab humiliation and instituted modernisation programmes to restore parity with one another. It was natural and politic that as new more powerful weapons — particularly aircraft and tanks — were acquired in the 1960s from foreign suppliers, the foreigners' experience should also be applied to organisations, methods and training. None of the Arab or Israeli contestants were well versed in modern warfare. Nearly all had acquired what knowledge they possessed from the old colonial British and French powers they had ousted. Lacking armament industries of their own, they now were dependent upon major arms producers for their sources of supply. It was inevitable that those sources should include some of the principals in the world-wide struggle between East and West and that there should be strings applied through the threat to withold resupply of ammunition, spares and technical advice if the recipients failed to toe the appropriate political line. Such a situation had a dominating effect upon the strategic and even the tactical policies of the recipients. Whilst not actual puppets of the supplying nations, in that they could flout them if prepared to take the consequences, there was no question but that, to a certain extent, they were in logistic thrall to them. All too often, a substantial team of 'technical advisers', particularly from the Eastern Bloc countries to Egypt and Syria, accompanied the equipment and this too greatly influenced the nature of warfare in the area.

When a worsening series of border incidents finally erupted on 5 June 1967 into another all-out war, a very strong build-up of Egyptian forces, comprehensively supplied by extensive depots linked with the Egyptian base by newly constructed cross desert roads and air bases, compelled the Israelis to forestall an impending invasion. It had to be done quickly and by surprise with the intention of overrunning the Egyptian Army before Syria and Jordan could mount diversionary operations on the northern and eastern frontiers and before the self-interested Great Powers could impose a cease-fire (as they had in 1956), with the threat of arms or fuel sanctions throttling their military breath.

In many ways the assumption by the Egyptians of a forward deployment of teeth arms and large tail depots close to the frontier in an offensive defensive posture, served the Israeli concept of a lightning stroke aimed at their opponent's teeth and tail. They aimed to isolate and starve out the enemy in the desert and, at the same time, to sustain a subsequent deep penetration of enemy territory, throughout Sinai, by living off booty. For, strong though the basically militia-type Israeli army was operationally, logistically it was weak. Simple as it had been to create reserve stocks close to the frontier before the attack, their subsequent delivery to far-ranging mechanised spearheads was uncertain. Israeli supply columns were not well organised, and neither properly disciplined nor adequately controlled. The justifiable care and attention lavished on the teeth arms had not percolated through to the tail units — an old story.

The nature of the stunning, swiftly executed blow by Israeli armoured forces which came hard on the heels of the almost complete obliteration of the Egyptian Air Force on its bases by pre-emptive air attack, overwhelming the Egyptian Army within 72 hours, is a matter of history. It was a tactical masterpiece. Less commendable were the various, arguably avoidable logistic crises which put those operations in jeopardy. For example, if the Egyptians had held more firmly to the northern flank as the Israelis plunged along the coastal road, they might easily have smashed the Israeli column which broke through the blocking position of the Jiradi Pass to become cut off at El Arish. Appalling traffic jams developed behind the front when the drivers of civilian type, two wheel drive trucks either refused to drive off the road or, when they did so, became stuck in deep sand. Drivers who, a few days ago, had been civilian truck and car drivers and who were none too compliant with military discipline, contributed to a breakdown in supply for which staff officers and loose traffic control had to take some of the blame. Fighting men at the front, looking over their shoulders for ammunition and fuel to sustain a dog fight as yet undecided, had reason for complaint — as did the commander of the armoured force which broke through to the vital Mitla Pass and found, just short of his objective, that ammunition (in short supply) was being wasted in shooting at enemy tanks already abandoned in good condition by their crews; that quite unnecessary fuel-consuming manoeuvres were being carried out when a more economic direct advance to the objective was feasible; and that neither meagre enemy stocks nor the Israeli supply echelons were likely to prevent his column running dry. Eventually those few tanks which had petrol towed those that did not to the objective to form an immobile road block which depended for success upon the enemy's failure to out-manoeuvre them. Of only nine Israeli tanks out of the 28 which came within two kilometres of the Pass to complete the journey, just four had a few drops of petrol left. The remainder of the battalion was strung out behind, broken down or bone dry.

On the other hand, there emerges from this campaign the tale of how the Egyptian supply columns, caught in the open by an almost unopposed Israeli air force or by rampaging tank groups, were shot to pieces without much chance of supplying their own vehicles. And of guns which had to be abandoned in droves. Undoubtedly, the superior tactics and combat prowess of the Israelis were the keys to their victory, but it has to be added that Arab morale also declined in proportion to the realisation that their lines of communication were being systematically destroyed and their mobility crippled. Much could be credited to unopposed aircraft operating over desert terrain, though the job would have been less easy if surface-to-air fire had been available to the stricken Egyptian columns, or if cover had been available.

The Yom Kippur War of 1943 was to produce some of the most intense fighting in the history of war and demonstrated very clearly how serious a problem the rate of ammunition consumption had become. As it was, neither side was adversely affected by logistic shortages in the early stages, mainly because both were within reasonably easy reach of their sources of supply and, the formidable Israeli Air Force was unable to strike the Egyptian ground forces because of the strength of their surface-to-air defences. In the north, where a numerically weak Israeli force fought with unparallelled heroism against an unexpectedly powerful and effective Syrian armoured onslaught, there were indeed anxious moments over ammunition supply and the need for replacement tanks. Had it not been for the self-sacrifice of the Air Force, who repeatedly savaged the Syrians, though at terrible cost to themselves, the Israeli armour might have been overwhelmed. But, in the end, fresh supplies appeared, reserve and repaired tanks were pushed into the line and the assault was repulsed. It says much for the progress made by the IDF over the six years since the Six Days War that they made so startling a recovery from what could only have been seen as a desperate situation on both fronts. Not only were the fighting troops supplied but much of their damaged armour was repaired on the battlefield, thereby greatly reducing their total losses. Deserving of special mention is the lightning Israeli reaction to the problems associated with air defence suppression. In close collaboration with the United States, radar defeating pods were produced and, by the time the Israeli counter-stroke across the Canal was ready to be launched, the Israeli Air Force was in a position to attack the previously formidable SAM defences and to give General Sharon the direct air support he badly needed. That Canal crossing itself is a brilliant example of logistic improvisation. Complete floating bridge-systems were towed across the face of the desert for many miles by tanks to make the crossing possible. Working in close co-operation with the Gillois amphibious bridging vehicles which, showing great logistic foresight, they had bought from the French against just such an eventuality, the Israeli engineers ferried and maintained a substantial armoured force across the Canal.

As for the Egyptians, they soon found that their fears of the Israeli Air Force were well founded once they ventured outside the umbrella of their static air defences and began to suffer casualties in the armoured battles east of the Mitla and Giddi Passes which they were unable to replace. In the north, the Syrians too found that their devestating losses from both ground and air attack were too great for them to replace, even though they were later to be reinforced by Jordan and Iraq. Mention has been made earlier of the question of the care of the human content of armies. No army in the world has developed this more carefully than the Israeli Defence Forces for whose tiny population every soldier lost is a serious blow. By 1982, in Operation *Peace for Galilee* (the invasion of the Lebanon), casualty evacuation was to be developed to so fine an art that soldiers were frequently in hospital in Israel within two hours of being wounded and the worst cases were given life-saving surgery in the air as they were flown to safety.

The Arab–Israeli Wars are the nearest thing so far seen to the sort of conventional warfare which might characterise a future conflict in Europe, albeit, on a lower scale, so the logistic lessons are essential matters for study.

Two important related factors may already have been lost sight of in the turmoil of speculation which attended post-war analysis of the Yom Kippur War. First, that after air power had been neutralised, the supply of modern mechanised forces across passable terrain was unlikely to be dangerously interrupted. (Though it has to be said that this is a situation much more likely to occur in the Middle East than in Europe where the conduct of the air battle will be so very sophisticated). Second, that untrammelled fire power in battles dominated by strong armoured forces might just possibly degenerate into a kind of stalemate in which the delivery of ammunition took precedence over the demands for fuel. This will be returned to later.

The Protracted War: Vietnam 1959-75

A very different state of affairs to those of the Middle East emerged in the early 1960s as, with premeditated diligence, the leaders of North Vietnam prepared to complete the conquest of what once had been French Indo-China. Taking the subjugation of South Vietnam was a prime objective, Ho Chi Minh and his generals also sought the dominance of the sovereign states of Laos and Cambodia as harbours for secure lines of communication that would open up numerous routes leading to the strategic centres of the south. The inland routes, along with ever enlarging channels of coastal supply through innumerable ports, inlets and rivers ensured generous supply of any forces the North infiltrated into a country whose long and almost indefensible frontiers were wide open to infiltration. Not only Viet Cong guerrillas but also considerable regular forces could come and go as they pleased. The logistic key to this strategy was the so-called Ho Chi Minh Trail — a misnomer if ever there was one since the sophisticated roads leading out of the north through Laos and Cambodia were anything but a beaten track through the wilderness.

Beginning in 1959, under General Vo Bam, 30,000 troops, engineers and labourers converted the original tracks which had maintained earlier campaigns into an extensive road system linking the North with well-stocked bases, located at the entrances to the major access to the South. In the next sixteen years of intensifying struggle against the South Vietnamese and their American, Australasian, Thai and Philippino allies, the 'Trail' was expanded into a road eight metres wide, and 12,500 miles long, supplemented by 3,125 miles of pipeline to carry fuel through mountains and across waterways. In due course 10,000 motor vehicles traversed the road reducing the time to move sufficient men, equipment and stores to the furthest point to less than a week for a journey that, in 1959, had taken six months on foot.

It was hardly surprising, therefore, that when Ho Chi Minh authorised the attack, the South Vietnamese were at once in serious trouble, and not only because of the relatively logistic weakness. For the American training teams which had come to their assistance after the French withdrawal had by no means finished their task and those troops who were prepared were, from the outset, inferior to the North in almost every respect. Highly mobile and well supplied, under General Vo Giap, the invaders could cut the South's lines of communication with impunity to place a stranglehold upon centres of population which were penetrated and remorselessly terrorised to the verge of collapse. But in addition to their quantitive and qualitative inferiority, the difficulties facing the forces of the South were exacerbated by naive policies and faulty doctrine. Only slowly did they recognise that the enemy was a very large, very well-supplied regular force instead of, as assumed, lightly armed guerrilla bands; and only gradually was the true immensity and threat of Ho Chi Minh discovered. On American advice the South Vietnamese fought a relatively limited anti-guerrilla campaign. Even when the importance of the Trail was realised, American policy still prohibited attacks upon it, and Laos and Cambodia, thus permitting an unchecked flow of supplies to the enemy. Furthermore, despite knowledge that the French had used armoured vehicles to some extent up to 1954, it was concluded that this was an infantry war in which the best way of moving unprotected men from one place to another was by air — mainly by light aircraft and helicopter of which the first, with a troop lifting capability, arrived in mid-1961 as a tangible direct involvement of Americans in the war.

To begin with the aircraft were types from the Korean War employed on tasks similar to those of that static conflict. Medical evacuation was, as usual, given high priority. But the emphasis upon troop lift and supply increased as the latest machines of higher capacity — such as the famous UH-1 Iroquois and the CH-37 Mojave helicopter and the twin-engine CV-2 Caribou fixed wing aircraft were introduced. By 1964 there were 250 Iroquois, 9 Mojave and 32 Caribou present as forerunners of a ground support force which, by the quality of their mobility, would come to dominate the war in years to come. Henceforward, in addition to their vital contribution to logistics and the gradual assumption too of an armed combat role, there appeared a coherent doctrine of 'Airmobility' associated with the emotive title of 'Sky Cavalry'.

Until 1967 indeed, air transport was seen as the only sensible way of maintaining *in situ* those isolated garrisons which had become surrounded by the enemy swarm. Many were the miniature Dien Bien Phu-type sieges which were sustained to the South's advantage by the ability of VSTOL and STOL (Vertical Take Off and Short Take Off and landing) aircraft to operate from pads and short air strips within tightly held perimeters of defence. But in 1967, after over five years under-employment of armoured land vehicles, economically, to keep open the lines of communication, the United States armoured teams produced a report entitled *Mechanised Armor Combat Operations, Vietnam* which expounded upon several highly successful actions by armoured forces to lift sieges, keep supply routes open and attack enemy centres. It also showed that large tracts of the country were suitable for tracked vehicle movement.

American Armor saw its influence eroded by the emergence of a strong, infantry-orientated caucus who postulated the theory that air mobility provided protection as well as logistic support free of ground interference. Armoured units sent to Vietnam were actually being divested of their vehicles and made to fight as infantry. Yet the reports' analysis of terrain showed that, with suitable organic (such as engineer and logistic) support, 61 per cent of the country in the dry season and 46 per cent in the wet was suitable for tanks with 65 per cent suitable all year round for the ubiquitous M 113 Armoured Personnel Carriers (APC) which did duty as a combat vehicle as well as a troop and supply carrier. It has to be added, however, that many sceptics (including those with Sky Cavalry and Infantry interest) belittled the report's findings, and pointed out that improved enemy anti-tank measures were likely to impair the use of armoured vehicles in the future. It was an old argument in the long-running debate surrounding the development of the tank, one which ignored the fact that operational helicopters were also meeting tougher resistance and that armoured columns were persistently improving their results, at acceptable cost, when given the chance of fighting supply convoys through and dealing heavy blows at located enemy positions.

Only gradually were ground supply operations stepped up as armoured soldiers applied lessons which, after all, had long ago been learnt by the British in Burma as well as by the French in Vietnam: that tracked vehicles with adequate engineer support could make sustained headway with decisive results through undeveloped jungle and paddy as the spearheads of relatively deep penetrations of enemy terrain.

Meanwhile the apostles of air power enjoyed a field day once restrictions on attacking North Vietnam, and, later, the Laos 'panhandle' along with the Trail, were marginally lifted in the aftermath of a North Vietnamese Army attack (NVA) on an American base in South Vietnam in August 1964. Yet at once the menace of heavy ground fire tended to reduce the effectiveness of low-level attacks because they forced the attackers higher. When American attacks were intensified and widened in scope, they met stiffening resistance from enemy fighters and SAM as ferocious air battles blossomed forth after the opening of Operation *Rolling Thunder* in March 1965.

Rolling Thunder, approved in February 1965 by President Lyndon Johnson, had political as well as operational and anti-logistic objects. By aiming attacks at purely North Vietnamese targets, such as vital railway bridges, ports and ammunition and supply dumps, it was hoped, over a period of twelve weeks, to drive the North Vietnamese to the peace conference table. Its failure was partly due to restrictions placed on air crew, for fear of inciting adverse world opinion, and very much due to an inability to inflict lasting damage on such key targets as the vital railway bridges. It was an old style fiasco, one which scarcely interrupted the flow of supplies through the port of Haiphong (by sea mining) and from China to the Ho Chi Minh Trail by air attack. Moreover the related operation *Steel Tiger* which simultaneously struck at tentacles of the Ho Chi Minh Trail in the Panhandle was hardly more effective. Such damage, sometimes locally heavy, as was inflicted rapidly was repaired by the ant-like activities of Bam's industrious engineers and labour force. Delays in delivery there were, but never were the fighting units deprived. It might have been a lot worse for the North, however, if American pilots had not been burdened by rules of engagement which allowed them only to attack moving transport in open country and forbade attacks on airfields. In consequence transport moved only under cover of night and parked openly in villages during the day. Incredibly, enemy aircraft had nothing to fear while on their bases.

Rolling Thunder, supplemented from 1968 until the end of American participation in 1973 by Operation *Commando Hunt*, only tampered with the Ho Chi Minh Trail in Laos. It never seriously threatened the North Vietnamese economy or NVA and Vietcong supplies in the field. A further handicap to the pilots engaged were their own logistic deficiencies. Whereas US Navy pilots flying, from off-shore located carriers at short range, could reach their targets with ease, their Air Force counterparts, based in Thailand not less than 500 miles from Hanoi, depended upon climbing to rendezvous with tanker aircraft in order to complete their missions. And the 2,500 miles which the gigantic B 52 bombers had to fly from Guam to North Vietnam to drop fifteen tons of bombs with, at times, questionable accuracy, were arguably wasted.

Indeed, the dropping of 643,000 tons of bombs during *Rolling Thunder* alone (from 1965 to 1968), with the attendant loss of 922 aircraft, was extremely suspect from the outset in the light of the political faint-heartedness which inhibited the total destruction of all stated targets. Vacillation lay at the root of American failure to mount the all-out strategic offensive which alone might have produced an enemy logistic collapse. Most enfeebling of all — to the South and its allies — was the rejection in moments of crisis of two separate pleas by General William Westmoreland, the Commander-in-Chief, to enter Laos and close the Ho Chi Minh Trail permanently. This refusal was crucial since no matter how well organised and munificient was the flow of American supplies to Vietnam, their use against so determined an enemy could never end the war unless, at the same time, his supplies were fully shut off — a task as far beyond the scope of air power as ever it had been in the past. The characteristically huge quantities of supplies handled by the United States Navy, Air Force, and from March 1965 until May 1972, the First Logistical Command, could not win the war merely by enabling vast destruction alone. So long as the United States Government condemned its troops to ineffectuality by denying them the benefits of their logistic superiority, and so long as the North pursued its strategy of constant pressure without outright confrontation, no end to the war was in sight.

Yet on 30 January 1968, General Giap then made the fatal miscalculation of changing the North's strategy of hit and run tactics by launching the so-called Tet offensive in a concerted series of all-out attacks upon the principal cities (including Saigon and Hué), route centres and bases. In so doing, he exposed the NVA and Vietcong not only to fierce retribution during open combat *en masse*, but also to an expenditure of resources beyond their capability to replace. As their entire logistic structure came under air attack and deliveries to the fronts were reduced by systematic blocking of the routes out of Laos, they drove themselves to exhaustion.

The sacrificial assaults by the massed ground forces of the North against well fortified and resolutely held Southern communication and supply centres led to appalling losses and also to the virtual neutralisation of the Viet Cong, whose lightly supported infiltration operations were hacked to pieces. Foremost in the defence were artillery, armoured vehicles and aircraft which were presented with ample visible targets at last. Inevitably, the uninterrupted supply of besieged positions, which also were local supply centres, posed the logisticians with many problems, difficulties which were often complicated by the systematic cutting of land routes by the Viet Cong and NVA, the menace of anti-aircraft weapons among the besiegers and low cloud which sometimes made air delivery extremely hazardous. Many supply operations turned into fierce battles. As usual, armoured columns managed to fight their way through in time (there were no 'Dien Bien Phus' in this campaign) and nearly all local crisises of supply were overcome by the bravery and skill of helicopter and transport aircraft crews skimming the earth to make their deliveries while suppressive fire was aimed at enemy air defences. The relief of Hue would have been a more extended affair had it not been for the work of APC and aircraft crews. Khe Sahn, the strongly defended centre established by General Westmoreland in the north west corner of South Vietnam as a base for an intended (but never attempted) invasion of Laos, to cut the Ho Chi Minh Trail at root, might well have fallen had it not been for air supply.

On 21 January, Khe Sanh came under attack as a prelude (perhaps a diversion) to Tet. For two months the battle raged, as the North aimed for 'a Dien Bien Phu' and the American defenders dropped 96,000 tons of bombs and fired 118,000 artillery rounds, besides all the other projectiles expended on nearby enemy positions. Nothing like this deluge came back from an opponent who was checked progressively by the defenders and then driven off by a massive relief operation in which airmobile tactics dominated — tactics which in themselves were extravagently demanding of a large logistic outlay to support multitudes of helicopters, which sometimes flew in swarms of 200. Needless to say, aircraft losses were heavy, reflecting the vulnerability of all such vehicles when operating in a close combat zone. It is worth pointing out that, throughout the duration of the war in Vietnam, total American helicopter losses amounted to about 3,000 plus the many damaged and demanding repair by a costly and dedicated maintenance organisation. There were those who argued that the job might have been done more cost effectively by more ubiquitous armoured units.

It was the American tragedy that, when so often on the verge of victory, they were frustrated by a shortage of political will at home which was compounded by an erosion of public support. It was the anti-Communist world's loss that the nature and extent of the North Vietnamese threat was never properly understood nor evaluated. Had it been shown earlier that it was not a nationalistic guerrilla movement but a predatory invading army which was carrying on the fight, sympathy for the North Vietnamese might have been otherwise directed. In which case, the permanent cutting of the Ho Chi Minh Trail, in conjunction with a complete naval blockade of the North, might have been implemented with decisive results.

Just how effective cross-border attack could be had been shown in 1967 when the United States air force struck hard at the North's principal port of Haiphong, destroying bridges, port facilities and dredgers, besides ships and stores. Almost at once an evacuation of non-essential civilians was ordered, the port's channel began to silt up and stores trapped by damage to internal lines of communication, were held up. An estimated 200,000 tons of supplies and equipment had to be dumped in the open — 80 per cent of all materials received for the war effort — due to the difficulties of port clearance and onward movement. But this was only a piecemeal American operation, not part of the wholesale assault upon the North's logistic system which the situation demanded. Yet the promise of such an attempt was amply indicated by subsequent piecemeal attacks which scored notable successes.

There were the major ground raids of 1970 into Cambodia, 1971 into Laos and the sea mining of ports in 1972 — each of them intended, ironically, to relieve pressure on the Americans after President Richard Nixon had decided to withdraw from military operations. Most revealing of all, the Operation *Toan Thang* raids against Cambodian sanctuaries uncovered a vast complex of depots which proved only too well how efficiently and with what deliberation the import of stores through the port of Sihanoukville, as well as along the Trail, had been conducted. They also revealed with what ease the NVA had managed to sustain its operations against Saigon via the Mekong River — an artery which had all along absorbed intense activity into Cambodia in April 1970 fought its way against patchy NVA opposition into a veritable Aladdin's cave of military stores and supplies. Concealed dumps containing all kinds of munitions, heavy weapons, trucks and fuel were linked by a comprehensive signal communication and hidden road system. Sufficient, it was claimed, 'to feed more than 25,000 troops for an entire year; individual weapons to equip 55 full-strength rocket units; and recoilless rifle ammunition for more than 9,000 average attacks against free world units. In all 11,362 enemy soldiers were killed and over 2,000 captured'. Nor was this all, as subsidiary *Toan Thang* raids fanned out across the country to capture and take away or destroy tens of thousands of tons of material accumulated over the years against the time of a renewed assault upon the South. Far less successful was the *Lam Son 719* raid of February 1971, when South Vietnamese Army formations, strongly supported by helicopters, at last struck at the Ho Chi Minh Trail in Laos. For after initial successes, which exposed to capture installations and stores dumps similar to those found in Cambodia, the NVA reacted with the ferocity of desperation and drove the raiders back. Casualties were heavy, including 168 helicopters lost and 618 damaged.

Further anti-logistic attempts to compel the North to come to terms were created by the isolation of the port of Haiphong in May 1972, in the aftermath of another major NVA offensive which had taken four years to assemble after the Tet defeat of 1968. This time it was achieved by the laying of thousands of sea mines from the air which, in conjunction with far more accurate air attacks upon the bridges on the route to China, cut the railway and made it necessary for the North to depend upon a far longer and more tenuous supply link via India and Burma. The key to guaranteed destruction of road bridges was to be found in the latest so-called 'smart' bombs which were guided to their targets by television cameras in the nose or by laser technology. Not only were the bombers able to stand off from these heavily defended targets but they could now strike them hard with deadly precision. For example, the robust Thanh Hoa bridge, which had withstood prolonged attack over many years, was finally demolished by a mere eight smart bombs and then detached from its abutments by a further 24; this in a three month period when no less than 106 bridges were destroyed in North Vietnam, causing not only a collapse of logistics but also ushering in a new era in anti-logistic warfare. Henceforward bridges would be prime targets in any conflict, simply because they were no longer, as once rated, too difficult or costly to destroy.

It was the supreme irony of a war which the Americans fought with their hands tied that, in December 1972 within a few days of an all-out attack upon all targets associated with the North Vietnamese war effort, they managed, at last, to reduce their opponent to impotence. By blotting out the vital supply centres of Hanoi and Haiphong, in conjunction with totally disrupting the vital rail and road links (with the exception of the Ho Chi Minh Trail), they strangled the NVA. The 'peace' at last agreed was concluded most cynically by both sides. The Americans admitted defeat in the aftermath of victory in order to break off an embarrassing political involvement. The North Vietnamese, in defeat, conceded little and remained intent upon renewing hostilities at the earliest moment after the stream of supplies could be renewed along re-established routes, with China and Russia ready to fill up the supply pipe line. Without compunction, the NVA set to work topping up its forward bases through a Ho Chin Minh Trail now safe from serious interdiction. Inexorably this engineered such a superior mobility over its opponents that it could concentrate forces and be supplied almost anywhere it chose. Almost inevitably the slower reacting South Vietnamese were out-manoeuvred and, with almost unimaginable speed, collapsed in 1975.

In truth, the Ho Chi Minh Trail really was 'the road to victory'. Yet it could so easily have been a memorial to defeat if it had been permanently severed from the outset — as was well within American military capacity.

The Gulf War — Struggle for a World Lifeline

After the Iraqis invaded Iran in 1980 the long ensuing war proceeded with varying degrees of intensity, seeming mainly, to the rest of the world, to pose a dire threat, through Islamic fundamentalism, to Middle East political stability and so to the security of the Persian Gulf area, with its vital oil sources and shipping route. It went without saying that none of the powers, least of all the great industrial ones, could afford to stand aside and see so crucial a region reduced to chaos. With one of the world's greatest logistic assets at stake it was essential either to end the war or confine it to the original combatants and keep the oil flowing. However, rather as in the Spanish Civil War, nations who paid lip service to restrictions upon arms deliveries took the opportunity to make vast and profitable deals. Both sides received sufficient and balanced quantities of arms and supplies to keep the war going without allowing one or the other a clear cut advantage.

It is not the intention here to describe the fighting in a war of attritional stalemate which has caused vast out-pouring of wealth, immense casualties and considerable political stress and strain. A war about which corroborative evidence is almost impossible to come by amid the smoke screens of circumlocution, propaganda ploys and commercial wheeling and dealing. It is ironic that both contestants have been compelled to expend their oil revenues to purchase the war materials required to prop-up their mutual antagonism. No reliable figures show what proportion of the many billions spent can be attributed to each supplier for each contestant. But while many nations have helped Iraq keep her logistic lead over Iran, with her three to one fanatical population advantage, it is plain that Britain, Argentina and France (among several others) have supplied both sides. But, as is usual in such destabilising confrontations, it has been Russia, with enormous shipments to Iraq, and the United States with considerable illegal deliveries to Iran, who have kept the feud in balance without feeling the need to bring it to an end with a fully enforced arms embargo.

The balance was also, of course, made possible by the destructive qualities of Iran's revolutionary movement which, in turmoil, badly damaged the Armed Services. The enormous quantities of modern weapons previously purchased by the Shah fell rapidly into disrepair when skilled technicians and operatives were lost or withdrawn. To make matters worse, the computer catalogue of spare parts was out of action for two years. Battle casualties probably contributed far less to dilapidation than mechanical breakdowns. Replacements became harder to come by rather more from the complexities of subversive and often fraudulent dealing than from arms embargoes to which few sellers paid heed. If all else failed, smuggling in all its duplicity on the grand international scale was perpetrated. Hand-to-mouth improvisations tended to rule in chaotic conditions.

The outcome became a stalemated war of attrition which effectively almost confined hostilities to the two original contenders despite the presence of Western naval forces in the Gulf to protect the trade routes. Though the Iranians threatened the closure of the Straits of Hormuz or attacks on other Gulf nations' oil resources, they rarely did much harm. Indeed they found it extremely expensive themselves to maintain the oil exports upon which they depend for survival. Even though the Iraqis achieved a significant air superiority with modern aircraft and missiles, this did not prevent numerous Iranian offensives on land and minor operations at sea. An uneasy 'cease-fire' now prevails.

Many causes have been suggested for the stalemate on land, where operations were contained within a long but relatively narrow belt on either side of the frontier — in much the same shape as the trench warfare zone of 1914 to 1918. Difficult terrain and some none too well developed local communication systems handicapped mobility. Yet there were many zones in which it might be practised by forces which, on paper, seemed to be capable of deep and decisive penetrations. That these did not take place has sometimes been ascribed to a lack of inspired generalship or the possibility that warfare is entering another phase in which defensive weapons effectively proscribe manoeuvre. There is indeed ample evidence to indicate that, even when tactical surprise was achieved, the vast weight of defensive firepower available to both sides was deadly in bringing a halt. Yet, although this suggests that both sides were adequately supplied at the front, the existence of crippling logistic difficulties, notably for the Iranians, cannot be dismissed as the real cause of immobility.

Static conditions minimise logistic problems because they make it easier to accumulate stocks close behind the front. Once the initial Iraqi attempts to overrun Iran were checked by an opponent who probed stronger than expected (and the Iraqis settled for a war of frontier attrition), the Iranians soldiered on in a state of such deprivation and confusion that it was impossible for them to sustain any prolonged offensives — let alone organise a pursuit in depth. Time and again the Iranians have wasted painstakingly acquired materials with appalling loss of life in attacks which were bull-headed and, most sinfully of all, inadequately supported logistically. Even when the Iranians seemed to be within sight of isolating the important port of Basra and seizing the Shat al Arab for good, their attacks faded away. Never did the great 'final offensive' promised by the Ayatollah materialise in all its grandeur — a disappointment for his fanatical followers, whose generals have by no means always planned operations badly and whose sacrificial bravery in action bears excellent comparison with the most determined troops in history.

The Falklands — Operation *Corporate:* A Study in Improvisation

It is arguable that when Argentine Marines were sent to spearhead the conquest of the Falkland Islands (Operation *Rosario*) on 2 April 1982, they went there in the belief that Britain would not attempt to retake the islands even if she was remotely capable of doing so. Some people would say that a political 'green light', had been shown by the British Government and others would point out that, for logistical reasons alone, the mounting of a successful amphibious operation (*Corporate*) at a range of 8,300 nautical miles from Britain was a tall order. No doubt the Argentines felt reasonably secure when, a month after their landing, they had managed, without distraction, to ship and fly in 9,000 troops along with 5,000 tons of equipment and stores and also to have extended the runway at Port Stanley's airfield by 200 feet to assist combat operations and the movement of freighter aircraft.

Everything about the British riposte in strength with the minimum delay revolved around logistic constraints. But if the decision to do so depended on wholesale improvisations in the absence of any preconceived plan for such an eventuality, it has to be stated that logistic contingency plans for dealing with the totally unexpected had been long in existence and had been practised. Furthermore, no modern logistic system, controlled by the latest management techniques and computers, is worth its salt if it cannot cope flexibly with the unanticipated. It was also a distinct bonus for the British that their naval forces and the spearhead troops of the Royal Marine and Airborne brigades were well-trained and fully accustomed, thanks to NATO exercises in Norway, to the problems of survival and fighting conditions even harsher than the bleak Falklands environment. But wonderful though it may have seemed to the uninitiated that the glamorous assault troops were ready to go at a moment's notice (as indeed prescribed by the normal rules of preparedness for war), far less praise was given to the logisticians and the thousands of men and women working flat out in depots, on transport, in ports and on airfields to prepare and deliver thousands of tons of material in a mere two or three days. In some instances, this was to ships which were engaged in peacetime pursuits. Of the 80 vessels with specific logistic roles which went to the Falklands, 50 were taken up from trade (STUFT) at very short notice, including three big passenger liners currently engaged in cruising. Such was the haste that, when the Task Force sailed under Rear Admiral John Woodward, no tactical plan had yet been settled because sufficient intelligence had not been assembled. In consequence, ship loading could not be fully tactical, even had there been time to do so. But it was one of the triumphs of the loading phase that virtually all the 3,800 tons of stores, 8,000 tons of ammunition and 1,250 tons of fuel, plus equipment demanded was on board on time — if not always in a desirable order.

It was of some benefit to the Task Force that it took four weeks to concentrate in the operational zone and that, almost at the midway point, lay the island of Ascension, whose anchorage and airfield, leased by the United States, were crucial to logistic support. By the time ships began arriving there, advance detachments had been flown in, communication systems established and a forward base to handle the transit of transport and combat aircraft, in particular, adequately stocked and staffed. In its role as a stores distribution centre, Ascension acted both as a unique staging post to the operational zone of South Georgia (which was recaptured from the Argentines on 25 April), and the Falklands, where British reconnaissance elements began probing in mid-April. It was at Ascension, that an extensive re-allocation of stores and equipment between ships took place, the work being carried out chiefly by helicopters and the sixteen landing craft belonging to two large Landing Platforms Dock (LPD). When the Task Force moved on southwards it was tactically loaded to suit the plan which finally had been hatched and which included the use of South Georgia as an additional staging post for

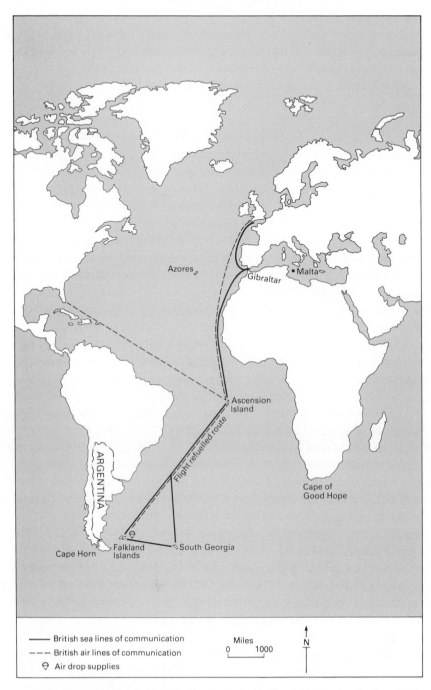

MAP 20.   Sea and air lines of communication to the Falkland Islands, April – June 1982

extremely valuable ships, such as the 67,000 ton liner, Queen Elizabeth II — which it was felt undesirable to sail anywhere near a potential threat from the enemy. In historical terms, the mounting and positioning of the force was something of a logistic miracle — a miracle made possible, in no small part, by the generous co-operation of the United States over the use of Ascension Island. That generosity and willingness to support a close ally, despite world opinion, was further reflected in the supply of desperately needed high technology equipment and air-to-air missiles. Once again, it had been shown that even the most sophisticated of nations can rarely meet all their own needs in emergency and that the cooperation of close allies may prove to be 'the nail' which saves 'the shoe' from loss.

The enemy menace to the Task Force and its stream of vessels in train was ever present. The South Georgia Task Force actually sank an Argentine submarine leaving the landing place on 25 April, invasion day — a potent threat even though it was actually engaged on a supply mission. Yet despite the possibility of attack by Argentine ships and aircraft en route, the Task Force, while taking deception measures, sailed straight to its deployment area to blockade the Falklands and begin a process of attrition before the planned date of landing, 19/20 May — an event which took place a mere 24 hours later.

The arrival of the Task Force off the Falklands effectively put an end to Argentine maritime traffic. But the blockade was never complete, since the bombing of Port Stanley airfield by carrier-borne Harrier VSTOL aircraft and two attacks by a single Vulcan bomber (whose long flight from Ascension necessitated no less than seventeen in-flight refuelling rendezvous) failed to put the strip out of action. To the end the Argentines managed to average two low level Hercules transport missions each night bringing in 470 tons of urgent stores and artillery and taking out 604 wounded men, with only one Hercules shot down. Indeed at no time were the Argentines seriously embarrassed by supply problems, monotonous as their diet was and hindered as they were by Falkland farmers when attempting to purchase sheep which grazed in plenty across the islands. It was in distribution to outlying defences that the Argentines found most difficulty, in a desolate land of meagre tracks, so meagre that sea and air supply were often the only efficient means of transport — both of which were largely denied the Argentines, who soon had no ships and few helicopters available.

The problems caused by extremely difficult terrain handicapped the better equipped British far less than it did their enemies, even though, for tactical and logistic reasons, they chose to make their initial, main landing at the well-sheltered San Carlos waters, 50 miles as the crow flies, from the heavily defended key objective of Port Stanley. A direct assault on Port Stanley had been ruled out. The risk of heavy casualties, a lack of fire support and the problem of ammunition supply for an opposed landing across unsheltered beaches, plus the unlikelihood of surprise being foremost among the factors leading to that decision.

Throughout the preliminary attritional struggle, from the moment the Task Force arrived off the Falklands, the British aim of weakening the enemy was restrained by the necessity of keeping the main strike force of two aircraft carriers intact while also protecting the logistic vessels in order to maintain adequate war replenishment. Attacks against enemy warships at sea and defence against land-based air attacks were central to this strategy which was served by two important enemy deficiencies. First his lack of long-range attack aircraft. Second, the fact that he possessed only two Hercules tanker aircraft to extend the reach of his mere 30 short-range attack aircraft capable of air refuelling. As a result, about half the Argentine fighter bombers were compelled at great peril and with difficulty, to operate at maximum range. A third factor was the preference of the Argentines for attacks on warships rather than supply vessels. Only one major supply ship, the 15,000 ton *Atlantic Conveyor*, was put down. However, this had such serious repercussions (as will be seen) as to suggest how fatally misdirected the Argentine air strikes had been. As a result naval operations in a battle which was far more consumptive of fuel and certain vital spare parts, rather than ammunition, were readily sustained. Refuelling ships at sea was routine; the delivery of such urgent items as were required by air drop into the sea of 44 flight-refuelled Hercules missions a unique achievement.

No sooner had land operations started, with the establishment of the bridgehead at San Carlos, than the pattern began to change. Although early ammunition expenditure on air defence and in the fight for Goose Green was moderate, the difficulty of advancing and being supplied across such difficult terrain became a major consideration. The movement ashore of up to 30,000 tons of stores and equipment ran into various local, unforeseen snags, not to mention determined enemy bombing, which delayed the essential build up prior to the march on Port Stanley. It was soon discovered that tracked vehicles, the 24 Volvo BV-202, could not move much faster than marching infantrymen, who found themselves committed to the 50 mile cross-country trek in bad weather carrying up to 54 kilogrammes on their backs. The loss of the *Atlantic Conveyor* on 25 May not only deprived the assault force of all its tentage and quantities of important engineering stores, it took with it six smaller Wessex helicopters and three big Chinooks, which were of crucial importance to heavy lift. Henceforward, the naval Sea King helicopters, of medium lift capacity, were severely overworked by a multiplicity of tasks. The single surviving Chinook, kept flying by maintenance marvels, was used for priority movement of ammunition and troops to a front which was at the end of ever lengthening lines of communication. In three weeks this machine carried forward 600 tons and 1,530 men and brought back 650 prisoners of war to San Carlos. Many were the painful decisions thrust upon the staff when it came to fixing priorities of lift. Often the troops, struggling across sodden ground in exacting weather, were called upon to subsist on combat rations, using only their small portable stoves for heating (since kitchens were left behind) and sheltering in the most rudimentary way. As the march progressed, the health and stamina of even the fittest, began to deteriorate. Among other complaints, up to 20 men a day reporting sick with the old-fashioned, crippling 'trench foot'. (The simple fact of the inadequacy of the soldiers' boots represents yet another 'nail' — and one which, in a more protracted campaign, could indeed have had consequences leading to ultimate failure.)

It was these narrow margins of supply which persuaded Major General Jeremy Moore, the Commander Land Forces, to chance opening a fresh, none too secure, forward supply base at Bluff Cove. This was a calculated risk which, although it led to the loss of two major logistic ships, with heavy casualties, nevertheless helped solve the equation of closing in quickly for the final blow at Stanley without leaving his men short of ammunition for vital fire support at a time when Admiral Woodward was warning him that 'the capabilities of the Fleet to support my operations were going to be a diminishing asset'. — a statement which concealed the truly remarkable efforts and improvisations by ships' companies and the maintenance vessels in keeping damaged or broken down ships constantly at sea in some of the most exacting, storm swept waters of the world. As a matter of routine, almost all work normally tackled in dockyards was done in the combat zone. Commenting upon contemporary Press statements that the battle for Stanley had been 'a close run thing', Moore has remarked that 'In the sense that Wellington used that phrase it was not a close run thing, for I did not think that there was ever any serious likelihood of Mendendez (the Argentine commander) and his troops defeating mine, though General Winter could have been another matter'. But he went on to say that the calculations relating to ammunition expenditure were a much nicer matter.

The picture of troops of both sides enduring the winter rigours on chilled rain soaked heights, crouched in waterlogged trenches or behind wind-blasted rocky outcrops is as revealing of Moore's worries as is that of the need on one occasion, prior to the final assault on the hills dominating Stanley, to postpone an attack for 24 hours due to a shortage of helicopters to move both ammunition and men to their assault positions. It was not just time and material in which Moore was trading but also his men's lives. Without intense fire support the casualty list among units, whose strength was diminishing, might place an unwarranted strain upon a helicopter evacuation service that had so far coped well flying back the wounded quickly to San Carlos. Few who arrived there alive for treatment prior to onward transmission to the hospital ship at sea were lost. Final evacuation by smaller vessels to the neutral country of Uruguay put the finishing touches to a triumph of medical performance.

Chapter 13

Retrospect and a Glance into the Future

As WE have seen, the history of logistics has been one long struggle between the demands of 'teeth' and 'tail' — a struggle that the teeth are inevitably losing as war becomes more and more complex and the demands of modern technology for an ever increasing measure of administrative support become irresistible. As that technology and the growth of automation enable fewer and fewer widely dispersed fighting men to wield the destructive power that previously involved many times their number, so does the network of logistic support and computer-based communications increase — inexorably.

Yet that same history has shown us that technology cannot unseat principle and those same principles which, when broken, led to Napoleon's failure after Borodino in 1812, and the scandalous administrative chaos of the British involvement in the Crimea in 1855 were the root causes of Hitler's downfall in Russia 130 years after Napoleon's debacle. In contrast, it was their successful application which brought triumph to Sherman in his legendary drive through Georgia in 1864 and to Slim in the Arakan in 1943 — the turning point of the Burma Campaign. Supremely well applied in Indo-China in the late 1940s and some ten years later in Vietnam, they enabled Ho Chi Minh and his generals to defeat the French and then to frustrate the best endeavours of the Americans for a considerable period until, at last, President Nixon realised that the only way to check Ho and bring him to terms was through the destruction of his bases and supply system — targets which their forces in the field had been denied for political reasons until too late.

Finally, in 1982, we find a gem of an operation, by no means devoid of risk, in which the highly professional application of the principles of administration, combined with the skill and quality of the forces involved, brought the British a crushing success in the South Atlantic against what many outside observers had previously regarded as formidable odds. Small though that operation may have been in terms of the numbers involved, it is worth remembering that its mounting took just about every ounce of logistic support the nation could raise without seriously affecting its principal commitment to the Atlantic Alliance — even then, without United States assistance, it could not have succeeded.

The part played by communications in all this runs like an unbroken lifeline. From the days of Jenghiz Khan, who exercised command and control by pony messenger from Mongolia to the Iron Gates of Hungary, to Admiral Sir John Fieldhouse's direct control over Admiral Woodward's task force, 8,000 miles from Whitehall, by satellite radio, we can follow a fascinating progression of steady development — a progression which steadily eroded the personal powers of the commander charged with the actual conduct of the campaign. In terms of history, HMS *Pickle*, which brought the news of Trafalgar to Portsmouth or the pigeon that carried the story of Waterloo to the City of London, are really very close to our own times. Yet, once the telegraph had been invented in 1837 and the practice of cable-laying, both over the land and under the ocean, had become common practice, the whole business of operational command and control in war became completely revolutionised. Curiously enough, it took a second world war to establish the use of radio as a tool for every level of command and administration. However, once that point had been reached, progress became unstoppable. The advent of the computer and the discovery of the micro-chip made possible new methods of management and control, so that today much of that side of our military life, as in industry, is becoming increasingly automated.

As this book has shown, no retrospective consideration of the logistics story can have any meaning without the inclusion of the growth and development of transportation. In the Peninsular War, even as he was suffering his greatest reverse in Russia through his neglect of the logistics factor, so did Napoleon suffer a further reverse at Wellington's hands for precisely the same reason — he relied too much on feeding his great armies off the land over which he fought or advanced, whereas Wellington's soldiers were supported by an elaborate Commissariat served by every mule, ox and waggon upon which he could lay hands. Within a matter of only a relatively few years, the railway would begin a new revolution — as we have seen in the American Civil and Franco-Prussian Wars and, later, in South Africa. Then came perhaps the most significant breakthrough of all — the internal combustion engine — just in time to play a major role in the First World War and to give us not only the load-carrying lorry but also the aeroplane and the tank (which brought with them their own built-in logistic burdens). Most important of all, these three new types of machine gave us the seeds of mobile warfare as we now know it, with all its attendant logistic demands.

Away from the battlefield, the transportation of troops by rail and steamship, which had become comonplace, was later to give way to air trooping. Even more significant was the new-found possibility of supplying whole formations in battle by air — dramatically demonstrated in Burma, not only with the Chindits but also in the Arakan, where that factor was to prove decisive. Despite all these advances, it

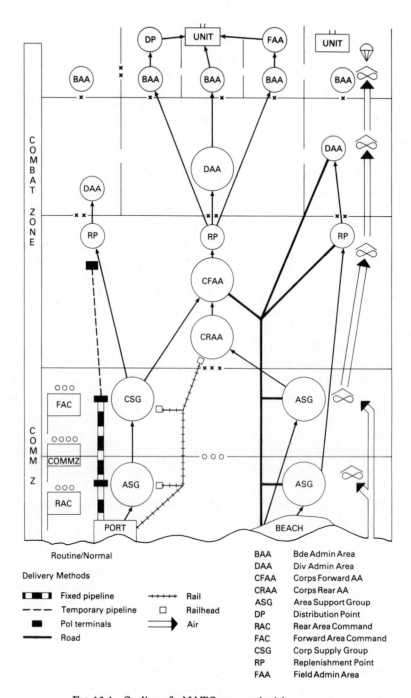

FIG 13.1 Outline of a NATO-type replenishment system

is a remarkable thing that there is still a place in war for the humble human porter! It is simply a matter of applying the most appropriate resources to the circumstances of the moment — like it or not, there are circumstances still in which the porter or, perhaps, the mule are the only practicable means of transportation (certainly there was porterage in the Radfan in South Arabia in 1964 and the story of the advance by foot to Port Stanley, with every man his own porter, in 1982, is proof enough of the occasional need). In the same way, it was many years before the horse disappeared from the supply echelons of both the German and Russian armies, despite the existence of a high proportion of mechanised transport and cargo aircraft.

And what of the future?

We have seen how, as sophistication and the power of individual weapons increase, so too does the ratio of man to killing power, and the battlefield grows increasingly sparsely populated. It follows, of course, that the importance of every single soldier in the forward area increases proportionately, as does the importance of his re-supply. Yet we know too that the power of the nuclear weapon or of massed artillery, together with the destructive power of modern air forces, is likely to reduce the surface of any future theatre of war to a shambles that will seriously inhibit logistic movement. Indeed, the combination of the loss of mobility with the threat of electronic attack against a complex system of command and control (including crucially important, automated logistic management systems) and an ever-present threat from the air, reaching to the full depth of the theatre of operations, bodes ill for the logistician. Modern ammunition is extremely heavy, particularly in the form of rockets for such equipments as Multiple Launch Rocket Systems (MLRS), and the quantities required daily to replace consumption, which will reach hitherto unknown rates of intensity, present a huge movement problem in themselves, even without the added hazards of route destruction. Similarly, vast quantities of fuel are needed to keep a modern mechanised army mobile. Even with the use of pipelines well forward, distribution to widely dispersed units must create serious problems. Quite apart from the question of distribution, there is also the matter of stockholding. Few governments today are prepared to sink the billions needed into the provision of adequate in-theatre stocks of replacement equipments, spares, ammunition and fuel. Quite apart from the fact that to do so is locking up huge capital sums in infrastructure as well as the actual stocks but the cost of individual items is now so appallingly high that, understandably, there is extreme reluctance to buy any more than is essential to equip the forces involved with their needs for more than a few days. Even these holdings are often depleted when economies are needed, because the cutting of stocks in war reserve is an invisible exercise to the public at large — but let no man think that this pernicious practice fools the enemy for one minute. The consequence of this situation is that incalculable sums are laid out on the development of highly sophisticated weapon systems and the means of supporting them, let alone on the expensive training needed to use them effectively. Yet the whole exercise might be described as a costly sham, since the means of sustaining battle for more than a very brief period will not exist within the theatre and re-supply from home bases will be a hazardous business at best (even if the stocks exist there) in the light of the sea and air threats to the lines of supply.

Given that the problems of logistic movement will affect both sides, it has to be said that he who fights on interior lines must have a substantial advantage. In all probability, the best that can be hoped for is a stalemate, forced upon both sides but even this is contingent upon the successful suppression of the enemy's logistics and the inhibition of the movement of his reinforcements.

So much for the short-term outlook. If we take what might be seen as a more fanciful look well into the future and consider what effect emerging technology might have upon the whole situation, the need is clearly to see in what way it might be able to eliminate those two 'nails' in the 'shoe' which are the chief cause of our current concern — fuel and ammunition. Great strides have been made in recent years in two electronic fields — superconductivity and the laser. If work can be progressed upon the first to the level at which it becomes feasible to give battlefield equipment all-electric propulsion, it is just conceivable that the question of fuel can be beaten. We know that it is already perfectly possible to create weapons by the use of the laser, although the power needed for this purpose is so great that the laser-powered gun is still something of a pipe-dream. Yet even in that field, scientists have been able to devise laser-powered devices which might be used in space for the destruction of enemy satellites. The transition from space to the earth's surface may not be so far away, after all. These thoughts, which are admittedly redolent of wishful thinking, are intended only to suggest that dramatic changes could be round the corner. In the meanwhile, and for the near-term future, we are left with the situation as it now is, with the future of conventional warfare in any but the most abbreviated form highly questionable, once the Super Powers become embroiled. To take a more optimistic view, even conventional war has become a futile option. The world in which we live offers untold opportunities for government to pursue their national aims without recourse to anything so utterly self-defeating — once more, the power of the tail will have defeated the teeth.

★   ★   ★   ★   ★

But what happens if nuclear weapons *are* employed?

Neither side, regardless of political posturing, can be trusted not to fire the first nuclear weapon, any more than they can be trusted not to initiate Chemical Warfare which might, incidentally, trigger a nuclear counter strike. Likely as not, the first explosion will be a low yield, anti-submarine depth charge at sea — not simply because that sort of warning shot of intention will damage only the marine environment, instead of people and property, but because it may be judged to be the best weapon for eliminating deep-diving submarines. At sea or over land, if the first cautionary blow is ignored, escalation with ever larger weapons over a widening area will almost certainly result. Maybe the first blasts will be from small, tactical warheads in the combat zone, the damage from any one of which will throw a large load upon medical repair and replacement services, let alone probably creating some local imbalance in the attritional contest. As front line targets are devastated, the call upon logistic services, whose main bases, ports, airfields and so on also will be struck, will become overwhelming. Almost at once the dividing line between military and civil priorities for help and support will disappear. Without even contemplating the unleashing of thermo-nuclear fusion weapons of absolute last resort, it is likely that the numerous relatively low yield fission weapons, of the type used against Hiroshima and Nagasaki, will impose upon civilisation a catastrophe of unprecedented scale.

Under these conditions continuance of formal war by peoples who turn to rescue work might be very difficult because, apart from the destruction of so many weapons and of large parts of the logistic structure of nations, as well as of armies, the humanitarian instinct would assert itself powerfully. Many individuals and communities, faced with unparalleled suffering and cries for survival, would turn aside from the fighting. Yet, as history repeatedly has shown, people striving for survival tend to come to blows. Within the turmoil of the fission nuclear exchange some groups will carry on fighting. Though communications shrivel and the bonds of centralised controls are loosened, it is more than likely that national strategies will collapse and give way to localised initiatives.

Yet amidst this tumultuous holocaust there remains the possibility that surviving cells of central governments will persuade themselves that the original, by now blurred, image of ideology or Grand Strategy justifies a thermo-nuclear fusion strike. If that happens the fires and irradiation caused by earlier fission attacks will themselves be engulfed by the ultimate deterrent which has failed to deter. The result will be the wiping out of civilisation as we know it but not, it may safely be assumed, of humanity itself. Life will continue for vastly depleted populations who have avoided the blasts and fireballs and escaped fatal doses of radiation. Here and there intact but isolated communities which have suffered little or no physical damage will look like oases in a desert world. They would lack much which was previously considered essential to everyday life. It is certain that destruction of electricity supply, industry, transport, bridges and routes, along with the sensitive distribution networks, will have killed orderly economic practices and reduced to almost nothing the replacement of materials and equipment as surviving stocks are consumed, worn out or destroyed during further outbreaks of combat. Food and fuels will be scarce and poorly distributed with dire shortages and surpluses of essentials, in one place, and the reverse in another nearby. Successful communities will manage to feed on a basic diet or warm themselves with locally gathered solid fuels. But liquid fuels will be extremely difficult to obtain due to the destruction of oil fields, the difficulties of restoring them to production, and the time it will take to rebuild sunken tanker fleets. Road and air transport will be at a premium, almost non-existent in most areas. Railways and ships, for the time being, will revert to sail and in due course coal burning vessels will reappear — most of them yet to be constructed.

In a majority of areas life will be as primitive as the Middle Ages, with only the few luckier communities enjoying something like the mid-19th Century standards. It really will be a question of the survival of the fittest in a period when, for example, health care and medical treatment will be reduced to the basics. The apparatus, the anaesthetics, antibiotics and much else taken for granted in the 1980s will no longer be available.

How long this extreme deprivation and chaos will last before the reknitting of the previous fabric even begins — let alone is achieved — is impossible to say, because the magnitude of likely moral and physical destruction is unimaginable. But in a world where a great store of knowledge and expertise has been, perhaps irretrievably, lost, where natural resources are in desperately short supply and where labour from small populations is largely without mechanical assistance, progress will be very slow. There will be all manner of distortions and set-backs as stronger and more able leaders, helped by cadres of surviving technicians, begin to rebuild essential communication, financial and supply systems. Very likely it will be two steps forward and one back as nearby communities link up and try to pool their resources. Unhappily, human nature being what it is, there must be doubt about hopes for unselfish, unified action for the common good. Ancient tribal jealousies and ideologies along with fear, hatred and greed may well be amplified rather than quelled *because* it is such a desperate situation. The mere hint of one community's self-sufficiency reaching the ears of a nearly deprived group may well be the spur to further hostilities, violence and waste.

It is perhaps asking for too much to believe that, at an early stage, some organisation, blessed by clear-sighted leaders and brilliant technologists, will emerge, ensconced in a defensible part of the world where it can establish and maintain a well-supplied base from which to expand outwards. Science fiction has often enough depicted a revolution of that nature in the aftermath of universal destruction. Scenarios of a higher breed thrusting into the wilderness with modern communication tentacles and superior transport systems, fuelled by unlimited power are emotionally very attractive. They are daunting in their technical, administrative and logistic magnitude — and will be miraculous if they come to pass.

*   *   *   *   *

If conventional warfare has become futile, nuclear war is far more so. It were better by far if the logistic skills and resources developed at such great cost over the years for warlike purposes should be devoted to the promotion of peace by helping to bring prosperity and stability to a new world in which problems are no longer solved by conflict.

Bibliography

In addition to those listed, many Official Histories relating to several wars have also been consulted. The lists of books which provide information of greater or less extent about logistic matters are almost as many as those written about war and related subjects: to include them all would be less than helpful. So the list below is of the books which have contributed substantially to the compilation of 'For Want of a Nail' and which may be of most assistance towards further study of military logistics and communications.

Anon. *The German Campaign in Russia (1940–1942)*. Dept. of US Army, 1955.

Anon. *The Rise and Fall of the German Air Force*. Arco.

Appleman, R.E. *US Army in the Korean War (June to November 1950)*. Dept. of US Army, 1961.

Baker, W.J. *A History of the Marconi Company*. Methuen, 1970.

Beadon, R.H. *History of the RASC (Vol 2)*. Cambridge, 1931.

Brereton, F.S. *The Great War and the RAMC*. Constable, 1919.

Brown, D. *The Royal Navy and the Falklands War*. Cooper, 1986.

Carter J.H. and Karne, D. *Maintenance in the Field (2 vols)*. War Office, 1952.

Churchill, W.S. *Marlborough, His Life and Times (2 vols)*. Harrap, 1947.

Creveld, M. van. *Supplying War*. Cambridge, 1977.

Dietrich, E.C. *The last Iliad: The Siege of Port Arthur*. New York University, 1978.

Durnford, A.W. *A Memoir*. Samson Low, 1882.

Dyer, G.C. *The Amphibians Came to Conquer (2 vols)*. US Government, 1969.

Emery, E. *The Red Soldier*. Hodder and Stoughton, 1977.

Fortescue, J. *The RASC; A History of Transport and Supply in the Army (Vol 1)*. Cambridge, 1930.

Fuller, J.F.C. *Machine Warfare*. Hutchinson, 1942.

      Decisive Battles of the Western World (3 vols). Eyre and Spottiswood, 1956.

Furneaux, D.F. *The Zulu War*. Lippincott, 1963.

Guderian, H.W. *Panzer Leader*. Joseph, 1952.

Herzog, C. *The Arab Israeli Wars*. Arms and Armour, 1982.

Hinsley, F.H. and others. *British Intelligence in the Second World War (4 vols).*
    Horne, A. *To Lose a Battle*. Macmillan, 1969.

Howard, M. *The Franco Prussian War*. Hart-Davis, 1968.

HMSO, 1977–1988.

Leighton, R. and Coakley, R. *Global Logistics and Strategy (1940–1943)*. Dept. of
    US Army, 1955.

Lewin, R. *The Other Ultra*. Hutchinson, 1982.

Macdonald, G. *The Mighty Endeavour*. Oxford, 1968.

Macksey, K. *Technology in War*. Arms and Armour, 1986.

Nalder, R.F.H. *History of the Royal Signals (1800–1955)*. R. Sigs. Institute, 1958.
    Signal Communications. War Office, 1950.

Ruppenthal, J. *Logistical Support of the Army (Vol 2)*. Dept. of US Army, 1959.

Seaton, A. *The Russo-German War 1941–1945*. Barker, 1971.

Sherman, W.T. *From Atlanta to the Sea*. Folio Society, 1961.

Slim, W. *Defeat into Victory*. Cassell, 1956.

Starry, D.A. *Armoured Combat in Vietnam*. Blandford, 1981.

Stone, N. *The Eastern Front, 1914–1917*. Hodder and Stoughton, 1976.

Summers, H.G. *Vietnam Almanac*. Facts on File Publications, 1985.

Terret, D. *The Signals Corps (3 vols)*. Dept. of US Army, 1956.

Tolson, J.J. *Airmobility 1961–1971*. Dept. of US Army, 1973.

Waddell, W. and Wood, N. *Air War — Vietnam*. Arms and Armour, 1978.

Woodham-Smith, C. *Florence Nightingale*. Constable, 1950.

Index